AMENDING CANADA'S CONSTITUTION

AMENDING CANADA'S CONSTITUTION

HISTORY, PROCESSES, PROBLEMS AND PROSPECTS

James Ross Hurley

Canada

Issued also in French under title: La modification
de la Constitution du Canada.
Includes bibliographical references.

Available in Canada through
your local bookseller
or by mail from
Canada Communication Group - Publishing
Ottawa, Canada K1A 0S9

Canadian Cataloguing in Publication Data

Hurley, James Ross

Amending Canada's constitution: history, processes,
problems and prospects

ISBN 0-660-16261-X
Cat. no. CP32-63/1995E

1.   Canada — Constitutional law — Amendments.
2.   Canada — Constitutional history.
I.   Canada. Privy Council Office. Policy Development
and Constitutional Affairs.
II.   Title.

JL27.H87 1996   342.71'039   C96-980057-6

Canada	Groupe
Communication	Communication
Group	Canada
Publishing	Édition

TABLE OF CONTENTS

PREFACE

IN THE SPRING of 1992, the Clerk of the Privy
Council, Secretary to Cabinet and Secretary to the
Cabinet for Federal-Provincial Relations, Paul Tellier,
and the Associate Secretary to the Cabinet for Federal-
Provincial Relations, Jocelyne Bourgon, agreed that
I should be relieved of the routine pressures of office
work for twelve months at some point after the
constitutional exercise then underway to write a book
on the law and processes of constitutional change in
Canada. In this way, I might be able to share with
others knowledge gained and insights developed in
what is now 20 years of working on the constitutional front in the Federal-Provincial Relations Office
and the Privy Council Office as constitutional advisor,
senior constitutional advisor and Director of
Constitutional Affairs.

After the dust of the 1992 referendum had settled, the then Deputy
Secretary to the Cabinet for Constitutional Affairs, Suzanne
Hurtubise, made the necessary arrangements that allowed for
the production of this work.

I wish to thank the Honourable Paul Tellier, Mme Bourgon
and Mme Hurtubise for the rare opportunity they provided me
and for the trust they demonstrated in my capacity to bring the
work to fruition.

Michael Wernick, the Assistant Secretary to the Cabinet for Policy
Development and Constitutional Affairs, provided not only
encouragement, but also read the draft carefully and made
numerous suggestions for strengthening the text.

Mary Dawson, the Associate Deputy Minister of Justice, and
F. J. E. Jordan, Senior General Counsel in the Department
of Justice, both vetted the document and made important
contributions.

In the Policy Development and Constitutional Affairs Secretariat, John McDowell read the text and provided helpful comments, while Leo Doyle was indispensable in undertaking research and tabulating material.

The assistance of the following people who, in 1993, provided information on constitutional resolutions proposed in the Senate, House of Commons and the legislative assemblies, is gratefully acknowledged: Gordon L. Barnhart, Clerk of the Senate and Clerk of the Parliaments; Robert Marleau, Clerk of the House of Commons; Peter Sibenik, Procedural Clerk (Research), Legislative Assembly of Ontario; Pierre Duchesne, Le Secrétaire général, Assemblée Nationale du Québec; Darryl Eisan, Research Officer, Government of Nova Scotia, Department of Intergovernmental Affairs; Loredana Catalli Sonier, Clerk Assistant (Procedural), Legislative Assembly of New Brunswick; W. H. (Binx) Remnant, Clerk of the Legislative Assembly of Manitoba; I. M. Horne, Q.C., Clerk of the Legislative Assembly of British Columbia; Charles MacKay, Clerk Assistant, Office of the Clerk, Legislative Assembly of Prince Edward Island; Robert Vaive, Deputy Clerk, Saskatchewan Legislative Assembly; Robert H. Reynolds, Parliamentary Counsel, and Grant Wagman, Assistant to the Parliamentary Counsel, Legislative Assembly of Alberta; A. John Noel, Clerk of the House, House of Assembly of Newfoundland and Labrador; Missy Follwell, Deputy Clerk, Yukon Legislative Assembly; David M. Hamilton, Clerk of the Legislative Assembly of the Northwest Territories.

I particularly wish to thank Professor J. Peter Meekison of the University of Alberta for reviewing the work. As the key constitutional advisor to Premier Lougheed in the period prior to patriation, Professor Meekison was the architect of the amending formula now in place.

This book would not have seen the light of day without the careful and patient work of Vidalia Velho who prepared the text for publication: I would like to take the opportunity of acknowledging her contribution and thanking her.

The contributions of others were essential to bring the book through the various final steps leading to publication. Without being exhaustive, it would be appropriate to mention a few who have played a critical role: Jacques Carrière and Claude Gagnon of the Translation Services, Privy Council Office; Jeane Carrière, Andrea Nugent and Lucile Basu of the Communications Support Directorate, Privy Council Office; Daniel Woolford; Toivo Roht of Thor Communications; Madeleine Choquette of Communications Choquette; and Leslie-Ann Scott and Jim Baxter of the Canada Communications Group.

The text of *Amending Canada's Constitution* was completed in the spring of 1995. Three noteworthy constitutional developments took place since then. They are discussed in the Addendum at the end of the book.

This work is intended to share knowledge and insights: it is not a kiss-and-tell book. The emphasis is on the law and processes of constitutional change, not on the advisability or otherwise of particular proposals for amendments. A rigorous attempt has been made to remain neutral and non-partisan. Special efforts have been deployed to ensure that the factual information contained in this work is correct. If, on either account, I have fallen short, the fault is mine and mine alone.

Whatever views might be expressed in the following pages do not necessarily reflect those of the Government of Canada.

James Ross Hurley

Ottawa, December 22, 1995

INTRODUCTION

FOR NEARLY a quarter of a century — from 1968 to 1992 — Canadians were involved in an almost constant debate on their constitution.

The debate was broad ranging and focused on a number of issues:

- whether — and how — the distribution of legislative powers between Parliament and the provincial legislatures should be realigned;

- the desirability of making changes to certain national institutions, including the Senate and the Supreme Court;

- the advisability of protecting or entrenching certain rights in the Constitution; and

- devising rules and processes for making changes to the Constitution — which involved the search for an amending formula.

This work is concerned with the last-mentioned issue: the method of amending the Constitution of Canada.

The events of the past 25 years have demonstrated that Canadians hold strong views on how the Constitution should be amended. Those views have high symbolic value and important practical consequences — whether it be, for example, Quebec's concern with a constitutional veto, Alberta's belief in the equality of the provinces or the desire of Canadians to participate in the amendment process.

This work is designed to provide a broad examination of the issue of constitutional amendment in Canada. The focus is on how the Constitution is amended — the law and process of constitutional change in Canada — and not on the desirability or specific nature of amendments that have been made or proposed since 1867.

The examination will begin with a consideration of the competing pulls of protection and flexibility that determine ultimately how states provide for the amendment of their constitutions. This will be followed by a review of how Canada's constitution was amended from July 1, 1867, to the time of patriation on April 17, 1982.

The long search for an amending formula that would permit patriation of the Constitution merits special attention and provides information that may surprise some. For example, an amending formula was proposed by a federal-provincial committee of attorneys general in 1936. It provided a unanimity procedure for some matters (including the office of the Queen and the use of French and English), a two-thirds/55 percent procedure for most matters concerning the federal government and all the provinces, and a provincial opting out procedure for some amendments. It appears to be a distant mirror of the formula now in place.

A detailed examination of the seven procedures comprising the current amending formula is provided, and the complexity of the issue of constitutional amendment is illustrated by reviewing what might be the appropriate procedure for various aspects of Senate reform and for abolition of the Senate.

There are two ways of achieving amendments since patriation: by legislation and by proclamation issued by the Governor General. The second method is the more difficult and constitutes the principal focus of the examination of the 1982 formula.

Whether or not it is easy to amend Canada's constitution under the amending formula adopted in 1982 is touched upon in two chapters, one of which examines the four amendments by proclamation achieved since patriation and the other of which examines the unsuccessful attempts at amendment over the same period.

How does one get from the authorization of an amendment by proclamation to the proclamation itself? The Constitution is not particularly forthcoming on this matter, but the precedents established to date are set out.

Finally, the processes and the laws that supplement the amending formula are reviewed and some tentative conclusions are offered.

A few words about vocabulary are in order. The word "formula" has been used repeatedly in Canadian history to designate an integrated set of procedures. The Fulton-Favreau formula and the Victoria formula, for example, each contained a number of distinct amendment procedures.

Some people now refer to the unanimity "formula" or the 7/50 "formula," but these are both procedures under the formula adopted in 1982. For the purposes of clarity, I have used the word "formula" throughout this work to describe a set of integrated procedures for amending the Constitution, and the word "procedure" to identify a specific method of amendment (for example, the unanimity procedure, the 7/50 procedure, the bilateral procedure).

Also, for greater clarity, I have used the current terms "federal government," "federal-provincial" and "first ministers" even when referring to historical periods when "the Dominion government," "Dominion-provincial" and "the Prime Minister and the premiers" were employed.

A comment on the word "dominion" and the term "first ministers" may be in order. The Dominion of Canada was in the vanguard in seeking ever-greater autonomy within the British Empire. When the Balfour Report of 1926 recognized that Canada and five other countries were independent communities but sharing a common sovereign, they were said to enjoy "Dominion status."

However, as an increasing number of Commonwealth states became independent republics after the Second World War, the once proud word "dominion" began to smack of the last phase of colonialism. The word fell out of favour, internationally and domestically. The word "federal" soon replaced the word "dominion" when used as an adjective.

During the Quiet Revolution in Quebec, Jean Lesage thought the English term "premier" connoted inferior status to that of the Prime Minister of Canada, and insisted on being called the Prime Minister of Quebec.

The premiers of Ontario and British Columbia did likewise. How then should one describe a meeting of four prime ministers and seven premiers? The term "first ministers' conference" was coined.

Of course, the question does not arise in French. "Prime minister," "premier" and "first minister" are all translated by the term "premier ministre."

There may be some confusion about the titles of some of the most important written documents forming part of the Constitution of Canada. The British North America Act, 1867 and the various British North America acts adopted over the years that amended it were retitled at the time of patriation in the Schedule of the Constitution Act, 1982. They became known as the Constitution Act, 1867, the Constitution Act, 1871, etc. There was one exception: the British North America Act, 1949 became the Newfoundland Act.

Finally, I wish to acknowledge my debt to various works prepared in the Federal-Provincial Relations Office and published by it, by the Privy Council Office or by *Options* over the past 20 years. On occasion, I have integrated a paragraph or two from those publications into this work, where appropriate, sometimes with minor alterations, sometimes without. In the case of the document published under my own name, I have included several pages in the current text: it did not seem advisable or necessary to reinvent the wheel. The Government of Canada holds the copyright to all those works as, indeed, it does to the current volume.

All of the material contained in the appendixes is in the public domain, or is unclassified, or has been declassified, or has been tabulated on the basis of material in the public domain. Some documents in the public domain are now difficult to find (such as the correspondence between Premier René Lévesque of Quebec and Prime Minister Pierre Elliott Trudeau in Appendixes 11 to 16). The appendixes should provide a fairly rich source of reference material for those wishing to delve more deeply into the question of the constitutional amendment process in Canada.

1

CONSTITUTIONS AND CONSTITUTIONAL AMENDMENT

IT IS IRONIC that a word of such high symbolic value and with such important practical consequences — "constitution" — should defy any attempt to provide a precise and complete definition of universal application.

CONSTITUTIONS

Reduced to a bare minimum, a constitution provides the essential framework for orderly government in a state. It establishes the organs of government and provides for the relations among those organs. Constitutional government is the opposite of capricious government and seeks — in varying degrees and with greater or lesser success — to reduce or remove uncertainty and arbitrariness from political life.

This does not mean that constitutions are necessarily imbued with liberal democratic values. A totalitarian constitution may indeed provide for orderly government while proscribing political dissent or permitting the oppression of individuals and classes of people through rule of law.

Constitutions may go beyond providing the bare bones for orderly government. They may also provide for the relations between the organs of government and the citizens, and for relations between the state and individuals. They may set out the responsibilities of the state towards citizens and individuals, and they may define the rights of citizens or individuals. They may even provide for the responsibilities of citizens, such as compulsory voting. They may attempt to be more comprehensive and to include social and economic charters that set out specific public policy goals for the community.

Where is the constitution to be found? Some states, such as the United States of America and France, spelled out fundamental aspects of their constitutions in a written document. The provisions of such constitutional documents are enforced by the courts. But no state has succeeded in codifying its full constitution in one written document.

The constitution in a broader sense also includes numerous laws of an organic or fundamental character, such as electoral laws, laws providing the conditions for the acquisition of citizenship or laws determining the age of majority. Such laws are enforced by the courts, as are such common law rules as the prerogative powers of the Crown and the privileges of the Senate and House of Commons, in the case of Canada.

Constitutional conventions also form part of the constitution. The conventions of the constitution are rules of constitutional behaviour which are considered to be binding by those who participate in public life, but which — unlike laws — are not enforced by the courts. Conventions are essentially political and the sanction for failure to respect them is political, not legal.

Because of their nature, conventions are usually quite concise and precise. Complexity or ambiguity would defeat the purpose of achieving a broad consensus among political actors on the meaning of a convention.

Conventions play a greater role in states with constitutions that are largely unwritten, such as the United Kingdom, than in states in which many fundamental aspects of the constitution have been set out in a formal document. However, even in the latter case conventions have an important role in supplementing the letter of the law.

Given the role of the courts in enforcing formal written constitutions and the laws of the state, it follows that certain judicial decisions also form part of the constitution in its broadest sense. Such decisions help clarify the meaning of various provisions of the written constitution and fundamental laws. However, the courts might decide not to restrict themselves to clarification, but to play an active role in determining how the text of the written constitution should be adapted, through judicial interpretation, to changing circumstances. Court decisions provide rules which are also part of the constitution in its broader meaning.

Thus, the constitution of a state may be found in a formal written document (although, as the British experience makes clear, this is not essential), in fundamental or organic laws, in the conventions of the constitution and in certain judicial decisions.

AMENDING THE CONSTITUTION

The circumstances of any given state are not static; over time, changing or amending the constitution is often desirable if not indeed imperative.

Judicial interpretation is one of the most flexible ways of adjusting a constitution to new situations, but it is limited to the interpretation of existing constitutional provisions and laws, and does not extend to the substitution of new ones. Furthermore, judicial interpretation escapes public control, since judges are not usually accountable to the people.

The conventions of the constitution, while deemed binding by political actors, are not legally enforceable and could be contravened in exceptional circumstances. However, conventions represent established customs, practices, maxims or precepts broadly accepted and supported by the public. Because the sanction for violating a convention is political, political actors must be reasonably confident of public support before transgressing a convention and achieving, thereby, constitutional change. Paradoxically, conventions are flexible in theory, but quite rigid in practice.

Fundamental or organic laws may be amended or replaced by subsequent laws. This method of amendment is highly flexible in theory and in practice. In most democratic states, laws may be amended by a simple majority of the members of the legislature present at the time the vote is held.

In some unitary states there are constitutional laws which are not codified in a special document. In the United Kingdom, for example, the Act of Settlement of 1701, the Acts of Union of 1707 and 1800 and the Catholic Emancipation Act of 1829 form part of the Constitution of the United Kingdom, but they are laws adopted by a simple majority in Parliament and can be altered or abrogated in the same way.

Sweden, like the United Kingdom, does not have a codified constitution. However, constitutional laws, such as the Instrument of Government Act of 1809, the Act of Succession of 1810, the Parliament Act of 1866 and the Freedom of Press Act of 1949, are subject to a special amendment procedure: changes may be instituted only with the approval of two successive parliaments, between which elections must occur.

The purpose of codifying certain basic rules in a "written" constitution is to highlight and clarify the consensus of a society on political relationships and to provide a stable framework for political life. It follows that written constitutions, unlike laws, are normally subject to an extraordinary amendment procedure that makes change possible, but not too easy.

In many unitary states, fundamental laws have been codified in a written constitution. Formal amending procedures for such constitutions are varied. For example, the Constitution of France provides that the Constitution may be amended by a bill passed by both assemblies of Parliament and approved by the people in a referendum, or by the submission of a proposal by the President to both assemblies convened in a congress where passage would require approval by a three-fifths majority of the votes cast. In the second case, no referendum is required. The Constitution of Ireland provides for passage of a bill to amend the Constitution by both houses of the national parliament, followed by a referendum.

The issue is somewhat more complex and pertinent in the case of federations. Federations arise when constituent units — whether they be called states, cantons, provinces or *Länder* — seek to create a political union to pursue certain defined common objectives without, however, wishing to vest all authority in a central legislature and government. Furthermore, in the case of many federations, an essential part of the agreement creating the federation is the protection of certain minority interests — regional, ethnic, linguistic or religious — against arbitrary or majoritarian changes.

Upon the creation of a federation, legislative powers are distributed between the federal authority and the constituent units. The way in which those powers are distributed will depend upon the particular circumstances of each federation. In general terms, the federal government is usually responsible for matters of common concern, such as defence, the economic union, currency and postage. The constituent units normally exercise jurisdiction over matters of more particular concern, such as education, highways and bridges, and municipal government.

Constitutional amendment procedures in federal states are designed, among other things, to ensure that the distribution of legislative powers between the federal and constituent governments cannot be altered too easily, thus providing stability and protection for the original federal compromise. A role is usually provided for the constituent units, either directly or through institutions that represent them, in the amendment procedure.

Thus, in the United States of America — the oldest federation in the world — amendments to the Constitution may be proposed by a favourable vote by at least two-thirds of both the House of Representatives and the Senate (which represents each state on the basis of equality) or by a convention called by the federal Congress upon the application of two-thirds of the states. The second method of initiating an amendment has never been successful because, while there have been some two dozen applications by state legislatures to Congress proposing a constitutional amendment, no proposal has ever been submitted by the required two-thirds of the states.

Once an amendment has been proposed, Congress may choose between two methods of ratification: either by the legislatures of three-quarters of the states or by conventions in three-quarters of the states. The second method was only used once (for the Twenty-first Amendment, which repealed prohibition).

This extraordinary procedure for proposing amendments and for ratifying them has not led to a great number of amendments. Although more than 9,100 proposals to amend the Constitution have been introduced in Congress since 1789, only 33 received the required degree of congressional support to be put to the states for ratification and only 26 were, indeed, ratified.

The Constitution of Australia has also proven rather "stable" over the years. In Australia, proposals for constitutional change must be initiated in the federal Parliament in the form of a law passed by an absolute majority of the two Houses of Parliament (or, in exceptional cases, by one House). The proposed law, so adopted, is then put to the people in a referendum. To pass, it must be supported by a majority of the electors voting in a majority of the states of the federation and by a majority of electors voting in Australia as a whole. Since 1901, 42 separate proposals for amendment have been submitted to the people for approval through 18 referendums, but only eight amendments have been ratified.

On the other hand, an extraordinary procedure does not necessarily make amendment rare or nigh impossible. Constitutional amendments in Switzerland may be initiated by the two Houses of the Federal Assembly or by popular initiative requiring the signatures of 50,000 voters (until 1971) or of 100,000 (since then). In either case, the proposal must be submitted to the people in a referendum. A double majority is required for ratification: a majority of voters in Switzerland as a whole and a majority of the cantons (that is, the constituent units). The result of the popular vote in each canton is regarded as the vote of that canton.

From 1848 to 1994, this seemingly cumbersome procedure resulted in 292 amendments being put to the people in 182 referendums: 150 were ratified and 142 were rejected.

Striking the appropriate balance between stability and adaptability in the procedures for constitutional amendment is normally a key issue when a federation is created.

CANADA'S CONSTITUTION

The British had established a precedent of providing a constitution for Canada in the form of a United Kingdom statute when the Quebec Act of 1774 was adopted. It was, in fact, the first time the British Parliament had ever enacted a constitution. It was replaced by the Constitutional Act of 1791 which in turn gave way to the Act of Union of 1840.

The British North America Act of 1867 was the fourth constitution for Canada enacted by the British Parliament in 93 years.
There was, at that time, no thought of providing a method of
amending the British North America Act (with some minor
exceptions which will be noted in chapter 2) other than through
a subsequent act of the United Kingdom Parliament.

The legal position was clear: only the United Kingdom Parliament
could amend vital parts of the Constitution of Canada. Gradually,
however, certain practices, conventions and processes emerged
that defined in what circumstances the British would enact
changes to the British North America Act.

The need for an alternative Canadian procedure for amending
the Constitution did not arise until Canada became — de facto
— an independent country in 1926. This gave rise to the patriation debate, which is discussed in chapter 3.

our Majesty's loyal subjects, the Hou
s of Canada in Parliament assembl
approach Your Majesty, requesting
graciously be pleased to cause to be
Parliament of the United Kingd
containing the recitals and c
ter set forth ;:

An Act to give effect to a request by t
and House of Commons of C

Whereas Canada has requested a
the enactment of an Act of the Parl
United Kingdom to give effect to
after set forth and the Senate an
anada in Parliament
Her Majesty

2

AMENDING CANADA'S CONSTITUTION 1867 TO 1982

IT IS USEFUL to distinguish between two separate issues. The first is how Canada, as a federation, handled amendments to its constitution in the absence of formal procedures entrenched in the Constitution itself. The second is how agreement was ultimately reached on amendment procedures that were enshrined in the Constitution — the so-called patriation debate which, as already noted, will be examined in chapter 3.

The two issues overlapped in time. The question of patriating the Constitution with an amendment procedure was initiated by the Balfour Report of 1926 and was not concluded until 1982. Yet important amendments to the Constitution were achieved without a resolution of the broader issue of agreeing on amending procedures. Such amendments included the transfer of jurisdiction over unemployment insurance to Parliament in 1940 and the "partial patriation" of the Constitution in 1949, which enabled the Canadian Parliament to amend certain parts of the Constitution through legislation without reference to the United Kingdom.

THE CONSTITUTION OF CANADA

Three of the British colonies in North America — the united province of Canada, Nova Scotia and New Brunswick — were legally brought together to form a federal union by a statute of the British Parliament in 1867.

The terms of the British North America Act, 1867 were largely the fruit of deliberations by elected representatives from the British North American colonies at the Charlottetown Conference in September 1864 and the Quebec Conference in October 1864. Those terms were debated by the legislative assembly of Canada, but not by those of Nova Scotia and New Brunswick.

Elected representatives of the three colonies met in London in December 1866 and, in collaboration with British authorities, prepared the final text of what would become the "written" Constitution of Canada. The contribution of British authorities was not negligible; for example, they proposed a deadlock-breaking procedure for the Senate. However, the essential terms of the distribution of powers between the federal and provincial governments clearly resulted from agreement among the British North Americans.

The British North America Act, 1867 was adopted as a statute by the British House of Lords on February 26, 1867, and by the House of Commons on March 8, 1867. It was given royal sanction on March 29, 1867, and came into force on July 1, 1867. As a British statute, it could be amended or, indeed, repealed, by subsequent action by the British Parliament.

The British North America Act, 1867 did a number of things:

■   It joined the provinces of Canada, Nova Scotia and New Brunswick in a federal union and set out the distribtion of powers between the federal and provincial governments.

■   It divided the old province of Canada into two new ones, Ontario and Quebec, and set out important elements of their provincial constitutions.

■   It established certain institutions of the new federal government: the Governor General, the Senate and the House of Commons.

■   It provided for the judiciary.

- It spelled out, for the first time in British history, some of the conventions of the Constitution respecting money bills.

- It entrenched a narrow range of rights in the Constitution: those respecting the use of English and French in federal and Quebec institutions on the one hand, and those respecting certain denominational school rights on the other.

But the British North America Act, 1867 was fundamentally concerned with the issue of joining provinces together in a federal union and the specific terms for the operation of federalism in the new country. The principles of responsible self-government which had been established through conventions and instructions to the governors over the previous 25 years were not spelled out (with the exception of some principles respecting money bills and the establishment of the Queen's Privy Council for Canada).

Instead, the preamble to the British North America Act, 1867 stated that the federating colonies had expressed a desire to be federally united "with a Constitution similar in principle to that of the United Kingdom." In so doing, it transferred to the new federal government and maintained in the provinces the constitutional conventions governing parliamentary responsible government. There was no mention in the written Constitution prior to 1982 of a prime minister or provincial first ministers. There was no mention of Cabinet, although sections 11 and 12 of the 1867 act did create the Queen's Privy Council for Canada and assigned a role to it. No provision was made for votes of confidence. No requirement that most of the members of Cabinet must sit in the elected House was to be found in it.

In short, the critical underpinnings of democratic, responsible government in Canada are to be found not in the "written" Constitution but in the constitutional conventions inherited from the United Kingdom.

Prior to 1982, the Constitution of Canada embraced more than the British North America Act, 1867 and its amendments, and the conventions of the Constitution. It also included certain other United Kingdom acts, such as the Statute of Westminster, 1931, the Letters Patent of the Governor General, imperial orders in council and federal and provincial laws of a fundamental or organic character. These laws were supplemented by decisions by the Judicial Committee of the Privy Council in London and by the Supreme Court of Canada. There was not a single comprehensive document that spelled out all the basic elements of the Constitution of Canada.

AMENDMENTS UNDER THE AUTHORITY OF THE BRITISH NORTH AMERICA ACT

The British North America Act, 1867 was a statute of the United Kingdom Parliament and, in principle, could only be altered by a subsequent act of the Parliament at Westminster. However, the British North America Act, 1867 actually contained a number of provisions that permitted constitutional change without further reference to Britain.

Section 92, which set out the exclusive legislative powers of the provinces, provided that the legislatures could amend the provincial constitution, except as regards the office of lieutenant-governor. However, the federal Parliament did not have an analogous power to amend many parts of its constitution which were set out in the British North America Act, 1867. Consequently, the British Parliament was called upon over the years to adopt rather technical bills, such as the clarification in 1875 of the privileges, immunities and powers of the Canadian Parliament or the Canadian Speaker (Appointment of Deputy) Act, 1895 to clarify the power of the Canadian Parliament to make provision for a deputy speaker in the Senate.

This was not a satisfactory arrangement. Section 91, which sets out the exclusive legislative powers of the Canadian Parliament, was amended by British statute in 1949 to allow Parliament to amend the Constitution of Canada (with the exception of certain matters intended to protect provincial powers, denominational school rights, and English and French language rights, and retaining the requirement of an annual session of Parliament and federal elections at least every five years in peacetime). This gave the Parliament of Canada a power analogous to that of the provincial legislatures to amend their own constitutions. For example, Parliament could adopt — subject to certain limits — a new formula for the representation of the provinces in the House of Commons without reference to the United Kingdom Parliament.

But the British North America Act, 1867 was also peppered with specific provisions that provided for particular amendments, not all of which are necessarily of great importance. For example, section 16 provides that, "until the Queen otherwise directs, the seat of government of Canada shall be Ottawa." Under section 35, Parliament can determine the quorum for the Senate.

Section 101, on the other hand, provided for a very important future change. It allowed the Parliament of Canada to establish a general court of appeal for Canada. Under this provision, Parliament established the Supreme Court of Canada in 1875. The Supreme Court of Canada was not, however, the court of last resort for Canada as long as appeals to the Judicial Committee of the Privy Council in London were permitted. When such appeals were abolished by a statute of the Parliament of Canada in 1949, the Supreme Court — a creation of Parliament — gained the final word on jurisdictional disputes between the federal and provincial governments.

Two powers of amendment under the British North America Act, 1867 appeared to highlight the special position of Quebec. Although all other provinces could amend their provincial electoral districts without restriction, Quebec did not have the same power. Of the 65 districts for the Quebec legislative assembly, 12 were set out in the second schedule to the British North America Act, 1867. Section 80 provided that the Quebec legislature could not alter the boundaries of those 12 districts unless a majority of the members representing those districts concurred in the changes at second and third readings. Ostensibly, this was designed as a protection for certain anglophone districts. This power of amendment was later exercised, as provided by the Constitution, and these initial limitations on the power of the Quebec assembly are no longer relevant.

The other power of amendment was, potentially, far more radical — on paper, at least. Section 94 allowed Parliament to make uniform laws respecting property and civil rights in the common law provinces, notwithstanding the constitutional distribution of powers. Quebec, with its civil code, was not subject to this provision. However, any federal law providing for uniformity was subject to the affected provinces' adopting the law. In effect, there was a provincial veto on the power and it was never exercised.

AMENDMENTS THROUGH CONVENTIONS

The fundamental conventions of the Constitution that underlie the operation of responsible parliamentary government in Canada have not changed significantly since Confederation. Most changes relate to Canada's gradual accession to independence. For example, the Governor General ceased, in 1873, to preside over meetings of Cabinet. Since 1952, all governors general have been Canadian. There was agreement at the Imperial Conference of 1930 that the United Kingdom would not exercise its powers of reservation and disallowance respecting Canadian bills and legislation: this convention "amended" sections 55, 56 and 57 of the 1867 act, which vested such authority in the United Kingdom government.

The convention that a government must resign or recommend an election if it is defeated on a matter of confidence is central to parliamentary government. It is, however, a little fuzzy at the edges. If a specific motion of no confidence is put to the House, there is no question about the consequences that must follow. However, if the government is defeated at third reading on a tax bill, the question is perhaps not so clear. Is any defeat on a tax bill a vote of no confidence? Canadian convention evolved in February 1968 when the minority Pearson government was defeated at third reading on a tax bill. The House was adjourned for a few days and, when it returned, the Government introduced a motion of confidence which was adopted and made clear that the Government did not have to resign.

There is debate in Canada on whether provisions of the Constitution can become spent or void by convention over time if they are not exercised in practice. A number of provincial governments have argued in recent years that the "unilateral" powers of the federal government to reserve or disallow provincial laws — powers which have not been exercised since the Second World War — are now spent and cannot be invoked. Section 90 of the British North America Act, 1867 provided that the federal government could instruct a lieutenant-governor to reserve royal sanction for a bill passed by the legislative assembly for consideration by the federal Cabinet — even though the bill might be clearly within provincial legislative jurisdiction. If the Government of Canada approved, the provincial law would be signed by the Governor General. If not, it would not come into effect.

Section 90 also provided that, even though a lieutenant-governor had given royal sanction to a provincial law, the Government of Canada could, within a year of receiving an authentic copy of the provincial law, "disallow" it, thereby annulling the law.

Some provincial authorities believe that a convention has arisen from the federal practice of not using the powers of reservation and disallowance for over 50 years (they had been rather vigorously exercised from 1867 to 1941), and that this convention has made them inoperative. The federal government has consistently rejected this interpretation and has offered, on a number of occasions, to amend the Constitution to remove the powers, but only if the provinces accepted a *quid pro quo*, such as the entrenchment of a charter of rights and freedoms in the Constitution which would bind the provincial legislatures.

The clearest statement of the federal position was provided in 1975. The Quebec Association of Protestant School Boards, in collaboration with nine other associations or organizations, submitted a petition on February 17, 1975, to the Governor General in Council asking that the Official Language Act of Quebec (known as Bill 22) be referred to the Supreme Court of Canada to determine its constitutionality or, as an alternative, that it be disallowed.

On July 18, 1975, Prime Minister Pierre Elliott Trudeau replied to K. Douglas Sheldrick, President of the Quebec Association of Protestant School Boards, saying that, although the scope and meaning of some sections of the Official Language Act of Quebec were unclear, it appeared that the act was generally within the legislative authority accorded by the British North America Act to Quebec.

He said little would thus be gained by a reference to the Supreme Court, although as provisions that were unclear were applied in specific circumstances, court challenges might be undertaken. On the issue of disallowance, the Prime Minister stated:

> It is only in rare cases that the federal government should avail itself of this power since its use represents a clear exception to the general principle that the federal and provincial legislatures are autonomous in their respective areas of legislative competence and are responsible for the policies they embrace.

The petition urges that the *Official Language Act* of Quebec should be disallowed because it is contrary to the public interest of Canada as a whole and because it is contrary to federal policy. The petition also urges disallowance on other grounds which, generally summarized, are that the legislation in question is 'unjust and unwise.' In the view of the federal government, the arguments submitted by the petitioners in this respect do not warrant the use of disallowance. Not every provincial law which is contrary to federal policy or to the public interest, or which is 'unwise or unjust' should be subjected to disallowance. The responsibility for such laws should ordinarily be left with the province unless other elements are present: for example, that their effect cuts directly across the operation of federal law or creates serious disorder particularly beyond the boundaries of the province enacting them.

For a convention to arise, it must be considered to be binding by the political actors to whom it applies, and no federal government has indicated a view contrary to the position enunciated in 1975. The powers of reservation and disallowance do not therefore appear to be spent as a result of a convention.

Similarly, there are those who felt that the power of the Queen to appoint four or eight additional senators on the recommendation of the Governor General — the "tie-breaking mechanism" developed at the London conference in 1866 and included in section 26 of the British North America Act — was a spent provision because it had never been invoked. However, when Prime Minister Brian Mulroney availed himself of this provision in 1992, he was sustained by the courts.

AMENDMENTS THROUGH JUDICIAL INTERPRETATION

Although the Supreme Court of Canada was established in 1875, Canada's court of final appeal until 1949 was the Judicial Committee of the Privy Council in London, England.

Until 1982 and the coming into force of the Canadian Charter of Rights and Freedoms, the majority of constitutional cases considered by the courts, and ultimately the Judicial Committee, concerned sections 91 and 92 and related sections of the British North America Act, 1867, where legislative powers are enumerated and distributed between Parliament and the provincial legislatures.

The Judicial Committee was acutely sensitive to the conflicting claims of the central and provincial authorities in Canada, and to the need to create a balance between these two levels of government. The Committee's legacy — the principle that both Parliament and the provincial legislatures are supreme in their respective legislative jurisdictions — is now one of the principal features of Canadian federalism.

The Judicial Committee not only resisted the centralizing tendencies built into the 1867 Constitution, but also, over time, shaped the constitutional distribution of powers in the most fundamental way.

The Judicial Committee established precedents that gave, for example, narrow interpretation to the principal federal powers, such as the "residual" and "trade and commerce" powers, and wide interpretation to the provincial power over "property and civil rights," which became, to all intents and purposes, an alternative residual power.

In 1949, Canadian appeals to the Judicial Committee were ended, and the Supreme Court of Canada became the court of final appeal.

Since 1949, the Supreme Court has presided over a general strengthening of government power at both the federal and provincial levels as Canadian society and the economy have become more complex and difficult to manage. However, the Court has been careful not to tilt the balance of power between Parliament and the provincial legislatures unduly one way or the other.

AMENDMENTS THROUGH FEDERAL AND PROVINCIAL LAWS

The federal and provincial governments were, of course, highly active in amending the Constitution in its broadest sense from 1867 to 1982 through statute law. Not only were there innumerable government reorganizations — departments were created, altered and abolished — but many laws affecting the rights of Canadians were adopted. The franchise was extended to women and to Aboriginal Canadians. The age of majority was lowered. The right to free education was established and the obligation for children to attend school was imposed. In 1960, Parliament adopted a bill of rights applying to areas of federal jurisdiction. In 1970, the Government invoked the War Measures Act, a federal law which curtailed the rights of Canadians.

Some federal laws amended the British North America Act, 1867. For example, the British North America Act (No. 2), 1975 provided Senate representation for the territories, and the British North America Act, 1952 provided a new formula for representation in the House of Commons. Under the authority of the British North America Act, 1871, a British statute, the Parliament of Canada enacted laws creating and constituting the provinces of Alberta and Saskatchewan in 1905. The 1871 act also confirmed the creation of Manitoba in 1870 by a law of the Parliament of Canada. However, the federal laws creating the three prairie provinces cannot be repealed or altered by the Parliament of Canada acting alone.

All of these laws were adopted by a majority of members present in the House at the time the vote was held. They were not, in short, subject to a special procedure.

AMENDMENTS ENACTED BY THE UNITED KINGDOM PARLIAMENT

Those parts of the Constitution which remained under the authority of the United Kingdom Parliament could only be amended by British statute. The British Parliament amended Canada's constitution 21 times prior to patriation (see Appendix 1).

Over the years, conventions or practices developed respecting the circumstances under which:

(a) the United Kingdom Parliament would act; and

(b) Canada would ask the United Kingdom Parliament to act.

In reviewing 14 amendments to the British North America Act, 1867 adopted between 1871 and 1964, the Government of Canada (in a 1965 paper published by the Minister of Justice, Guy Favreau) identified four principles that had governed the amendment process:

- No act of the United Kingdom Parliament affecting Canada would be passed unless requested and consented to by Canada, and every amendment requested by Canada was enacted by the Parliament at Westminster.

- After 1895, Canada invariably sought amendments by the British Parliament by means of a joint address of the Senate and House of Commons of Canada to the Crown.

- The British government would not act on a provincial request for an amendment, on the grounds that it should not intervene in the affairs of Canada, except at the request of the federal government (representing all of Canada).

- The Canadian Parliament would not request "an amendment directly affecting federal-provincial relationships without consultation and agreement with the provinces."

Two matters should be noted. The British did, on at least two occasions prior to 1926 (in 1920 and 1924), refuse to act on Canadian requests for an amendment respecting the extra-territorial operation of federal laws.

However, it could be argued that those requests were improper, since Canada was still a colony of the United Kingdom, which retained jurisdiction over Canada's foreign affairs.

The second matter is the question of provincial consent. The federal government did, in fact, secure the unanimous support of the provinces for three amendments dealing with the distribution of powers (the transfer of exclusive jurisdiction over unemployment insurance to Parliament in 1940, the granting of authority to Parliament in 1951 to legislate respecting old age pensions, subject to provincial paramountcy, and the extension of Parliament's power in 1964 to cover supplementary benefits to old age pensions). It also secured unanimous consent for a new scheme of constitutional subsidies to the provinces (1907) and for the mandatory retirement of provincial court judges at age 75 (1960).

However, even when making the effort to secure unanimous provincial consent, the federal government was not always prepared to agree it was necessary. In speaking on the unemployment insurance amendment in 1940, Prime Minister William Lyon Mackenzie King stated: "We have avoided the raising of a very critical constitutional question, namely, whether or not in amending the British North America Act, it is absolutely necessary to secure the consent of all provinces, or whether the consent of a certain number of provinces would of itself be sufficient" *(Canadian House of Commons Debates,* 1940, pp. 1117–18).

The Government of Canada published another paper in 1978, *The Canadian Constitution and Constitutional Amendment,* in which it reiterated the first three principles set out in 1965, reformulating them as observations rather than principles. But it qualified the fourth by saying, "although not constitutionally obliged to do so, the Government of Canada, before asking Parliament to adopt a Joint Address, sought and obtained the consent of all provinces on the three amendments (1940, 1951 and 1964) that involved the distribution of powers."

The question of the degree of provincial consent required prior to adoption of joint addresses requesting amendments to the British North America Act was ultimately resolved by the Supreme Court of Canada at the time of the patriation of the Constitution (see chapter 4).

The British North America Act, 1871 confirmed the authority of the Canadian Parliament to create new provinces in the territories and to extend existing provinces in the territories.

AMENDMENTS THROUGH IMPERIAL ORDERS IN COUNCIL

Section 146 of the British North America Act provided that the British government could admit Newfoundland, Prince Edward Island, British Columbia, Rupert's Land and the North-Western Territory into the Canadian federation on a joint address from the Canadian Parliament and, in the case of the three colonies, on addresses from the colonial legislatures.

Prince Edward Island (1873), British Columbia (1871) and Rupert's Land and the North-Western Territory (1870) were admitted under this provision. However, Newfoundland was admitted under the terms of a British statute, the British North America Act, 1949.

acio... 'e

our Majesty's loyal subjects, the Ho...
s of Canada in Parliament assemb...
approach Your Majesty, requesting...
graciously be pleased to cause to be
Parliament of the United Kingd...
containing the recitals and...
ter set forth :

An Act to give effect to a request by t...
and House of Commons of C...

Whereas Canada has requested a...
the enactment of an Act of the Par...
United Kingdom to give effect to...
ter set forth and the Senate an...
...nada in Parliament...
...Majesti...

THE SEARCH FOR AN AMENDING FORMULA 1926 TO 1982

A N IMMEDIATE CAUSE of Canada's accession to independence in 1926 was the report of a Canadian House of Commons committee, on June 18 of that year, on alleged scandals in the Customs Department.

That report set in train a dramatic series of events:

- the Conservative Official Opposition in Ottawa, with 116 seats in the House, moved to condemn the conduct of the Government over the alleged scandals;

- the Liberal government, with only 101 seats, feared losing the support of the 28 Progressives, Labour members and Independents who had sustained the Government since the general election of October 29, 1925;

- William Lyon Mackenzie King, the Liberal Prime Minister, asked the Governor General, Lord Byng, for a dissolution of Parliament following the adjournment of the House in the early hours of June 26;

- Lord Byng refused Mr. King's request and the Government resigned;

- Arthur Meighen, the leader of the Conservatives, was asked to form a government on June 28, but this new government was defeated three days later;

- Mr. Meighen asked Lord Byng for a dissolution, which was granted;

- in the ensuing election, Mr. King made the role of the British-appointed Governor General and — in particular — Lord Byng's refusal to grant him (Mr. King) a dissolution a key election issue;

- Mr. King won a solid majority in the general election of September 14, 1926, and ensured, thereby, that the status of the Governor General in the "dominions" would have to be addressed by the Imperial Conference which was to meet in London in December of that year.

THE BALFOUR REPORT

The Imperial Conference of 1926 appointed Lord Balfour, a former British prime minister, to preside over a committee to examine the relationship between Great Britain and the six dominions (Canada, Australia, South Africa, New Zealand, the Irish Free State and Newfoundland). The Balfour Report of December 1926 concluded that Britain and the six other self-governing countries were independent communities within the Empire, equal in status and in no way subordinate one to another, but united by a common allegiance to the Crown and freely associated as members of the Commonwealth.

The Balfour Report recognized the fact of the independent status of the dominions, but it was not a legal enactment. It was left to a committee of legal experts to examine the changes which might be necessary to give legal effect to the Balfour Report and to report to another Imperial Conference in 1930. The report of the legal experts would provide the basis for a law of the United Kingdom — the Statute of Westminster of 1931 — which would become the legal basis for the independence of the six dominions.

Although the Commonwealth of Australia Act of 1900 (which was a United Kingdom statute) provided for its own amendment by referendum in Australia without further reference to the United

Kingdom, the British North America Act of 1867 (with some exceptions discussed in chapter 2) did not. Therefore, the Balfour Report made it essential for Canadians to reach agreement on procedures or a "formula" to permit them to amend the Constitution of Canada in Canada and to remove the British North America Act from the legislative jurisdiction of the Parliament at Westminster.

THE "PATRIATION" DEBATE

The search for an amending formula became known as the patriation debate.

Agreement on amending procedures would allow Canadians to "patriate" the Constitution. The words "patriate" and "patriation" were devised by Canadians (as an alternative to "repatriate" or "repatriation") to acknowledge the legal reality that the British North America Act, 1867, although largely developed by British North Americans in British North America, had never been legally domiciled in Canada and subsequently sent abroad. Hence, legally, the Constitution could not be repatriated or brought back home again after an absence. This legal distinction did not affect French language usage in Canada, which consistently employed the word "rapatriement."

The patriation debate, launched by the Balfour Report in 1926, would be marked by many attempts to resolve the issue and would last 56 years. Canada would become, with the adoption of the Statute of Westminster in 1931, an independent state in all respects except that the British Parliament would retain legislative authority over the British North America Act and its amendments, until the patriation issue was concluded in 1982.

THE FIRST EXERCISE (1927)

The first attempt to resolve the question of devising amending procedures for those parts of the Canadian constitution that could not be amended in Canada occurred at a meeting of the Prime Minister and the premiers of the provinces in Ottawa in 1927. Patriation with an amending formula was only one item on a broad agenda. The conference was strictly an exercise in executive federalism — that is, discussion among the representatives of the executive branch of the federal and provincial governments with no legislative or public participation.

The federal government recommended that in the event of "ordinary" amendments, the federal government should consult the provincial legislatures and the consent of a majority of the provinces should be obtained; in the event of vital and fundamental amendments involving provincial rights, the rights of minorities or rights generally affecting race, language and creed, the unanimous consent of the provinces would be required.

The federal proposal meant not only that amendments affecting the distribution of legislative powers and denominational school rights would be subject to unanimity, for example, but also that any future attempt to entrench a charter of rights in the Constitution which would, by definition, place limits on the powers of the provinces would also be subject to the unanimity rule.

While some provinces supported the federal proposal, others felt that a purely Canadian procedure would make amendments too easy to achieve and preferred the status quo of amendments made only by the Parliament at Westminster. No general agreement was reached.

THE SECOND EXERCISE (1931)

In April 1931, a federal-provincial conference was held in Ottawa, at the request of Ontario and with the support of other provinces, to address the issue of constitutional amendment.

The provinces were particularly concerned that the then pending Statute of Westminster not be so construed as to permit the powers of the provinces to be curtailed, lessened, modified or repealed.

As a result of these representations, the Parliament of Canada adopted a joint address to the King requesting that a provision of the Statute of Westminster provide that nothing in the statute should be deemed to apply to the repeal, amendment or alteration of the British North America Act and its amendments and that Parliament and the provincial legislatures would continue to be restricted to their respective legislative powers.

When the Statute of Westminster was adopted and proclaimed in December 1931, it retained British legislative jurisdiction over the British North America Act and its future amendment.

This exercise was essentially one of executive federalism in Canada. While there was debate on the issue in Parliament, the joint address reflected the position agreed upon by the Prime Minister and the premiers and was adopted as such.

THE THIRD EXERCISE (1935)

A special committee was established by the House of Commons in February 1935 to study and report on the best method of amending the British North America Act so that the federal Parliament might be given adequate power to deal effectively with economic problems which were essentially national in scope.

The mandate of this committee arose out of concern that, at the height of the Depression and with a dust bowl undermining agriculture on the prairies, there was an imbalance between the fiscal resources of the federal government and the legislative powers of the provinces, which were responsible for social policy.

The committee addressed two key issues: the need for specific amendments to deal with economic problems confronting Canada and the broader question of agreement on amending procedures. The committee sought the views of the provincial governments on amendment procedures, but was rebuffed. In the circumstances, the committee did not recommend any form of amendment procedure and proposed instead that a federal-provincial conference be convened on an urgent basis to consider amendments to the distribution of powers and a clarification of powers of taxation.

This was a unilateral federal legislative exercise which sought, without success, to establish a dialogue between the provincial governments or executives and a legislative committee of Parliament.

THE FOURTH EXERCISE (1935–36)

The Federal-Provincial Conference of the Prime Minister and the Premiers in 1935 established a sub-committee of attorneys general which considered the work of the House of Commons committee referred to above. This group in turn established, in January 1936, a federal-provincial committee of officials: the Continuing Committee on Constitutional Questions.

The committee approved an amending procedure that was remarkable in a number of respects:

- matters concerning the federal government only could be amended by an act of the Parliament of Canada, but these matters were, in fact, extensive, including:

    - the office of Governor General and the offices of lieutenant-governor;

    - the constitution of the Privy Council;

    - the constitution, membership and powers of the Senate (except for the representation of the provinces in the Senate);

    - the constitution, membership and powers of the House of Commons (except for the representation of the provinces in the House); and

    - the Consolidated Revenue Fund;

- matters concerning the federal government and one or more, but not all, provinces could be amended by an act of Parliament with the assent by resolution of the legislative assembly of each province concerned;

- most matters concerning the federal government and all of the provinces (including most of the federal and provincial legislative powers) could be amended by an act of Parliament with the assent by resolution of the legislative assemblies of two-thirds of the provinces representing at least 55 percent of the population of Canada, but amendments respecting two matters — property and civil rights in the province and matters of a merely local or private nature in the province — would be subject to provincial opting out (that is, the amendments would not apply to dissenting provinces);

- specially protected matters could only be amended by an act of Parliament with the assent by resolution of the legislative assemblies of all the provinces, including:

  - the vesting of executive power in the Queen;

  - the number of senators and the representation of the provinces in the Senate;

  - provisions for the representation of the provinces in the House of Commons;

  - certain exclusive provincial legislative powers (including jurisdiction over provincial offices and officers, provincial lands and timber resources, municipal institutions, solemnization of marriage in the province, administration of justice in the province, the imposition of punishment for enforcing provincial law, education and the use of English and French languages federally, in Quebec and in Manitoba).

This detailed proposal did a number of things that, given the procedures ultimately adopted in 1982, are significant:

- it distinguished between specially protected matters that would require unanimous consent; matters subject to a more flexible formula that required support not only by a special majority of the provinces (two-thirds), but also a national demographic majority (55 percent); and matters requiring only the consent of Parliament and the provinces concerned;

- it provided for provincial opting out of amendments respecting certain provincial legislative powers; and

- amendments would be achieved through concerted action by the legislative assemblies and Parliament.

This exercise was, par excellence, an example of executive federalism. Nothing came of the committee's recommendations in the short term, although, as noted, some concepts would resurface.

THE FIFTH EXERCISE (1949)

The federal government attempted and succeeded in the "partial patriation" of the Constitution in 1949. Although the provinces had the power, under section 92(1), to amend their own constitutions, Parliament did not have a similar power. Thus, amendments to the British North America Act by the United Kingdom Parliament were required to clarify the privileges, immunities and powers of the Canadian Parliament (1875), to provide for territorial representation in Parliament (1886), to create a deputy speaker for the Senate (1895), to extend the life of Parliament in time of war (1916) and to postpone the redistribution of seats in the House of Commons during a time of war (1943). A limited power to amend the Constitution of Canada was granted to the Parliament of Canada by a 1949 British statute under a new section 91(1) of the British North America Act. However, this power did not extend to:

■ the exclusive legislative powers of the provinces or the rights and privileges of the provincial legislatures and governments;

■ provisions of the Constitution respecting the use of the English and French languages; or

■ the requirement of an annual session of Parliament and the limit of five years on the life of a Parliament (but the life of Parliament could be extended in time of real or apprehended war, invasion or insurrection if not opposed by more than one-third of the members of the House of Commons).

The matters excluded from the power of Parliament to amend the Constitution of Canada would remain under the authority of the British Parliament until agreement could be secured on full patriation of the Constitution.

The unilateral decision by Ottawa in 1949 to abolish appeals from the Supreme Court to the Judicial Committee of the Privy Council in London was a further example of partial patriation of the Constitution. As noted in the Introduction, judicial interpretation is one of the methods of amending or adapting the constitution of a state to changing circumstances. By unilateral legislative action, the Government of Canada established the Supreme Court of Canada as the court of last resort for the federation and the ultimate arbiter of constitutional disagreements between the federal and provincial governments.

THE SIXTH EXERCISE (1950)

Having secured a "partial patriation" of the Constitution through unilateral federal action, Prime Minister Louis Saint-Laurent sought to complete the job by convening a federal-provincial conference which met in Ottawa in January and in Quebec City in September 1950.

No agreement was reached on amending procedures during this exercise in executive federalism. However, the discussions were notable in one respect. The provinces were highly critical of the unilateral nature of the "partial patriation" of 1949 and the new section 91(1) which, they felt, went too far. Prime Minister Saint-Laurent agreed that section 91(1) could be repealed, but only in the context of agreement on an overall set of procedures to amend the Constitution. Ultimately, section 91(1) was repealed at the time of patriation in 1982.

The principle of the delegation of legislative authority was also discussed by governments in 1950. Only Parliament can legislate on matters of exclusive federal jurisdiction and only provincial legislative assemblies can legislate on matters of exclusive provincial jurisdiction. If Parliament and the legislative assemblies could delegate their exclusive legislative powers to each other, it would allow for a great deal of flexibility in practice: some provinces could delegate jurisdiction over post-secondary education to Parliament, for example, and Parliament could delegate powers over seacoast fisheries to certain provinces without having to resort to a cumbersome amendment procedure applicable to all provinces.

The Supreme Court of Canada was to rule, however, that such delegation would undermine the constitutional distribution of powers between the federal and provincial governments and was therefore not possible under Canada's existing constitutional arrangements. The Supreme Court also was to rule that Parliament and the legislative assemblies of the provinces could delegate limited powers of subordinate legislation or regulation to third parties, whether they be their own agencies, the agencies of the other order of government or non-governmental bodies. For example, Parliament could delegate regulatory powers over interprovincial trade (an exclusive federal legislative power) to the Prince Edward Island Potato Marketing Board (a provincial agency) and the provinces could delegate certain regulatory powers to federal agencies.

The advantage of being able to delegate legislative authority is that it provides for great flexibility. The disadvantages are that it could lead to confusion over the respective responsibilities of the federal and provincial governments and that the delegating body retains the unilateral power to take back the powers it has delegated at any moment. In short, it is not as permanent an arrangement as a constitutional amendment transferring jurisdiction from one order of government to another, and could lead to uncertainty.

Nonetheless, as we shall see, governments demonstrated interest, in subsequent years, in the concept of delegation of legislative authority, particularly as a device to get around rigid amending procedures which might make constitutional amendments transferring legislative jurisdiction impossible to achieve in practice.

THE SEVENTH EXERCISE (1960–61)

Prime Minister John Diefenbaker announced at the First Ministers' Conference in July 1960 that he wished to secure agreement with the provinces on amendment procedures that would lead to patriation of the Constitution. The federal and provincial attorneys general, under the chairmanship of E. D. Fulton, the federal minister, pursued the issue.

Initially, the federal government suggested that the British should terminate their authority over Canada's constitution and provide that amendments be made on the basis of unanimous consent by Parliament and the provincial legislatures. It was thought that once the complete amending formula had been transferred to Canada, a suitable — and more flexible — amending formula could subsequently be agreed upon and enacted with unanimous consent in Canada. As we shall see, Prime Minister Pierre Elliott Trudeau made a similar proposal in March 1976.

However, governments decided to seek agreement on an acceptable formula forthwith, before asking the British to take action.

General agreement among governments emerged on a formula that would confer a general power on the Parliament of Canada to amend the Constitution of Canada by federal law, subject to the following procedures:

■ laws related to the powers, rights and privileges of the provinces, to the use of the English and French languages, to the minimum representation ("senatorial floor") of a province in the House of Commons or to the constitutional amendment procedures would require the unanimous consent of the provincial legislatures;

■ a law relating to one or more, but not all, provinces would require the consent of the legislature of every province to which the amendment applied;

■ a law respecting education would require the consent of the legislature of all provinces, except Newfoundland, and a law affecting education in Newfoundland would require that province's consent; and

■ a law affecting any other provision of the Constitution would require the consent of at least two-thirds of the provinces representing at least 50 percent of the population.

Therefore, amendments would always be initiated in Parliament, and the Senate and House of Commons could each exercise a veto.

The first procedure in this formula would make amendments to the distribution of legislative powers very difficult to achieve. To overcome the rigidity of the unanimity rule, it was agreed to supplement the amending formula with a specific amendment respecting the distribution of powers.

Under a new section 94A of the British North America Act, 1867, Parliament would be empowered to delegate the power to make laws in any area of federal legislative jurisdiction if at least four provinces agreed to the delegation, and four provinces (or fewer under certain circumstances) could delegate provincial legislative jurisdiction to Parliament over provincial prisons, local works and undertakings, property and civil rights or local or private matters. However, whatever was delegated could be recalled at any time by Parliament or the provincial legislatures.

Under the terms of the new section 94A, the delegation of legislative jurisdiction would be the exercise of a legislative power: it would be a legislative supplement to the amending formula to provide greater flexibility in practice, but it would not be part of the formula.

Questions about the power of Parliament to achieve amendments without provincial concurrence under section 91(1) (Parliament's capacity to amend the Constitution in all areas not covered by the new procedures) remained unresolved and the "Fulton formula" of 1960–61 (with its adjunct respecting legislative delegation) was not acted upon.

THE EIGHTH EXERCISE (1964)

At the First Ministers' Conference at Charlottetown in September 1964, Prime Minister Lester B. Pearson and the premiers agreed to resolve the patriation issue without delay.

In October 1964, attorneys general, meeting under the chairmanship of Guy Favreau, the federal minister, agreed on a modified version of the "Fulton formula" that would clarify the federal unilateral power to amend the Constitution of Canada (section 91[1]) and integrate both it and the provincial power to amend provincial constitutions (section 92[1]) into the formula. The federal unilateral power to amend the Constitution was restricted to matters relating to the executive government of Canada and the Senate and House of Commons.

Agreement was also reached on including a French version of the new act respecting the amending formula and the delegation of legislative authority in a schedule that would make it (the French version) official. The British North America Act of 1867 and the amendments to it adopted by the British Parliament in English only would continue to be official in that language alone.

Unanimous agreement was reached in October 1964 by first ministers on this revised proposal, which became known as the "Fulton-Favreau formula" (see Appendix 3). The proposal had been developed exclusively through the operation of executive federalism — that is, through negotiations between the Government of Canada and the provincial governments.

However, the Government of Quebec had established the practice of seeking legislative approval of proposed constitutional amendments before giving its definitive consent. The government of Premier Jean Lesage submitted the Fulton-Favreau proposal to the legislative assembly in January 1965, but it soon became apparent that approval would not be secured easily. A *colloque* on the issue was organized at the Université de Montréal on March 18, 1965. Pierre Laporte and René Lévesque, ministers in the Lesage government, defended the Fulton-Favreau formula.

Mr. Lévesque maintained that it would merely put into law the existing practice: it would be neither easier nor more difficult for Quebec to achieve a *statut particulier* after patriation on the basis of the proposed formula.

The two ministers were opposed by Professor Jacques-Yvan Morin of the law faculty. The latter had no problem with the "rigidity" of the Fulton-Favreau formula as such, as long as a new distribution of powers were secured beforehand that would provide Quebec with all the exclusive and shared legislative powers it would need to ensure its own self-fulfilment within Canada. If such a new set of arrangements were not put in place prior to patriation, he feared the Fulton-Favreau formula would become a straitjacket that would prevent Quebec from achieving the powers he deemed essential for its future progress.

Professor Morin clearly won the hearts and minds of the students, and it soon became apparent that public opinion in Quebec was leaning in his favour. In these circumstance, Premier Lesage wrote to Prime Minister Pearson in January 1966 to say that he would no longer seek the consent of Quebec's legislative assembly to the Fulton-Favreau formula, which was a precondition for that province's acceptance of the terms of patriation.

This exercise had been confined to executive federation until Quebec turned to the legislative assembly and the *colloque* at the Université de Montréal permitted a degree of public participation.

THE NINTH EXERCISE (1968–71)

The Quiet Revolution in Quebec began in 1960 and quickly picked up steam. Notwithstanding the euphoria surrounding centennial celebrations in 1967 and the success of Expo 67 in Montreal, tensions within Confederation were apparent and separatist sentiments — and even acts of terrorism — were on the rise in Quebec.

The separatist ghost at the federalist banquet could no longer be ignored after General de Gaulle cried "Vive le Québec libre!" from the balcony of Montreal's Hôtel de ville on July 24, 1967.

Prime Minister Pearson, nearing his retirement, had no desire to reopen the constitutional file. In the absence of federal leadership on the issue, Premier John Robarts of Ontario convened a conference on the Confederation of Tomorrow in Toronto, November 27 to 30, 1967. The federal government declined to attend such a conference convened under provincial auspices.

Premier Robarts, recognizing that nothing concrete could be achieved without the participation of the federal government and that the provinces would hold strongly divergent views — support for the status quo to pressure for radical reform in the case of Quebec — decided to turn the conference into a public education exercise.

He introduced, for the first time in Canadian history, television cameras in a meeting of the executive heads of government (albeit without the participation of the federal government). As it turned out, the gamble paid off: the conference aroused a great deal of public interest and the premiers — many of whom were strong and colourful personalities, such as Joey Smallwood of Newfoundland and W. A. C. Bennett of British Columbia — gained a national platform to expound their views on Canada's future. It was an exercise in executive federalism, with the public able to observe but not participate.

The federal government clearly lost political points through its non-participation. Prime Minister Pearson, who had planned a first ministers' conference on reform of the criminal code for February 1968, announced that the agenda of that conference would be expanded to include the Constitution. He also decided that the conference would be televised. The Minister of Justice would be the key aide to the Prime Minister on both issues before the conference — reform of the criminal code and the Constitution. The incumbent, Pierre Elliott Trudeau, would emerge two months later as Mr. Pearson's successor as Prime Minister of Canada.

In February 1968, the federal and provincial governments began the first-ever federal-provincial comprehensive review of the Constitution. Parts of the proceedings were public and televised. The issues raised were far ranging and dealt with rights and freedoms (including language rights), national institutions, the distribution of powers, regional disparities and patriation with an amending formula.

The "Victoria formula" that emerged three years later from intergovernmental negotiations (see Appendix 4) represented an attempt to find a more flexible approach to amendment than the Fulton-Favreau formula of 1964, which required unanimous consent for key issues, such as the distribution of powers. The federal government was convinced that a formula which did not offer protection to Quebec — as the sole province with a francophone majority and a civil code — would not fly. The federal government was also convinced that protection offered to Quebec (for example, a constitutional veto) could not be denied to Ontario, which had a larger population and provided a larger proportion of the gross national product.

In looking for models that treated Ontario and Quebec, but no other province, in a special way, federal authorities took note of the existing formula for representation in the Senate:

■ Ontario and Quebec had equality of representation in the Senate, with 24 senators each;

■ The four Western provinces had 24 senators combined (six senators each); and

■ The Maritime provinces also had 24 senators combined (10 for Nova Scotia, 10 for New Brunswick and four for Prince Edward Island).

The symmetry of the Senate arrangements was spoiled by the addition of six extra seats for Newfoundland in 1949 and one for each of the two territories in 1975. Nonetheless, the distribution of Senate seats provided the inspiration for the Victoria formula, which divided Canada into four regions for the purposes of amending those parts of the Constitution that could not be amended by Parliament acting alone (the executive government of Canada and the Senate and House of Commons, with certain restrictions), by the provinces acting alone (the provincial constitutions, with certain restrictions), or by Parliament and the provinces concerned in the case of bilateral or multilateral amendments.

The general procedure for amendments would require the approval of:

■ the Senate (with a suspensive veto of three months which could be overridden by a second vote in the House of Commons);

- the House of Commons (which would have an absolute veto);

- the legislative assembly of any province having or having had at any time 25 percent of the population (this would provide a permanent veto for Ontario and Quebec, even if in the future Quebec's population fell below 25 percent, and it would not preclude any province that became very populous in the future from gaining a veto);

- the legislative assemblies of at least two of the four Atlantic provinces; and

- the legislative assembly of at least two of the four Western provinces that have, according to the latest general census, at least 50 percent of the population of the Western provinces.

A few observations are in order:

- Amendments would be made by proclamation issued by the Governor General under the Great Seal of Canada when authorized by the appropriate number of legislative bodies, and not by a federal law with provincial concurrence as proposed in the Fulton-Favreau formula.

- There was a reticence about identifying Ontario and Quebec by name as the only two provinces that would exercise a veto: the Victoria formula spelled out the names of the four Atlantic provinces and the four Western provinces, but nowhere are Quebec and Ontario mentioned directly.

- The procedure for legislative authorization in the Atlantic provinces would allow for adoption of an amendment approved by provinces representing a minority of the population (Prince Edward Island and Newfoundland), even though opposed by provinces representing the majority (Nova Scotia and New Brunswick).

- The procedure for approval in the Western provinces — with its demographic qualification — was more democratic, but the reason for the qualification was dictated by politics and not democratic theory: British Columbia, with a rising population and bright future prospects, wished to be treated as a fifth region with its own veto. The population qualification was designed to recognize the special strength of British Columbia and to ensure that an amendment not supported by that province could only pass if approved by the three Prairie provinces.

■   The Victoria formula introduced the concept of a suspensive veto for the Senate (the Senate had an absolute veto under the Fulton-Favreau formula).

Discussions on the amending procedures took place in the context of a much broader examination of constitutional renewal. First ministers launched the process at a conference that was largely televised in February 1968, but it was an open-ended exercise. First ministers gave a mandate to committees of ministers and officials to pursue discussions on specific items; they were to report back to first ministers who would deliberate and then provide a new mandate to ministers or officials as the case might be.

The process was essentially an exercise in executive federalism, with public involvement limited to the televising of plenary sessions of first ministers. Initially, the federal government had been reluctant to open up the constitutional debate, and did so largely in response to Premier Robarts's Confederation of Tomorrow Conference. But the introduction of television at the plenary sessions soon changed the dynamics.

Premiers began to use their televised opening statements as an opportunity to raise non-constitutional issues and to criticize the federal government in areas of exclusive federal jurisdiction (for example, monetary policy and freight rates). As the process continued over three years, the federal government became concerned that the debate was absorbing a great deal of the time of elected officials and public servants, that the numerous meetings of first ministers, ministers and officials were not without cost, and that — after three years — there was nothing yet to show for the investment of time, effort and resources. Between February 1968 and September 1970, there were five meetings of first ministers, eight meetings of ministers, twelve meetings of officials and fourteen sub-committee meetings of officials.

Furthermore, the federal government was of the view that premiers were using the televised plenary sessions of first ministers to become regional spokesmen on national issues under federal jurisdiction and that a temporary respite from the high frequency of meetings would be welcome.

Accordingly, the Minister of Justice, John Turner, visited provincial capitals in January 1971 to seek agreement on a modest package of constitutional changes and an amending formula that would permit patriation of the Constitution as a first step in the process of constitutional renewal. The process could subsequently be pursued in Canada, with no further reference to the United Kingdom.

The package ultimately submitted to first ministers at Victoria, British Columbia, in June 1971 contained provisions respecting political rights, language rights, a commitment to the principle of equalization, provincial participation in the appointment of justices of the Supreme Court of Canada and the amending procedures that became known as the Victoria formula. The package also included a new section 94A which would expand the capacity of Parliament to legislate in the area of social policy, subject to provincial paramountcy. No new legislative powers for the provinces — a matter of special interest to Quebec at the time — were included.

Although the proposed amending formula was "flexible," first ministers agreed on a "rigid" procedure to implement patriation of the Constitution:

- all provincial legislative assemblies and the two Houses of Parliament would have to authorize the proclamation of the constitutional package (including the amending procedures) by the Governor General;

- the United Kingdom would legislate to recognize the validity of the Governor General's eventual proclamation and to terminate British legislative authority over Canada's constitution; and

- the Governor General's proclamation would be issued on a date to coincide with the effective date of the British law.

The Victoria conference concluded on June 16 with an agreement in principle by all first ministers on the "Canadian Constitutional Charter, 1971," or, more popularly, "the Victoria Charter." It was to be reported to all participating governments for consideration and they had until June 28 to signify acceptance of the Charter as a whole. Quebec indicated on June 23 that it could not recommend the Charter to the National Assembly because the provisions of the revised section 94A on income security allowed for a degree of uncertainty not in keeping with the objectives of constitutional review.

A general election was held in Saskatchewan on June 23, 1971. In view of Quebec's decision not to proceed with the Charter, the new government in Saskatchewan took no action to confirm or reject it.

A special joint committee of the Senate and House of Commons (the Molgat-MacGuigan Committee) worked concurrently from 1970 to 1972 on constitutional renewal and patriation with an amending formula, but when it reported in 1972, the time was not ripe to pursue the issue.

THE TENTH EXERCISE (1975–77)

Following a successful resolution of differences between the federal and provincial governments in the area of social policy, Prime Minister Trudeau felt that the climate might again be ripe for reaching agreement on the patriation of the Constitution.

Accordingly, during a private meeting to discuss energy policy with the premiers in April 1975 at 7 Rideau Gate (the Government of Canada's official guest house just outside the grounds of the Governor General's residence, Rideau Hall), the Prime Minister raised the possibility of patriating the Constitution.

There was an agreement in principle among first ministers on the desirability of patriating the Constitution with an amending formula and of leaving the issue of substantive changes to the Constitution aside until after patriation had been achieved. This agreement was subject to Quebec premier Robert Bourassa's condition that patriation would have to be accompanied by "constitutional guarantees" for the French language and culture. It was also agreed that discussions would take the Victoria amending formula as the point of departure.

The process adopted for pursuing the issue was unique in a number of respects. Discussions would be "secret": there would be no public announcement that the patriation debate had been opened up again. Furthermore, discussions would take place through a series of bilateral meetings between the Secretary to the Cabinet for Federal-Provincial Relations, Gordon Robertson, supported by federal officials, and the premier of each province (or a minister designated by the premier), supported by provincial officials.

Three problems began to emerge as Mr. Robertson travelled across the country:

- various provincial governments felt that patriation would be more meaningful and more acceptable if certain substantive changes already agreed upon in the Victoria Charter of 1971 were established in the Constitution at the same time;

- some of the western premiers felt that the procedure for consenting to amendments in the Western provinces should be the same as in the Atlantic provinces: that is, the 50 percent of the population qualification in the Western provinces (designed to recognize British Columbia's special demographic strength) should be dropped; and

- federal and Quebec officials had difficulty in agreeing on how to handle the "constitutional guarantees" for the French language and culture.

The last issue was particularly difficult to resolve. After lengthy discussions, the federal authorities submitted a draft to Quebec in November 1975 which would constitute a negative imperative: "neither the Parliament nor the Government of Canada, in the exercise of their respective powers, shall act in a manner that will adversely affect the preservation and development of the French language and the culture based on it" (see Appendix 5, Part IV of the draft Proclamation). The effectiveness of this approach and, indeed, the approach itself were questioned by some in Quebec City.

There were leaks from Quebec City about the secret negotiations early in the new year. Premiers from other provinces who had not participated in bilateral discussions since the period of May to July 1975 asked for a report on the current state of play. In the circumstances, the Prime Minister spoke to Premier Bourassa on March 5, 1976, to ascertain his position. Premier Bourassa made it clear that the guarantees he envisaged might well relate to changes in the distribution of powers to provide for Quebec jurisdiction over matters deemed essential for the French language and culture. The federal government remained opposed to opening up a discussion on the distribution of powers prior to patriation, although it was willing to envisage a constitutional provision respecting agreements between the federal and provincial governments on the exercise of their powers in areas of special concern for the French language and culture.

Prime Minister Trudeau decided to report to all premiers and to share with them the federal draft that had been drawn up on the basis of discussions to that date. The draft would:

- secure patriation on the basis of the Victoria formula (with no change respecting consent by the Western provinces);

- establish in the Constitution some changes that had been agreed to in the Canadian Constitutional Charter, 1971 respecting the Supreme Court of Canada, language rights in areas of federal jurisdiction and the reduction of regional disparities; and

- entrench in the Constitution the negative imperative regarding the French language and culture and underline the capacity of the federal and provincial governments to reach agreements on the exercise of their powers, particularly in the fields of immigration, communications and social policy.

Failing agreement with Quebec, the Prime Minister wrote to the premiers on March 31, 1976, to set out "three alternatives" for consideration (see Appendix 5). He noted that the Government of Canada "is not prepared to contemplate the continuation" of British legislative authority over Canada's constitution and said patriation could be achieved by means of an address of the two houses of the Canadian Parliament to the Queen asking for appropriate legislation by the British Parliament to terminate its jurisdiction over Canada.

- Under the first alternative, the British would end their authority over Canada's constitution and provide that amendments to those parts of the Constitution not currently amendable in Canada could be made on the unanimous consent of Parliament and the legislatures until a permanent formula were established.

- The second alternative would be the same as above, but with a "permanent" formula, perhaps along the lines of the Victoria formula, set out in the Constitution and to come into effect at such time as approved by the legislatures of all the provinces.

- The third alternative would be the same as the first, but with the whole federal draft set out in the Constitution and to come into effect when the entirety of its provisions had been approved by the legislatures of all the provinces.

A senior official in Quebec City asked the British consul whether the British would act upon a unilateral request from the Parliament of Canada. The consul communicated with the High

Commissioner in Ottawa. The British determined that the appropriate way to get a policy position on the matter would be through a question in the Parliament at Westminster. As befitted the relations between two sovereign states that were close allies, British officials consulted with federal officials in Ottawa on a possible question and the reply to it.

On June 9, 1976, a Member of the British Parliament, John Cartwright, placed a written question on the order paper at Westminster respecting the issue. On June 10, the British Secretary of State, Roy Hattersly, replied:

> The British North America Acts, which contain the Constitution of Canada, can be amended in certain important respects only by Act of the United Kingdom Parliament. The Canadian Prime Minister has expressed publicly the desire of the Canadian Government that this power of amendment should be a matter of Canadian competence and should no longer be exercisable by the United Kingdom Parliament. If a request to effect such a change were to be received from the Parliament of Canada it would be in accordance with precedent for the United Kingdom Government to introduce in Parliament, and for Parliament to enact, appropriate legislation in compliance with the request.

During the course of a meeting with the premiers on June 14, Mr. Trudeau asked them for their views on his letter of March 31, 1976. They asked for more time to respond and said the issue would be on the agenda of the annual premiers' conference in Alberta in August of that year.

Officials from Quebec travelled across the country during the summer to secure broad provincial support for the preferred position of Quebec: that patriation should not occur without simultaneous amendments to the Constitution, particularly with respect to the distribution of powers. The premiers were unable to finalize a common position at their annual conference, and Premier Peter Lougheed of Alberta, chairman of the conference, informed the Prime Minister they would meet again in Toronto on October 1 and 2 to do so.

On October 14, 1976, Premier Lougheed wrote to the Prime Minister to say that there was consensus among the premiers on the objective of patriation. They also agreed that patriation should not be undertaken without a consensus being developed on an expansion of the role or jurisdiction of the provinces in the following areas: culture, communications, the Supreme Court of Canada, spending power, Senate representation and regional disparities.

With respect to the amending formula, Premier Lougheed noted:

> Considerable time was spent on this important subject and the unanimous agreement of the provinces was not secured on a specific formula. Eight provinces agreed to the amending formula as drafted in Victoria in 1971 and as proposed by you in your draft proclamation. British Columbia wishes to have the Victoria formula modified to reflect its view that British Columbia should be treated as a distinct entity with its own separate veto. In this sense it would be in the same position as Ontario and Quebec. Alberta held to the view that a constitutional amending formula should not permit an amendment that would take away rights, proprietary interests and jurisdiction from any province without the concurrence of that province. In this regard, Alberta was referring to matters arising under Section 92, 93 and 109 of the British North America Act.

It was clear that there was no longer support by the premiers for the limited exercise Mr. Trudeau had launched in April 1975. Furthermore, the popularity of the Prime Minister had dipped precipitously in the polls since the spring and, whatever the legal position, he no longer had the political legitimacy to pursue unilateral patriation as proposed in his letter of March 31.

The election on November 15, 1976, of a Parti Québécois government committed to holding a referendum on sovereignty-association presented further difficulties. In a letter to the premiers on January 19, 1977, Prime Minister Trudeau set out the federal position. In his view, the October 1976 position of the premiers was either too much or too little. It was too much in relation to the initial agreement in principle of April 1975 on a limited patriation exercise and it was too little in raising some, but not all, of the distribution of powers items that might form part of an eventual comprehensive and coherent approach to constitutional reform. Mr. Trudeau made a revised proposal for a limited exercise that would set aside the distribution of powers for a subsequent phase — but effectively, this brought the exercise to an end.

THE ELEVENTH EXERCISE (1978–79)

Having abandoned intergovernmental discussions, the federal government decided to establish its own position on constitutional renewal and patriation before engaging the provinces once again in negotiations.

After intensive work by officials and a Cabinet committee, the federal government published on June 12, 1978, *A Time for Action,* which set out its approach to constitutional change. Reform would be carried out in two phases. The first phase would cover matters under federal jurisdiction, and the second would cover areas in which the cooperation and consent of the provinces would be required.

On June 20, 1978, the Government of Canada tabled Bill C-60 (the Constitutional Amendment Bill) in the House of Commons. This represented the federal government's position on the first phase of renewal in areas under federal jurisdiction. Bill C-60 would:

- replace the Senate with a new body, the House of the Federation;

- enlarge the Supreme Court of Canada, provide for provincial participation in the appointment of Supreme Court judges and stipulate that only Quebec judges could rule on matters concerning Quebec civil law;

- provide for certain federal-provincial mechanisms (there would be an annual meeting of first ministers; certain payments to the provinces would be protected from sudden and arbitrary termination; there would be consultation with the provinces on the appointment of lieutenant-governors and on invoking the federal "declaratory power");

- clarify the role of the monarchy;

- ensure that the functions of Cabinet and the Prime Minister were spelled out in the Constitution; and

- set out a charter of rights and freedoms binding on the federal order of government that provinces could opt into.

Bill C-60 was sent to a special joint committee of the Senate and House of Commons. Two parts of the bill attracted a great deal of criticism: the attempts to clarify the role of the monarchy and the position of the Governor General were denounced as anti-monarchical; and the proposed House of the Federation was highly complex and unacceptable to many, including some senators on the special joint committee from the Government's own caucus. Indeed, senators established a separate Senate committee on the Government's constitutional initiative.

The special joint committee adopted a resolution asking the federal government to refer to the Supreme Court Parliament's capacity to amend or abolish the Senate. The Government of Canada announced on September 14 that it would make a reference to the Supreme Court on the matter.

There were already two British North America acts enacted by the Parliament of Canada to amend the Senate. The British North America Act, 1975 (No. 2) provided for the appointment of one senator each to represent the Yukon and the Northwest Territories in the Canadian Senate. This was enacted under the authority of the British North America Act, 1886 of the United Kingdom Parliament, which empowered the Canadian Parliament to provide from time to time for the representation of the territories in the Senate and House of Commons. It was a proper exercise of the legislative powers of Parliament under the Constitution of Canada.

The second amendment was more problematic. The British North America Act, 1867 provided that senators would have tenure for life. The Canadian Parliament, by the British North America Act, 1965, reduced tenure to the age of 75 years. The Supreme Court of Canada, in its ruling of December 21, 1979, declared that "the imposition of compulsory retirement at age seventy-five did not change the essential character of the Senate" and was, therefore, within the legislative competence of Parliament.

However, in the same judgment, the Supreme Court assessed Parliament's power to achieve fundamental change in the Senate or to replace it and concluded: "In our opinion, its fundamental character cannot be altered by unilateral action by the Parliament of Canada and section 91(1) does not give that power."

Oddly enough, the Supreme Court addressed another amendment issue at almost the same time in the Forest case. On December 13, 1979, the Supreme Court passed judgment on Manitoba's power to amend section 23 of the Manitoba Act, 1870 respecting the use of French and English in that province. In 1890, the legislature of Manitoba abolished the compulsory use of French in the journals and records of the legislative assembly — a provision which reflected the obligations of section 133 of the British North America Act, 1867 placed on Parliament and the legislature of Quebec.

Paragraph 131(4) of Bill C-60 would have repealed section 23 of the Manitoba Act, 1870 on the use of French and English if the Charter of Rights and Freedoms were entrenched through adoption by all provinces. It would also have repealed section 133 of the British North America Act, 1867, but the new charter would make the same provision applicable to both Quebec and New Brunswick, although not to Manitoba.

It is one of the not infrequent ironies of Canada's constitutional development that the federal government was prepared to acquiesce in the unilateral abolition of French language rights in Manitoba by the provincial legislature while at the same time it was involved, through financial support, in the challenge of Georges Forest of St. Boniface, who claimed Manitoba's unilateral abolition of French language rights in 1890 had been unconstitutional.

As part of the first phase of constitutional change, the Government of Canada published a discussion paper, *The Canadian Constitution and Constitutional Amendment.* The paper reviewed the Fulton-Favreau formula and the Victoria formula, and examined the possibility of supplementing the Victoria formula with an "appeal procedure": if sufficient provincial legislative assemblies supported an amendment so that it would pass in the four regions and Parliament were opposed, an appeal to the people through a referendum could be held if the provinces so requested; and if three regions and Parliament were of one mind, an appeal to the people in the dissenting region through a regional referendum could be held. The paper also examined the possibility of resorting to referendums exclusively for certain constitutional amendments and raised the issue of popular initiative whereby an amendment proposal could be initiated if a certain minimum percentage of registered voters supported it.

While the federal government was pursuing its "phase one" approach to constitutional renewal, the premiers met for their annual meeting from August 9 to 12, 1978, at Regina and Waskesin Lake, Saskatchewan. They stated in their communiqué on constitutional reform that "the division of powers is the key issue in constitutional reform, and should be addressed in conjunction with other matters." They set out the issues upon which there was a consensus among the premiers and they commented on the federal initiative. In particular, they opposed changes to the monarchy, called the House of the Federation unworkable, expressed some concern about entrenched rights and sought to protect provincial jurisdiction over resources.

Prime Minister Trudeau convened the premiers to a first ministers' conference in Ottawa from October 30 to November 1, 1978. He proposed an agenda for constitutional renewal that would embrace the key elements of Bill C-60 and the principal concerns raised by the premiers. All participants agreed on the agenda and a concentrated series of discussions that would lead to a second first ministers' conference on the Constitution in February 1979.

The process adopted was one of executive federalism. Negotiations were conducted in private by the Continuing Committee of Ministers on the Constitution (CCMC), supported by the Continuing Committee of Officials on the Constitution (CCOC), which represented the federal and provincial governments. Each government had two ministers on the CCMC.

The CCMC, supported by the CCOC, would meet three times: at Mont Ste-Marie, Quebec, from November 23 to 25; in Toronto, Ontario, from December 14 to 16, and in Vancouver, British Columbia, from January 22 to 24, 1979. At the beginning of each session, ministers would review each item on the agenda and provide a mandate for a sub-committee of officials to pursue discussions on each item. The sub-committees would take matters as far as they could within the mandate given them and report back to ministers during the latter part of each session. A special meeting of officials was held in Ottawa on January 11 and 12, 1979.

Quebec participated in the discussion of all matters save the issue of patriation with an amending formula, which, it argued, should not be discussed until after agreement had been reached on the substance of a new Constitution.

At the Toronto meeting, ministers arrived at a general consensus on a formula that would require unanimity for the amendment of matters on a short list (including the formula itself and provincial ownership and jurisdiction over natural resources), and the consent of Parliament and at least seven provinces representing at least 85 percent of the population of Canada for most matters of general application.

The 7/85 procedure, which became known as the "Toronto consensus," was designed to accommodate the principle of the equality of the provinces: no province was explicitly accorded an individual veto. As a practical matter, however, the high population qualification would guarantee that both Ontario and Quebec would exercise a veto. The first discussions on this approach centred on a 7/75 procedure, but since demographic trends suggested that Quebec might soon dip below 25 percent of the population, it was changed to 7/80 and then to 7/85 when it was suggested that Quebec might, under some scenarios, fall below 20 percent.

The Toronto consensus did not represent a full agreement among governments. Alberta, with the backing of its legislative assembly, said the amending formula should "reflect the principle that existing rights, proprietary interests and jurisdiction of a province cannot be taken away without the consent of that province." British Columbia preferred that a reconstituted Senate (rather than the legislative assemblies of the provinces) approve amendments.

At the Vancouver meeting in January 1979, Alberta presented an alternative amending formula the principal feature of which was a general amending procedure requiring the support of the Senate (suspensive veto only), the House of Commons and two-thirds (i.e., seven) of the provincial legislative assemblies representing at least 50 percent of the population. However, a province could dissent and opt out of any amendment affecting the powers, rights, privileges, assets, property or natural resources of the province. This alternative became known as the Vancouver formula or the 7/50 formula and formed the basis of the formula ultimately adopted in 1982. As noted earlier, opting out of some amendments affecting the provinces was a feature of the formula proposed by officials in 1936.

When first ministers met on February 5 and 6, 1979, any semblance of consensus on the amending formula issue was gone. Four formulae were submitted to first ministers for consideration:

■ the Toronto consensus;

■ the Vancouver formula;

■ the Victoria formula; and

■ the Fulton-Favreau formula.

First ministers also considered draft provisions on the separate but related issue of the delegation of legislative authority. Ultimately, full agreement on an amending formula was not secured. Indeed, at the close of the conference, there was unanimous agreement on only one item: the federal government accepted the joint position of the provinces that no attempt should be made to alter the provisions of the Constitution respecting the monarchy.

There were two schools of thought as to why the February 1979 conference ended in failure. Some argued that public opinion polls made it clear that Prime Minister Trudeau, in the fifth year of his mandate, was expected to be defeated in the upcoming federal elections. Furthermore, it was felt that the Leader of the Opposition, Joe Clark, would be more sympathetic to provincial aspirations and that better arrangements, from a provincial perspective, might be struck with a new Conservative government. Thus, there was little incentive to resolve the constitutional question before the elections.

Others argued that failure should be attributed to the process on two accounts. The first problem with the process was that first ministers aimed at achieving "a consensus" on each item on the agenda. While consensus seemed to be a somewhat flexible notion, it amounted in practice to unanimous agreement by first ministers on the explicit legal texts for each item: it was, in fact, a very rigid process.

The second problem was that there were twelve broad issues on the agenda, many of which were, in themselves, highly complex — such as the question of a charter of rights and freedoms and a sharing of jurisdiction in the area of telecommunications. Various delegations engaged in a form of horse-trading symbolized at one point by the expression "Rights for Fish," by which the Prime Minister alleged that the Premier of Newfoundland would not agree to a charter of rights unless his province was provided with appropriate jurisdiction over the fisheries. When the conference ended in failure, the Prime Minister himself seemed to suggest that he would have been willing to decentralize legislative powers significantly — but only if he could get agreement on a charter of rights and on patriation.

THE TWELFTH EXERCISE (1980)

When Mr. Clark assumed power on June 4, 1979, no new public initiative on the Constitution was announced. Rather, exploratory discussions on the 1978–79 constitutional agenda were held privately by the CCMC, supported by the CCOC, in Halifax on October 22 and 23, 1979, and by the CCOC in Toronto on November 15 and 16, 1979, in anticipation of a first ministers' conference on the Constitution in February 1980. However, the Government was defeated on a vote of no confidence on December 13, 1979 and in consequence a new exercise was not formally launched.

Following the federal election on February 18, 1980, attention focused on the upcoming referendum in Quebec.

In its May 1980 referendum, the Government of Quebec sought a mandate from the people of the province to negotiate sovereignty-association with the rest of Canada. During the referendum campaign, Prime Minister Trudeau and the majority of premiers from the other provinces told Quebecers that rejection of the sovereignty-association mandate could and would lead to constitutional renewal. In the event, approximately 60 percent of Quebecers voting in the referendum refused to support the mandate sought by the provincial government.

Intensive negotiations — in the classic Canadian tradition of executive federalism behind closed doors — were held by the federal and provincial governments on a twelve-item agenda during the summer of 1980. The agenda included:

- a constitutional preamble or statement of principles (including the issue of Quebec's distinct society);

- patriation with an amending formula;

- a charter of rights and freedoms;

- institutional reform (the Senate and the Supreme Court);

- increased provincial authority over natural resources, offshore resources, fisheries, communications and family law; and

- increased federal authority over the economy.

The leaders of Canada's Aboriginal peoples were encouraged to make representation to governments on these issues.

When first ministers met in September 1980, they failed to achieve unanimous consent — the litmus test for agreement at that time — on any of the items on the agenda.

On the eve of the September 1980 First Ministers' Conference, a secret memorandum to the federal Cabinet on the state of negotiations and the federal position for the conference was leaked to the other provinces and the press by the Quebec delegation. This document, popularly called the "Kirby Memorandum" because it had been prepared by Michael Kirby, the Secretary to the Cabinet for Federal-Provincial Relations, created consternation.

The section of the Kirby Memorandum dealing with the amending formula (see Appendix 6) proposed that the federal government might consider joining what had emerged during the summer as a majority position on the Vancouver formula (7/50 with opting out) — if that majority position held — on the following conditions:

- opting out would not be available on certain matters of universal applicability, such as Senate reform;

- on matters of special concern to Quebec (the Supreme Court and the use of English and French), where there would be no opting out, there should be a special procedure that would ensure Quebec was party to any change; and

- there should be no obligation to provide compensation for provinces that opt out of amendments.

Part of the reason why the federal government decided it could support the Vancouver formula was that it believed a charter of rights would be entrenched at the time of patriation and therefore would not be subject to opting out at a future time. Furthermore, Parliament would have a veto over all subsequent amendments and could hold out for unanimity if it did not wish to contemplate any province opting out.

A special feature of the Kirby Memorandum proposal was that, for the first time, a federal government was seen to contemplate popular initiative as part of a permanent formula.

It was proposed that, whether a consensus formed around the Alberta proposal or another, the federal government might wish to raise the possibility of citizens being able to initiate referendums in the event of negative action or lack of action by Parliament or legislatures on an amendment proposal. This would support the view that sovereignty ultimately resides in the people.

For example, if seven provinces approved an amendment and Parliament did not, 3 percent of the federal electorate could initiate a national referendum; if a majority of electors voting approved, the result would be binding on Canada.

On the other hand, if Parliament approved an amendment and no province or an insufficient number of provinces approved it, three percent of the provincial electorate in each province that had not acted affirmatively could initiate a provincial referendum. If referendums were carried in a sufficient number of provinces to bring the total of assenting provinces to seven, the amendment would be adopted.

The Conference was marked by a high degree of tension and an inability to reach unanimous consent on any one item. The provinces met privately at the Château Laurier and, with Quebec holding the pen, produced a common stand for the provinces, popularly called the "Château consensus." It was a rather rough document that required further refinement (see Appendix 7). It called for adoption of the Vancouver formula as the general amending procedure (identified in the document as the "Alberta" amending formula) and stated there should be "financial arrangements between governments" on matters subject to opting out. But it also called for adoption of the Victoria amending formula for other unspecified matters. How the two formulae would be combined was not clear.

Although the provinces unanimously agreed to the Château consensus, their agreement was conditional on the whole package being implemented. When the federal government refused to join the consensus, provinces no longer considered themselves bound. This allowed Ontario and New Brunswick to abandon the consensus position following the failure of the September conference.

In assessing the exercise, the federal government concluded that the process was in large measure responsible for failure: there were too many complex issues on the table and the level of consent required was too high. It decided that unilateral federal action was necessary to break the logjam.

THE THIRTEENTH EXERCISE (1980–81)

In October 1980, Prime Minister Trudeau decided to seek unilateral patriation of the Constitution and constitutional change on the basis of a "peoples' package" comprising:

■ a charter of rights and freedoms;

■ a constitutional commitment to the principle of equalization and the reduction of regional disparities; and

■ patriation with a process for adopting an amending formula within two years of patriation.

"Unilateral" patriation referred to a joint address of the two Houses of Parliament to the Queen asking that the United Kingdom Parliament terminate its legislative jurisdiction over Canada's constitution and authorize the proclamation by the Queen in Canada of certain changes to the Constitution of Canada.

Although the Government of Canada had previously sought provincial consent for some amendments before adopting a joint address, the Government maintained that it was not legally required to do so.

The process for adopting a permanent amending formula within two years under the terms of the joint address was quite complex (see Appendix 8).

Immediately after patriation, unanimity would have been required to amend the Constitution for an interim period not to extend beyond two years. During the interim period, governments could seek unanimous agreement on an amending formula and, failing such agreement, if seven provinces representing 80 percent of the population agreed on an alternative, that alternative and the Victoria amending formula (or any other formula preferred by the Government of Canada) would be put to the people in a referendum. However, in the absence of unanimous agreement on an alternative or of a referendum, the Victoria amending formula — which was set out in the unilateral resolution — would automatically come into force after the expiry of the two-year period. Needless to say, this focused public examination on the Victoria formula.

The Victoria formula which would come into effect failing agreement on an alternative or a referendum allowed for ratification of amendments by resolutions adopted by Parliament and the requisite number of provincial legislatures or through a referendum sanctioned by Parliament. In the latter case, the amendment would have to be supported by a national majority and a majority in the requisite number of provinces for an amendment under the Victoria general procedure.

Two provinces — Ontario and New Brunswick — supported "unilateral" patriation, but the majority of provinces were opposed. In Parliament, the federal initiative was supported by the New Democratic Party, but opposed by the Conservative Party. The New Democratic Party caucus ultimately split, with MPs from Saskatchewan joining the forces opposed to the federal plan. Joe Clark, Leader of the Opposition, moved on October 22, 1980, that the Vancouver formula — and not the Victoria formula — be the formula for amending Canada's constitution. A special joint committee of the Senate and House of Commons was created to study the proposed joint address. The federal government initially sought to have the joint address examined without the glare of television and disposed of before Christmas, but political pressure within the committee and Parliament forced it to revise its position on both counts. Hearings began on November 6, 1980, and did not conclude until February 9, 1981. For the first time in Canadian history, the special joint committee submitted a constitutional proposal to televised public parliamentary hearings. The result was to create populist support for the "unilateral" proposal in spite of opposition by most provincial governments. The charter of rights became the focus of attention and succeeding groups argued in favour of entrenched rights.

The eight dissident provinces challenged the "unilateral" patriation attempt through references to the courts of last resort in Manitoba, Quebec and Newfoundland. They also published a document called the *Constitutional Accord: Canadian Patriation Plan* on April 16, 1981, which called for patriation on the basis of the Vancouver formula initially developed by Alberta, complemented with a constitutional requirement for reasonable compensation by Canada to any province that availed itself of the opting-out provision, and special provisions respecting the delegation of legislative authority. However, no other action should accompany this patriation proposal (i.e., there should be no entrenchment of a charter of rights). (See Appendix 9.)

A number of premiers were opposed to an entrenched charter of rights. Premier Sterling Lyon of Manitoba was perhaps the staunchest and most vocal defender of the position that legislatures should remain supreme in law-making and should not be constrained by a charter enforced by non-elected judges. The New Democratic Party feared that a charter might make programs to favour the disadvantaged more difficult to achieve. And Premier René Lévesque of Quebec, committed to sovereignty-association, did not wish to strengthen the bonds of the existing union with a charter.

Premier Lévesque was sharply criticized by Claude Ryan, leader of the Liberal Party of Quebec and Opposition Leader in the National Assembly, for signing the Constitutional Accord of April 16, 1981, because, in so doing, he effectively abandoned Quebec's traditional demand for a veto. Mr. Ryan felt that Quebec should have a veto so that it could play a positive role in Canada's future constitutional evolution rather than removing itself from the application of future amendments by opting out. However, if Premier Lévesque wanted a common front of the dissident eight against an entrenched charter, he had to support the Vancouver formula, a position not popular in Quebec.

In the references launched by the dissident provinces, the courts of last resort in Manitoba and Quebec ruled in favour of the federal government and its unilateral proposal, but in Newfoundland ruled against it. The federal government decided to put a "definitive" unilateral patriation package to the Supreme Court of Canada.

The federal government secured adoption of a resolution by the House of Commons on April 23, 1981, and by the Senate on April 24, 1981, on the text of a joint address to the Queen which would be put to a vote without further amendment if the Supreme Court of Canada found it to be within the competence of Parliament. It was important to have the exact text in hand before asking the Supreme Court to rule upon it; and it was important to ensure that no changes would be made to it following the Supreme Court's ruling, which might call into question, once again, its constitutionality.

The unamendable text adopted in April incorporated certain amendments and it provided for a somewhat different two-year process for adopting a permanent amending formula (see Appendix 10):

■ it would allow for provinces to opt into the English and French language rights provided for under the Charter during the interim period;

■ the alternative formula favoured by seven provinces with at least 80 percent of the population would have to be supported by the legislative assemblies of those provinces and not merely by the governments as permitted under the original proposal;

■ detailed rules for the holding of the referendum on the provincial alternative and the preferred federal option were spelled out, whereas the original proposal had provided that Parliament could make the rules for the referendum; and

■ detailed rules were spelled out for the holding of a referendum sanctioned by Parliament under the "permanent" amending formula, rather than leaving the matter to Parliament.

One other important amendment introduced into the joint address by the federal government was a provision to affirm and strengthen provincial jurisdiction over natural resources. It reflected the "best efforts" draft negotiated during intergovernmental discussions in the summer of 1980. In particular, it would empower provinces, subject to federal paramountcy, to legislate with respect to extra-provincial trade in the area of natural resources — a matter of special concern to the New Democratic Party government of Premier Allan Blakeney of Saskatchewan. The federal government believed that it might be possible thereby to win the Premier's support and to heal the rift within the federal New Democratic Party caucus.

A reference to the Supreme Court of Canada was launched on April 28, 1981. The Court ruled, on September 28, 1981, that "unilateral" patriation was legal, but inconsistent with the convention of the Constitution which required the "substantial" consent of the provinces — more than the support of two, but less than the support of ten. The Court majority declared, on the issue of a convention of the Constitution:

> If a consensus had emerged on the measure of provincial agreement, an amending formula would quickly have been enacted. To demand as much precision as if this were the case and as if the rule were a legal one is tantamount to denying that this area of the Canadian Constitution is capa-

ble of being governed by conventional rules. It would not be appropriate for the Court to devise in the abstract a specific formula which would indicate in positive terms what measure of provincial agreement is required for the convention to be complied with. Conventions by their nature develop in the political field and it will be for the political actors, not the Court, to determine the degree of provincial consent required. It is sufficient for the Court to decide that at least a substantial measure of provincial consent is required and to decide further whether the situation before the Court meets with this requirement. The situation is one where Ontario and New Brunswick agree with the proposed amendments whereas the eight other provinces oppose it. By no conceivable standard could this situation be thought to pass muster. It does not disclose a sufficient measure of provincial agreement.

The decision of the Supreme Court came at a time when tensions were high: the personal animosity between some premiers and the Prime Minister had poisoned the atmosphere and feelings of western alienation were strong. One scholar who had followed the work of the Supreme Court over the years qualified the decision on the convention as "bold statecraft based on questionable jurisprudence." Mr. Trudeau, after leaving office, criticized the decision on a number of grounds. The political actors were, he said in *Fatal Tilt: Speaking Out About Sovereignty*, sharply divided: the federal government, Ontario and New Brunswick maintained that provincial consent was not necessary; seven of the remaining provinces had argued that unanimity was required, and this was the question that had been put to the Court; only Saskatchewan argued that there should be substantial consent.

Mr. Trudeau concluded:

> No doubt believing in good faith that a political agreement would be better for Canada than unilateral legal patriation, they [the majority of the Supreme Court judges] blatantly manipulated the evidence before them so as to arrive at the desired result. They then wrote a judgment which tried to lend a fig-leaf of legality to their preconceived conclusion.
>
> It has often been remarked by commentators — to the point of having become, so to speak, conventional wisdom, echoed as usual by the media — that in taking their stand the

majority judges provided the framework within which a political settlement eventually became possible. Having rejected unilateralism and unanimity, the Court embraced the "Canadian way," supporting both sides and forcing a political compromise.

The decision by the majority did not conform to the definition of a convention as a concise and precise rule of political behaviour considered binding by those who participate in public life — but it did provide the basis for bringing the actors back to the table.

THE FOURTEENTH EXERCISE (1981–82)

In an attempt to respect the conventions of the Constitution identified by the Supreme Court, the Prime Minister convened a three-day first ministers' conference on November 2, 1981, to seek broad support by governments for the terms of patriation.

The Government of Canada had two options at the outset of the conference:

- it could try to win over three "moderate" premiers (Messrs. Buchanan of Nova Scotia, Blakeney of Saskatchewan and Bennett of British Columbia) to the proposal then before Parliament and meet thereby the test of substantial provincial consent, while isolating the three premiers (Messrs. Lévesque of Quebec, Lyon of Manitoba and Lougheed of Alberta) who were thought to be rock solid in their opposition to the parliamentary package; or

- it could try to break the common front of the dissident eight, thereby opening up the way for negotiations on a compromise.

The conference had been convened for three days, from November 2 to 4. Towards noon on November 4, it was clear that a stalemate had developed. Prime Minister Trudeau then made a radical suggestion. The British should not be asked to legislate changes for Canada, he suggested. Rather, they should provide the legal and constitutional basis for resolving two key issues in Canada by Canadians. Under this proposal, the British would sanction two referendums in Canada:

■   One referendum would ask Canadians whether they wanted the Charter. To pass, it would have to receive support
by a majority of Canadians and a majority in each of the
four regions (Atlantic, Quebec, Ontario and the West).

■   The other referendum would ask Canadians whether they
wanted the Victoria formula or the Vancouver formula
and, to pass, the same special majority would be required.

On the Charter, the issue was simple: yes or no. On the amending formula issue, it would have been possible for the Western
and Atlantic regions, for example, to support Vancouver and for
Ontario and Quebec to support Victoria, leading to a stalemate.
In this case, unanimity would become the general amending
formula.

Premier Lévesque, without consulting his colleagues in the dissident group of eight, said that he could accept the new Trudeau
proposal. The other provinces, all opposed to referendums, were
aghast. Mr. Trudeau adjourned for lunch and announced to the
press that there was a new "alliance Québec-Canada."

During the luncheon period, it became clear there were problems. The House of Commons and the Senate were committed
to vote on the joint address (as submitted to the Supreme Court)
with no further amendments. If the Conference ended in failure and the federal government could not respect the convention of substantial provincial consent identified by the Supreme
Court, Parliament could be asked to proceed legally and adopt
the joint address.

However, if the federal government withdrew the joint address
already before Parliament (supported by Ontario and New
Brunswick) and introduced a new one supported only by Quebec,
the whole process would open up again and the outcome was
by no means certain.

His colleagues in the group of eight dissident premiers believed
that Premier Lévesque's quick acceptance of Prime Minister
Trudeau's referendum proposal without consulting them amounted to breaking ranks and effectively released them from their
common front. When the conference resumed in the afternoon,
premiers asked that it be extended for one more day. Several
provincial authorities negotiated with each other and the federal government during the course of the evening and the night.

By the morning of November 5, a compromise was reached. The federal government would accept the Vancouver formula (but with no obligation for reasonable compensation in the event of opting out). The provinces would accept the Charter of Rights and Freedoms, but fundamental freedoms (such as freedom of expression), legal rights and equality rights would be subject to a "notwithstanding clause." This meant that provincial legislatures (and, indeed, Parliament) could expressly contravene those rights and the contravention could operate for up to five years. At the expiry of the contravention, a new declaration would have to be made to maintain it but, since general elections had to be held within five-year periods, it was probable that the contravention would figure in and be debated during the election.

Following a breakfast meeting of the eight dissident provinces on November 5, all provinces accepted the compromise, except Quebec. At a signing ceremony later in the morning, the Prime Minister and the premiers of seven provinces signed an agreement to provide the basis for patriation of the Constitution. Ministers signed on behalf of Nova Scotia and Manitoba, and Quebec did not sign.

Manitoba's signature was conditional on the legislative assembly's agreeing to minority language education rights. However, in the election of November 17, 1981, the Lyon government was defeated and the new Pawley government withdrew the condition by means of a telephone conversation of which there is no written record.

On November 5, 1981, all governments — except that of Quebec — signed an agreement to resolve the constitutional issue. Several points related to process and substance are worth noting:

- the agreement was worked out by governments behind closed doors following a court decision;

- the agreement included an amending formula and (in the Charter) a notwithstanding clause that had not been subjected to public scrutiny during the unilateral process; and

- some subsequent adjustments were made to the agreement through executive consultations before the two Houses of Parliament were asked to adopt the constitutional resolution. For example:

- all governments agreed, after November 5, to add a provision to the amending formula requiring reasonable federal compensation to a province that opted out of any future amendment transferring jurisdiction over education or other cultural matters to Parliament; and

- the Premier of Manitoba dropped a condition that the provincial assembly determine whether the Charter's minority official language rights should apply in that province.

In short, notwithstanding the strong involvement of the people in the unilateral process, governments reverted to executive federalism when they adopted a multilateral process. But there were two notable exceptions.

The "unilateral" resolution that had been submitted to the Supreme Court recognized and affirmed the Aboriginal and treaty rights of the Aboriginal peoples of Canada. This was dropped on November 5 as a condition for provincial support. The resolution had also contained an absolute guarantee of the equal application of the Charter's rights and freedoms to male and female persons. This was made subject to the override or "notwithstanding" clause.

When Aboriginal leaders and women's groups subsequently protested, the Prime Minister said he would restore the original provisions if the Aboriginal and women's groups could convince the nine premiers who signed the November 5 agreement to do so. Both the Aboriginal peoples and women mobilized their resources and campaigned vigorously across the country. One by one, each premier agreed and, when the Constitution was finally "patriated" on April 17, 1982, it included Aboriginal rights and gender equality rights without an override. It has been argued that Aboriginal leaders and women's groups became, through this experience, significant political actors in the constitutional debate.

RECAPPING THE PATRIATION DEBATE

On the eve of patriation, the precedents for handling the issue of patriation with an amending formula (with or without substantive change) were complex:

- in 1935–36, 1950, 1960–61 and 1964, the *agenda was restricted* to patriation with an amending formula and the process was one of *multilateral executive federalism;*

- in 1968–71, 1978–79 and 1980, *the agenda was comprehensive* and the process was restricted to *multilateral executive federalism;*

- in 1975–77, *the agenda was very narrow* and the process was one of *secret bilateral executive federalism;*

- in 1935 and 1970–72 there were *"unilateral" parliamentary committees* to make recommendations on how to resolve the issue;

- in 1949, the agenda was limited to *partial patriation* and the process was *unilateral action by Parliament;*

- in 1976 and 1978, there were federal proposals for *unilateral action by Parliament;*

- in 1980–81, the agenda was narrow in scope ("the peoples' package") and the *process was unilateral with broad public involvement through televised parliamentary hearings;* and

- in November 1981, the agenda remained narrow in scope but the process reverted to *multilateral executive federalism* until November 5 and thereafter involved further executive accommodation *as well as direct lobbying action* by two major groups.

Prior to the November 1981 First Ministers' Conference, provinces — with Quebec in the lead — and Aboriginal organizations had been lobbying the British government and British parliamentarians vigorously in opposition to the federal unilateral initiative. During the highly volatile debate in Canada, a British legislative committee under the chairmanship of Sir Anthony Kershaw questioned whether and under what circumstances Britain would have to comply with a request from Canada.

Following the general agreement in Canada except for Quebec, in November 1981, British qualms were dissipated.

A patriation package which differed from the package upon which parliamentary hearings had been held in 1980–81 (it now included the "notwithstanding clause" and a new amending procedure) was introduced in the House of Commons on

November 20, 1981 and adopted on December 2, 1981. It was introduced in the Senate on December 3, 1981 and adopted on December 8, 1981. No public hearings were held on the new patriation package. No legislative assembly (save Alberta's, which debated the November 5 agreement for one day on November 10) examined the package, held public hearings or authorized it. On March 29, 1982, the Parliament of the United Kingdom enacted the Canada Act 1982. Under the terms of that act, the Constitution Act, 1982 was proclaimed on April 17, 1982, in Ottawa.

The Queen presided over the patriation ceremony in front of the Peace Tower on April 17, 1982. The day was overcast and it rained during the ceremony. The public could, of course, attend, but the crowd was small. In Quebec, attempts to mount a massive protest were unsuccessful.

QUEBEC AND PATRIATION

Following his isolation from the November 4–5 consensus, Premier Lévesque wrote to Prime Minister Trudeau on November 25, 1981, to say that Quebec's agreement to the April 16 accord on the Vancouver formula no longer stood and that Quebec would assert its veto over patriation and the formula for subsequent constitutional change (see Appendix 11). He provided a copy of an order of the Executive Council of Quebec opposing patriation without Quebec's consent and submitting a reference to the Quebec Court of Appeal on whether Quebec had a veto by convention over any joint address relating to Quebec's legislative powers and the status or role of the legislature or Government of Quebec in Canada. He asked Mr. Trudeau to act as he did in 1971 when Quebec refused to authorize the Victoria Charter and he indicated on what basis he would be prepared to approve patriation.

Mr. Trudeau replied on December 1, 1981, stating that, on the basis of the Supreme Court of Canada's decision of September 28, 1981, Quebec did not have by law or convention a veto over patriation (see Appendix 12). He then reviewed the federal government's consistent efforts since the Victoria exercise to ensure that Quebec would have a constitutional veto and stated: "We only abandoned this after your government did." He pointed out that he had changed the amending formula agreed to on November 5 to incorporate a requirement of financial compensation to a province that opts out of an amendment respecting "education or other cultural matters" to protect matters of special concern to the people of Quebec. He concluded that the Premier could propose that the amending formula be changed — after patriation.

Mr. Lévesque responded on December 2, 1981 (see Appendix 13), by noting what he called a flagrant contradiction: the Prime Minister, while saying that Quebec had no veto, stated that previous attempts to resolve the patriation issue had been unsuccessful because no government of Quebec had agreed to the previous constitutional proposals of the Government of Canada. He asked the Prime Minister to suspend any action on the joint address until the Quebec Court of Appeal and, ultimately, the Supreme Court of Canada could respond to the reference on the Quebec veto. The National Assembly of Quebec had, by resolution adopted on December 1, 1981, set out the conditions on which Quebec could accept patriation of the Constitution. One of those conditions dealt with the amending formula and maintained that the amending formula should provide a veto for Quebec (the preferred position of Mr. Ryan) or should be the formula of April 16, 1981, with obligatory and reasonable compensation in all cases of opting out (the position Mr. Lévesque had accepted earlier in the year).

In his reply of December 4, 1981 (see Appendix 14), Prime Minister Trudeau reminded Premier Lévesque that he had signed the accord of April 16, 1981 and abandoned thereby a veto for Quebec. He also reminded him that the Supreme Court, in its decision of September 28, 1981, had said that it was for political actors, not the Court, to determine the degree of provincial consent required for patriation. In the circumstances, he refused to delay action on the joint address.

The Constitution was duly patriated with the proclamation of the Constitution Act, 1982 on April 17, 1982. The Supreme Court of Canada subsequently — on December 6, 1982 — ruled that Quebec did not have a veto, by convention or otherwise, to protect it from the patriation plan.

On December 17, 1982, Premier Lévesque wrote to Prime Minister Trudeau to take note of the Supreme Court decision and to remind him of the conditions set out in the December 1, 1981 resolution of the National Assembly for accepting patriation of the Constitution. He asked the Prime Minister to seek adoption by Parliament of an amendment resolution that would give Quebec a veto or else compensation in all cases of opting out and would restore Quebec's exclusive jurisdiction in the area of language of education (see Appendix 15).

Prime Minister Trudeau responded on December 24, 1982, to say that the amending formula could not be changed by unilateral action. He said he would be prepared to unite with Quebec to seek a Quebec veto or its equivalent (i.e., compensation in all cases of opting out) if Quebec returned to the constitutional table in good faith and accepted formally the Constitution Act, 1982 (see Appendix 16).

This brought to an end the correspondence between Premier Lévesque and Prime Minister Trudeau on how to resolve Quebec's concerns on the patriation issue and the question of the amending formula. Quebec made clear, however, that it would not participate in post-patriation constitutional discussions until after its own concerns had been addressed.

our Majesty's loyal subjects, the Hou
s of Canada in Parliament assembl
approach Your Majesty, requesting
graciously be pleased to cause to be
Parliament of the United Kingd
containing the recitals and c
ter set forth :

An Act to give effect to a request by t
and House of Commons of C

Whereas Canada has requested a
the enactment of an Act of the Parl
United Kingdom to give effect to
ter set forth and the Senate an
nada in Parliament
Majest

4

THE AMENDING FORMULA ADOPTED IN 1982

THE AMENDING FORMULA adopted at the time of patriation is quite complex. Set out in Part V (sections 38 to 49) of the Constitution Act, 1982 (see Appendix 17), it is made up of seven distinct procedures. Opinions may vary, however, on the precise number of procedures. Some would group the three variants of the 7/50 procedure together as one, for a total of five procedures, while others would hold that the adoption of a resolution twice by the House of Commons to override a Senate veto constitutes another procedure.

THE PROCEDURES COMPRISING THE 1982 FORMULA

1. The 7/50 Procedure

Unless another procedure was provided, most general amendments to the Constitution would require the consent of the Senate, the House of Commons and the legislative assemblies of two-thirds of the provinces representing at least 50 percent of the population of all the provinces, according to the most current general census. This procedure is popularly referred to as the 7/50 formula (section 38).

A 7/50 amendment resolution can be introduced in the Senate, the House of Commons or a provincial legislative assembly (section 46[1]). The amendment is officially "initiated" when the first resolution authorizing it is adopted. A resolution authorizing an amendment can be revoked (by another resolution) at any time before the amendment is proclaimed (section 46[2]).

Certain time limits apply to this procedure. The amendment cannot be proclaimed before one year has expired from the date of adoption of the resolution initiating the amendment, unless every provincial legislative assembly has adopted a resolution of assent or dissent before the expiry of the year. This means that even though the requirements for a 7/50 amendment might be met within three months of its "initiation," proclamation must await the expiry of one year if any one legislative assembly refuses to take action one way or the other (section 39[1]).

Furthermore, no 7/50 amendment can be proclaimed after three years have expired from the date of "initiation" (section 39[2]).

No 7/50 amendment can be proclaimed without the consent of the House of Commons, which has a veto over all such amendments. No other legislative body, acting alone, can veto a 7/50 amendment. The Senate has a suspensive veto on such amendments. If, within 180 days (roughly six months) after the House of Commons has adopted a resolution authorizing a 7/50 amendment, the Senate:

■   rejects the resolution;

- adopts an amended or different resolution from that passed by the House of Commons; or

- does not take any action on the resolution approved by the House of Commons,

the House of Commons may override the Senate's veto or inaction by adopting its original resolution a second time (section 47[1]). For the purposes of calculating the period of 180 days, periods when Parliament is prorogued (the period between the end of one session of Parliament and the opening of a new session with a speech from the throne) or dissolved for the purposes of a general election are not counted. However, periods when the House of Commons is adjourned (weekends and vacation periods, for example) are not excluded from the 180 days (section 47[2]).

Because of the three-year time limit for 7/50 amendments, the House of Commons must take reasonably timely action in approving such amendments so that, if the Senate decides to exercise its suspensive veto, there will still be time to present the resolution a second time in the House and ensure its adoption within the constitutionally mandated time limit.

Because of the 50 percent population qualification, the 7/50 procedure does not treat all provinces the same way. Ontario and Quebec acting together can block an amendment supported by Parliament and the eight other provinces. Similarly, Ontario, British Columbia and Alberta in concert could veto an amendment supported by Parliament and the seven other provinces because of their combined demographic weight. But it would take four Atlantic provinces acting with a common purpose to veto an amendment supported by Parliament and the six other provinces — and the veto would be based on the failure to have seven provinces onside rather than the failure to meet the 50 percent of the population test.

There is no role provided in the 7/50 procedure for the assemblies of the territories or, indeed, for any other body, association or group, save for the Queen's Privy Council for Canada and the Governor General.

Such 7/50 amendments are authorized by resolutions, not laws, so they are not subject to three readings and, of course, they do not receive royal assent. However, the text of a resolution can be referred to a committee for hearing. Although the roles of the Senate and the House of Commons are distinct, the two Houses could agree to send the text of a resolution to a special joint committee of the two Houses to facilitate the amendment process.

Although the 7/50 procedure is the "general" method of amending the Constitution, section 42 provides that it is the only method to be used for amendments to the Constitution of Canada in relation to:

■ the principle of proportionate representation of the provinces in the House of Commons;

■ the powers of the Senate and the method of selection of members thereto;

■ the number of members by which a province is entitled to be represented in the Senate and the residence qualifications of senators;

■ the Supreme Court of Canada (except for its composition);

■ the extension of existing provinces into the territories; and

■ notwithstanding any other law or practice, the establishment of new provinces.

The reference to the Supreme Court of Canada in section 42 raises questions. Section 52 of the Constitution Act, 1982 defines the Constitution of Canada as including the Canada Act 1982 of the British Parliament, the Constitution Act, 1982 and the acts and orders set out in the schedule to the latter (see Appendix 2). The Supreme Court of Canada was created by act of Parliament and is not specifically included in the formal definition of the Constitution of Canada. Although the intent was to protect the existing Supreme Court under this procedure, it is not clear whether this has been achieved.

Amendments under the 7/50 procedure are made by proclamation issued by the Governor General under the Great Seal of Canada when the necessary conditions have been met. It is "the Queen's Privy Council for Canada" (that is, the Cabinet) which advises the Governor General to issue the proclamation "forthwith" when the conditions have been met (section 48). It is Cabinet, not the Governor General, which must determine whether all the authorizing resolutions are identical and whether the time limits have been respected.

A resolution of assent may be revoked at any time prior to the proclamation authorized by it under this procedure or the next four procedures for amendments made by proclamation.

2. The 7/50 Procedure with Opting Out

If a general amendment derogates from the legislative powers, the proprietary rights or any other rights or privileges of the legislature or government of a province, the legislative assembly of a province could opt out of the amendment and it would not apply to that province (section 38[3]).

To pass, such an amendment must be supported by Parliament and seven provinces representing at least 50 percent of the population, but up to three provinces with less than 50 percent of the population could opt out.

Any amendment that derogates from provincial powers, rights and privileges must be supported by a special majority: a majority of the members (and not merely a majority of those present at the time of the vote) of the Senate, the House of Commons and the legislative assemblies of the provinces must authorize the amendment by resolution. Unless an absolute majority of the membership in each of the required number of legislative bodies adopts the resolution, it does not pass (section 38[2]).

In order to exercise its right to opt out of an amendment in this category, a provincial legislative assembly must express its dissent by a resolution supported by a majority of the members of the assembly (and not merely a majority of those present at the time of the vote) prior to proclamation. The same assembly may also, prior to or after the proclamation, withdraw its dissent and authorize the application of such an amendment to the province by resolution, provided that a majority of the members of the assembly adopt the resolution (section 38[4]).

If a province decided to opt out of an amendment transferring, let us say, legislative jurisdiction over health care to Parliament, the distribution of powers would be formally amended to reflect the new federal power, but the amendment would not apply in respect to the opted-out province.

Among the federations of the world, this provision allowing a limited number of constituent units to opt out of an amendment of general application is unique.

The other rules respecting 7/50 procedure — such as the time limits — apply to the opting out procedure.

3.   **The 7/50 Procedure with Opting Out and Compensation**

There is a specific variant to the 7/50 procedure with opting out. Section 40 provides that if an amendment transfers provincial legislative powers relating to education or other cultural matters from provincial legislatures to Parliament, Canada shall provide reasonable compensation to any province to which the amendment does not apply.

The purpose of this provision is to avoid double taxation for the provision of the same service. If, for example, the federal government increased its rate of taxation to pay for post-secondary education following an amendment transferring this matter to Parliament, Canadians throughout the country would have to pay the new tax, including Canadians in the opted-out province. The opted out province would also have to raise revenues from its own sources to continue to finance post-secondary education in the province. Thus, to avoid having the same people contribute to both a national scheme (in which they would not participate) and a provincial scheme, Canada would provide compensation to the province.

The compensation would be "reasonable" and would represent approximately what the federal government would have spent in the province had it not opted out of the national scheme. The precise formula for working out the amount would depend upon the nature of the program and the relevant variables in the province and elsewhere in Canada. In short, there is a certain degree of flexibility and it would be up to federal and provincial authorities to devise an appropriate formula. If, however, the compensation appeared to be clearly "unreasonable," the compensation appeared to be clearly "unreasonable," the province could appeal to the courts.

The compensation itself could take a number of forms, such as cash payments or tax points transferred to the province. Again, there is flexibility.

While it is fairly clear what would constitute an amendment relating to education, it is far less clear what would be covered by "other cultural matters." Traditionally the federal government has asserted a narrow definition while Quebec has argued in favour of a very broad definition related to the development of its society. If federal and provincial authorities were unable to reach agreement in a particular case, resort could of course be had to the courts.

The question arises: why does the compensation clause not apply to all transfers of provincial legislative jurisdiction to Parliament, since the double taxation argument holds true for all such transfers? The answer is that Prime Minister Trudeau did not want the formula to encourage provinces to opt out of future amendments and felt that a constitutional guarantee of compensation might do so because there would be no price to pay. As noted in chapter 3, he finally decided, after the agreement of November 5, 1981, on patriation, and with the support of nine premiers, to include a guarantee of compensation in respect of education and other cultural matters, as a way of providing special recognition for Quebec, which had, in 1975, asked that patriation be accompanied by guarantees respecting the French language and culture.

Although there is no guarantee of compensation respecting transfers other than those related to education and other cultural matters, nothing precludes the possibility of Canada's deciding, in specific cases, to do so. But the decision would be political and would not be subject to a constitutional challenge.

The 7/50 procedure with opting out and compensation is subject to the same rules as set out for the second procedure above.

Needless to say, just as the opting-out provision is unique among the federations of the world, so is the compensation provision.

4. **The Unanimity Procedure**

Section 41 provides that amendments to the Constitution of Canada require the unanimous consent of the Senate, the House of Commons and the legislative assembly of all of the provinces if they are in relation to:

■ the office of the Queen, of the lieutenant-governor General or of the lieutenant-gj83

overnor;

■ the right of a province to a number of members in the House of Commons not less than the number of senators representing the province at the time of patriation;

■ the use of the English or French language (except for provisions applying to one or more, but not all, provinces);

■ the composition of the Supreme Court of Canada; or

■ the procedures for amending the constitution.

Again, it should be noted that the Supreme Court of Canada was created by act of the federal Parliament and this act is not included in the formal definition of the Constitution of Canada set out in section 52 of the Constitution Act, 1982. It is not clear, therefore, whether the current composition of the Supreme Court of Canada is protected by the unanimity rule or whether this procedure applies only to the amendment of whatever composition of the Supreme Court is eventually entrenched in the Constitution.

Clearly, the intent was to protect Quebec's current right, under federal statute law, to three of the nine justices of the Supreme Court.

"Unanimity" amendments could be introduced in the Senate, the House of Commons or the legislative assembly of any province. There is no minimum or maximum time limit for ratification of these amendments, unlike 7/50 amendments — although nothing would prevent any legislative body from making its resolution authorizing a unanimity amendment subject to proclamation occurring within a specified period of time.

Otherwise, unanimity amendments are authorized by resolutions adopted by the Senate, the House of Commons
and the legislative assemblies of the provinces, in the
same manner as 7/50 amendments. The Senate has a suspensive veto of 180 days over these amendments. And the
amendments are made by proclamation issued by the
Governor General under the Great Seal of Canada on the
advice of the Queen's Privy Council for Canada. The advice
must be tendered "forthwith" when the conditions for the
unanimity amendment have been met.

5.   The Bilateral and Multilateral Procedure

Section 43 provides that an amendment to the Constitution
of Canada in relation to a provision applying to one or more,
but not all, provinces requires the consent of the Senate,
the House of Commons and the legislative assemblies of
every province to which the amendment applies. Section
43 specifically notes that this procedure applies to any alteration of the boundaries between provinces and any amendment to any provision that relates to the use of the English
or the French language within a province.

While section 43 is often referred to as a "bilateral" procedure involving Ottawa and a particular province, it can
in fact involve Ottawa and more than one province at a
time (for example, alterations to boundaries between
provinces), in which case it is more properly described as
a multilateral procedure.

Bilateral/multilateral amendments are not subject to minimum and maximum time limits and do not require votes
by a majority of the members of the legislative bodies
involved. Otherwise, they are subject to the same rules as
7/50 amendments and the Senate is limited to a suspensive veto.

6.   The "Unilateral" Federal Procedure

Subject to the foregoing procedures, section 44 provides
that Parliament may exclusively make laws amending
the Constitution of Canada in relation to the executive government of Canada or the Senate and House of Commons.

Unlike all the foregoing amendments, which are made by
proclamation when authorized by the appropriate resolutions,
section 44 amendments are introduced as bills in either

the Senate or the House of Commons and must pass three readings in each House. The Senate has an absolute veto over such amendments (as does the House of Commons). The amendment bill as adopted by both Houses must then be presented to the Governor General for royal sanction.

Changes to the formula for the representation of the provinces in the House of Commons (subject to certain constitutional limits) are achieved by federal law under this procedure or under the authority of section 51 of the 1867 act.

7.   The "Unilateral" Provincial Procedure

Subject to the first five procedures set out above, section 45 provides that the legislature of each province may exclusively make laws amending the constitution of the province. This is a statutory process similar to the "unilateral" federal procedure, except that the provincial legislatures are unicameral (that is, composed of only one House) and therefore require adoption only by the legislative assembly. Royal sanction is, of course, given by the lieutenant-governor.

OBLIGATORY REVIEW OF THE 1982 FORMULA

Section 49 of the Constitution Act, 1982 requires that the Prime Minister of Canada convene a constitutional conference composed of himself and the provincial first ministers to "review" the provisions of the full amendment formula adopted in 1982 before April 17, 1997.

Although first ministers have reviewed specific procedures of the 1982 formula at constitutional conferences since patriation of the Constitution on April 17, 1982, they have never undertaken a full review of the whole formula. A conference to achieve this end is therefore required before the expiry of 15 years from the date of patriation, but the requirement is very flexible:

■   the conference could be private or public;

■   the agenda could be restricted to the amending formula or it could include other constitutional matters;

■ the conference could stand alone or it could be tagged onto another meeting of first ministers;

■ the conference must include the federal and provincial first ministers and could include — although this is not required — other persons (for example, the government leaders of the territories or representatives of the Aboriginal peoples of Canada).

First ministers are required to review the formula, but there is no requirement to take any further action. There is no penalty provided by the Constitution if first ministers fail to meet to review the formula.

APPLYING THE RIGHT PROCEDURE TO AN AMENDMENT PROPOSAL

At first blush, the amendment procedures in the 1982 formula seem to be fairly straightforward. However, when one turns to specific amendments, difficulties, ambiguities and uncertainties come to light. An examination of potential amendment proposals respecting the Senate may best illustrate this point.

1. Property Qualifications for Senators

Under section 23(3) and (4) of the Constitution Act, 1867, senators must hold at least $4,000 worth of real property over and above their debts and liabilities in the province they represent. In 1867, this was a considerable sum and was intended to ensure that senators represented the propertied classes in Parliament.

In 1995, the property qualification is no longer highly significant and, furthermore, is no longer in keeping with democratic values in Canada. If this qualification were to be removed, which amending procedure would be the appropriate one to use?

Since the issue does not relate to the powers of the Senate, the method of selecting senators, the number of senators representing a province or the residence qualifications of senators — matters subject to the 7/50 procedure — it would appear that the unilateral federal procedure (a law adopted by Parliament) could be used to abolish the property qualification.

However, abolition of the property qualification would have a special impact on Quebec. Quebec — and Quebec alone — is divided into 24 "electoral divisions" for the purposes of representation in the Senate. Quebec senators must meet their real property qualifications or their residence qualifications in the electoral division they represent (section 23[6] of the 1867 act). Thus, all Quebec senators currently could meet the residence qualification in Hull, let us say, while meeting their property qualification in an electoral division elsewhere in the province.

Removal of the property qualification would, in the case of Quebec, change the current residence option for Quebec senators and oblige them to take up residence in the electoral division they represent. This would constitute an amendment in relation to a provision that applies to one, but not all provinces, and would be subject to bilateral action. Thus, it could be argued, the removal of the current property qualification for senators might require two amendments:

- a bilateral Ottawa-Quebec amendment by proclamation issued by the Governor General to remove the requirement that Quebec senators meet their property or residence qualifications in the electoral division they represent;

- a federal law under the unilateral power of Parliament to remove the property qualification from the conditions required for appointment to the Senate.

2. Senate Reform and a Quebec Veto

Because Quebec — and Quebec alone — is divided into 24 electoral divisions for the purposes of representation in the Senate (section 22 of the 1867 act) and because Quebec senators must meet their property or residence qualification in the division they represent (section 23[6]), it could be argued that a scheme for Senate reform that sought to provide, for example, an equal representation of 10 senators each for all provinces might require not only a 7/50 amendment, but also a bilateral amendment with Quebec.

Indeed, in the days leading up to the constitutional meeting of April 30, 1987, at Meech Lake, the Government of Alberta had made clear it would not attend if Quebec insisted on a veto over Senate reform. It was only after the Government of Canada shared with Alberta the argument to the effect that Quebec might already have an effective veto over many proposals for Senate reform because of the 24 electoral divisions and the unusual property and residence qualifications in that province that Alberta dropped its objection and agreed to the Meech Lake meeting.

3. Abolition of the Senate

The 7/50 procedure applies to specific aspects of Senate reform, such as the powers of the Senate and the method of selection of senators. But if one wished to abolish the Senate completely rather than reform it, what would be the appropriate procedure to use?

In this case, one would have to begin by asking whether abolition would materially alter or affect any matter subject to the unanimity procedure — the most "rigid" of the amending procedures. And, as it transpires, it would indeed materially affect a matter subject to the unanimity rule: the amending formula itself.

The Senate has a suspensive veto of 180 days over amendments achieved through proclamation issued by the Governor General. If the Senate exercises its veto, the amendment is blocked unless the House of Commons considers the amendment a second time and readopts its resolution. The suspensive veto was designed to ensure, among other things, that the Senate could not block an amendment to abolish it or replace it with a new institution. The Senate also has an absolute veto over amendments achieved by federal statute law.

Abolition of the Senate would remove an actor from the operation of the amending formula adopted in 1982 and, since changes to the amending formula are subject to unanimous consent, it could be argued that abolition would be subject to unanimity, the most rigid procedure in the formula.

4. Increasing Territorial Representation in the Senate

The number of senators representing each province in the Senate is subject to the 7/50 procedure although, as noted above, changes affecting Quebec's representation might, under certain circumstances, also be subject to a bilateral amendment.

It might appear to be an oversight that the amending formula adopted in 1982 does not provide for how the representation of the territories in the Senate is to be achieved and, once achieved, how it could be modified.

In fact, the representation of the territories in the Senate is a matter within the exclusive legislative authority of Parliament under the terms of the Constitution Act, 1886.

Thus, representation for the territories in the Senate could be altered by federal statute law. However, a radical increase in territorial senators could, at some point, be challenged as a violation of the federal principle.

5.   **The Retirement Age of Senators**

It is not clear what procedure would apply if it were thought advisable to reduce the retirement age of senators.

In 1867, senators were appointed for life. The Parliament of Canada reduced tenure from life to age 75 when it adopted a federal law entitled the British North America Act, 1965 (retitled the Constitution Act, 1965 in 1982). In the Senate reference of 1979, the Supreme Court of Canada ruled that the fundamental character of the Senate could not be altered by unilateral action by the Parliament of Canada, but it upheld the federal statute of 1965: "The imposition of compulsory retirement at age seventy-five did not change the essential character of the Senate."

It would probably be constitutional for Parliament to further reduce the retirement age to 70 by a federal statute. However, there is a possibility the courts might find that an attempt to reduce dramatically the retirement age to, say, 55 might constitute a change to its essential character and be beyond the unilateral power of Parliament.

An attempt to replace the fixed age for retirement with a fixed mandate of, let us say, ten years might constitute a change in the method of selecting senators. If this were the case, it would be subject to the 7/50 rule. On the other hand, since tenure is not mentioned in section 42 — the 7/50 procedure — there is an argument that it is covered by section 44 — the unilateral power of Parliament — since the two procedures are exhaustive.

6. The Election of Senators

Senators are currently summoned by the Governor General on the advice of the Prime Minister (section 24 of the 1867 act). It would require a 7/50 amendment to replace this method of selecting senators with a requirement that they be elected.

Alberta adopted a law to provide for the popular election of persons to represent the province in the Senate. Though not constitutionally bound to do so, Prime Minister Brian Mulroney did recommend that the Governor General appoint Stan Waters to the Senate on June 16, 1990, following his selection by the people of Alberta. Prime Minister Mulroney also appointed persons to the Senate whose names had been submitted by the provinces during the Meech Lake ratification period.

There is nothing to prevent Parliament from adopting a law respecting popular consultation on Senate appointments, but the only binding procedure under the Constitution of Canada will be the procedure now in place until it is altered by a 7/50 amendment.

RESOLUTIONS

The formula adopted in 1982 provides a legislative model for initiating and ratifying amendments. It is the resolutions adopted by the appropriate number of legislative bodies that authorize the issuance of a proclamation by the Governor General amending the Constitution of Canada. While the legislative model could be supplemented by other processes — such as executive federalism or popular participation — the resolutions alone provide the legal basis for amending the Constitution.

Resolutions, therefore, merit special attention. Four aspects are of particular interest:

■ Should there be preambles?

■ Should all legislative bodies adopt identical texts?

■ Should all legislative bodies adopt the text of the amendment in both English and French?

■ Are resolutions severable?

1. Preambles to Resolutions

The legislative body which initiates the procedure to amend the Constitution may include a preamble in the resolution that proposes the amendment. Or a resolution containing such a preamble may be suggested and agreed to in the course of intergovernmental discussions on a proposed amendment to the Constitution.

Such preambles may, among other things, recite the legal authority for making the amendment and historical events leading to it, or the reasons why the amendment is desirable; or they may indicate how the amendment follows from past commitments or underline a political intention to take some action in the future. Nevertheless, preambles are not part of the amendment, and it is probably not essential, therefore, that all legislative bodies adopt the same, or any, preamble in passing amendment resolutions.

It cannot be said with complete certainty what legal effect, if any, might be given to a preamble in a resolution proposing a constitutional amendment that was approved by the required number of legislative bodies along with the proposed amendment itself. The preamble might be looked upon by the courts as a useful aid to interpretation if the text of the amendment was ambiguous. On the other hand, if the preamble had not been approved by a sufficient number of legislative bodies — either because they did not deal with it or because they used different preambles — the courts would likely refrain from taking any version into consideration.

In these circumstances, it would seem prudent to treat preambles with care. Some legislative bodies including, for example, the legislative assembly of Alberta, prefer, as a matter of principle, to avoid them. From all this, it seems desirable for all concurring governments to use the same preamble or none at all.

2. Approval of Identical Amendment Texts

It almost goes without saying that the precise text of an amendment should be approved in identical terms by the necessary number of legislative bodies. It is conceivable that a legislative assembly might "authorize" a proclamation by the Governor General under section 38, 41 or 42 in very general terms, and thus delegate to the Queen's

Privy Council for Canada the power to choose the final wording of an amendment or, perhaps, a suitable text in the other official language. It would appear, however, that there would have to be precise wording in the authorizing resolution to this effect, and it would still remain for consideration whether sections 38, 41 and 42 permit a delegation of this kind. The better view is that legislative bodies should adopt the precise text of an amendment: anything else would be open to challenge. In any event, there would seem little to be gained by such an indirect approach. The more prudent course, then, would be passage of the resolution by the legislative bodies in question with the amendment itself expressed in definitive wording and in all cases in identical terms. Ensuring that the text is identical in all cases raises the question of coordination and suggests the utility of, but does not legally require, some form of executive federalism. To date, the federal Department of Justice has fulfilled the role of ensuring that constitutional texts are identical.

3. Approval in English and French

The Constitution Act, 1982 exists in both English and French versions. Section 57 of the act stipulates that the two versions are equally authoritative. The intention seems clear that there be English and French versions of any amendments to the 1982 act, and that these versions, like those of the act as a whole, be equally authoritative. Furthermore, all amendments to the Constitution made by unilateral action by Parliament under section 44 must be adopted in both languages under the terms of the Charter of Rights and Freedoms.

Thus, it can be argued that the Senate, the House of Commons and a sufficient number of provinces should approve both an English and a French version of any amendment. It could be argued, on the other hand, that as long as the provinces have, in sufficient numbers, approved the substance of an amendment in at least one of the official languages, the Queen's Privy Council for Canada could advise the Governor General to proclaim the amendment in the two languages, both versions becoming authoritative. To remove any doubt, and to avoid a potential dispute respecting the wording of the other language version or any challenge in the courts, it would seem preferable for the legislative bodies concerned to give approval to versions in both languages, whether directly or by inclusion of the text in the other language in a schedule.

Prior to 1982, much of the Canadian constitution was enacted in English only by the United Kingdom Parliament. Although translations in French exist, none is authoritative at present. Section 55 of the Constitution Act, 1982 requires the Minister of Justice to prepare and bring forward a French version of all portions of the Constitution for which such a version does not now exist "as expeditiously as possible," for enactment by proclamation pursuant to the procedure then applicable to an amendment of the same provisions of the Constitution. Since the English text has already been entrenched, it would only be necessary to adopt, by resolution, the French text of amendments to give effect to section 55. The procedure to be followed for adoption would depend upon whether the text itself would be subject to a bilateral, a multilateral, a 7/50 or a unanimity amendment.

The federal Department of Justice appointed a French Constitutional Drafting Committee to provide a draft official French version for the purposes of section 55. The report of that committee was tabled in Parliament on December 18, 1990, and was circulated to the provinces in preparation for proceeding with a resolution. However, political circumstances have kept this matter in abeyance.

4.   Severability of Resolutions

In an ideal world, it might seem preferable for every constitutional resolution to be restricted to a single issue which in turn should be subject to only one of the amendment procedures in the formula adopted in 1982.

In practice, such a neat and tidy approach is not always possible. Some issues are subject to more than one procedure. For example, if one wished to entrench the Supreme Court of Canada in the Constitution, the 7/50 rule with its three-year time limit for ratification would be brought into play. But if entrenchment also involved setting out the composition of the Supreme Court, those provisions dealing with composition would be subject to unanimous consent and there is no time limit for unanimity amendments. Thus, the full constitutional resolution would be subject to the constraints of both the 7/50 and the unanimity procedures.

As a political matter, actors in the amendment process may decide to proceed with a "package" of amendments including both 7/50 matters and unanimity matters. If so, the whole "package" would be subject to dual constraints: one would have to achieve unanimous consent within three years. This was the case with the Meech Lake Accord of 1987.

There were those who argued during the Meech Lake ratification process that, since unanimity was being sought on the whole amendment resolution, the three-year time limit did not apply because there is no time constraint for unanimity matters. This position was not correct: the Constitution explicitly provides a three-year time limit for matters subject to the 7/50 rule. That legal requirement cannot be changed by the political decision of actors involved in the amendment process to link a unanimity item with a 7/50 item and thereby waive the time constraint.

If an amendment resolution contains both 7/50 and unanimity elements, the question then arises: can the resolution be severed so that 7/50 matters can be proclaimed when the necessary number of legislative bodies have authorized them and the unanimity items can be proclaimed at any time after the expiry of three years when, at last, all legislative bodies have taken the necessary action?

The answer is: it depends.

The Meech Lake Accord was drafted as an unseverable whole, reflecting the political will that the various amendments be adopted as a single package. The resolution read:

> NOW THEREFORE the (Senate) (House of Commons) (legislative assembly) resolves that an amendment to the Constitution of Canada be authorized to be made by proclamation issued by Her Excellency the Governor General under the Great Seal of Canada in accordance with the schedule hereto.

In any event, the 7/50 and unanimity provisions respecting the Supreme Court in the Constitution Amendment, 1987 were drafted as an integrated whole and to sever them would have been difficult even if severability had been contemplated by the parties. The intent of the political actors was clear: Meech was a "seamless web."

However, it is possible to draft a constitutional resolution authorizing a number of amendments and to provide that the amendments are severable for the purposes of proclamation.

On March 21, 1990, the Government of New Brunswick sought to foster adoption of the Meech Lake Accord in the provinces that had not yet ratified it by introducing a "companion resolution" that would address concerns raised during the debate on Meech. The "companion resolution" contained a number of amendments, but none could be proclaimed prior to the coming into force of Meech (that is, the Constitution Amendment, 1987). Furthermore, the resolution was drafted to allow for severability: an individual amendment could be proclaimed once the necessary conditions had been met even if the appropriate level of support for other amendments in the "package" had not yet been achieved. The resolution read:

> NOW THEREFORE the Legislative Assembly resolves that amendments to the Constitution of Canada be authorized to be made by proclamation issued by His Excellency the Governor General under the Great Seal of Canada in accordance with the schedule (hereto entitled Constitution Amendments) or any provision thereof, on the adoption of the resolutions required for such amendments, but only after the *Constitution Amendment, 1987,* comes into force.

The notion of severability was reinforced by the citation clause for the "companion resolution" which read:

> This schedule or any provision thereof may, if proclaimed, be cited as the *Constitution Amendment, (year of proclamation) (number, if necessary).*

However, this model was not adopted by first ministers when they developed a "companion resolution" in their communiqué of June 9, 1990, aimed at resolving the impasse on the Meech Lake Accord. Their "companion resolution" was not severable: it was, as in the case of Meech, all or nothing.

5

AMENDMENTS PROCLAIMED SINCE 1982

THERE HAVE BEEN four amendments to the Constitution of Canada made by proclamation since patriation on April 17, 1982. The first, the Constitution Amendment Proclamation, 1983, occurred in 1984 and was concerned with Aboriginal rights. The second, the Constitution Amendment, 1987 (Newfoundland Act), dealt with the entrenchment of the denominational school rights of the Pentecostal Assemblies in Newfoundland. The third, the Constitution Amendment, 1993 (New Brunswick), established the equality of the English-speaking and French-speaking communities in New Brunswick. The fourth, the Constitution Amendment, 1994 (Prince Edward Island), relieved Canada of the obligation to provide steamboat service to the Prince Edward Island upon completion of a "fixed link" joining the Island to New Brunswick.

THE CONSTITUTION AMENDMENT PROCLAMATION, 1983

The patriated Constitution contained a provision requiring a first ministers' constitutional conference before April 17, 1983, on the identification and definition of Aboriginal rights to be included in the Constitution (Part IV, section 37 of the Constitution Act, 1982). Representatives of the Aboriginal peoples of Canada and elected representatives of the two territories were to be invited to participate in the discussion of matters directly affecting the Aboriginal peoples and matters that, in the opinion of the Prime Minister, directly affected the territories.

This constitutional requirement for a first ministers' conference on Aboriginal issues set into motion a process involving seventeen participants: the federal government, the ten provinces, two territorial governments and the four Aboriginal associations (the Assembly of First Nations, the Inuit Committee on National Issues, the Native Council of Canada and the Métis National Council). However, the territorial governments and Aboriginal organizations had no formal role in the ratification of any amendment which might result from the process.

There were originally only three Aboriginal associations participating, but political pressure and a pending court action resulted in the Métis National Council (formerly part of the Native Council of Canada) being invited to participate as a separate group. Quebec attended as an observer but was not willing to agree to any amendment until its own constitutional agenda had been addressed.

In preparation for the 1983 First Ministers' Conference, a series of multilateral conferences was convened at both the official and ministerial levels and involved the participation of the seventeen parties. These early multilateral meetings focused on concepts and ideas rather than on draft proposals. It was not until the First Ministers' Conference that draft wording was actually proposed.

The multilateral meetings leading to the 1983 First Ministers' Conference were private and the conference itself was partly private and partly televised. The process could best be described as one of *extended executive federalism* — because all parties around the table represented governments or, in the case of the Aboriginal participants, what might be called "governments in waiting."

The 1983 Constitutional Accord on Aboriginal Rights was signed on March 16, 1983, by the Government of Canada and nine provincial governments (all except Quebec which, while not opposed to the proposed amendment, would not be an active player until after its own demands had been resolved). The Accord was also signed (under the heading "and with the participation of:") by the four Aboriginal organizations and the government leaders of the territories.

The 1983 Conference on Aboriginal Constitutional Matters resulted in the 1983 Constitutional Accord, which set out the first amendment to the Constitution Act, 1982. The scope of sections 25 and 35 was expanded to apply to existing and future land claims agreements. In addition, section 35 was amended to ensure that the rights referred to in that section apply equally to male and female persons. A new section 35.1 was created to ensure that a first ministers' conference with Aboriginal participation would be convened prior to any amendments to the provisions of the Constitution which directly affect the Aboriginal peoples.

The most striking amendment was the addition of the new Part IV.1 and the new section 37.1, which required at least two further first ministers' conferences to deal with Aboriginal constitutional matters. The last of these conferences was to be held by April 17, 1987.

It was the first amendment agreed to under the new amending procedures and there were some glitches that had to be worked out. For example, the citation clause in the proposed amendment stated: "This Proclamation may be cited as the *Constitution Amendment Proclamation, 1983.*" It was only when the Governor General's proclamation was being drawn up over a year later that it was concluded that it would have been more appropriate to identify the amendment as the Constitution Amendment, 1983, the proclamation being a separate instrument bringing the amendment into force.

Furthermore, it was subsequently concluded that it would have been preferable to identify the amendment as the Constitution Amendment, *Year of Proclamation* and to fill in the actual year at the time of proclamation. Since it was a 7/50 amendment and could not be proclaimed until a year had elapsed from the date of adoption of the resolution initiating it unless all provincial assemblies adopted resolutions of dissent or assent in less time, and since Quebec would take no action on the matter, proclamation could not occur prior to 1984.

A practice firmly established during this process, however, was that once there was agreement on the nature of an amendment, the federal Department of Justice would be asked to translate the intent into a legal draft in English and French upon which other governments and participants would comment.

The ratification process was low-key and timely, but there was little public participation. It was "initiated" when Nova Scotia adopted the first resolution on May 31, 1983. In just over six months (that is, on December 2, 1983), it was adopted by Parliament and all provinces except Quebec.

There was one day of hearings in Manitoba, but no other legislative body provided for hearings. The resolution was debated for only one day and adopted unanimously in Newfoundland, Prince Edward Island, Saskatchewan, Alberta and British Columbia. It was debated for one day only in Nova Scotia, but the vote was split (36 to 4). In New Brunswick, there were two days of debate and the vote was split (41 to 1). There were four days of debate and unanimous adoption in Ontario and Manitoba. The House of Commons debated the amendment for two days and the Senate for five days; in both cases, it was adopted unanimously. Because Quebec took no action, the amendment could not be proclaimed until after May 31, 1984 (i.e., until after a year had elapsed from its initiation).

The federal Department of Justice drew up the text of the proclamation, in collaboration with the Federal-Provincial Relations Office. The provinces, territories and Aboriginal organizations were not involved in developing this text, which was largely a technical instrument to bring the amendment into force.

Proclamation of the Constitution Amendment Proclamation, 1983 occurred in Ottawa on the grounds of Rideau Hall, the Governor General's residence, on June 21, 1984.

THE CONSTITUTION AMENDMENT, 1987 (NEWFOUNDLAND ACT)

When Newfoundland entered Confederation in 1949, the Terms of Union were set out in the schedule to the Newfoundland Act (known, prior to 1982, as the British North America Act, 1949).

Term 17 of the Terms of Union provided that rights respecting denominational schools, common (amalgamated) schools and denominational colleges existing by law in Newfoundland at the time of Union were entrenched in the Constitution: in particular, the right to public funding on a non-discriminatory basis.

The Pentecostal Assemblies did not enjoy by law such denominational school rights in 1949, but over the succeeding years they did establish schools which were duly recognized. They wanted to provide constitutional protection to these acquired rights and the Government of Newfoundland was agreeable.

Discussions were held with the federal government on an amendment to Term 17 to extend entrenched denominational school rights to the Pentecostal Assemblies. The federal Department of Justice prepared a legal text in English and French to achieve this end.

The Constitution Amendment, *Year of Proclamation* (Newfoundland Act) was introduced into the House of Assembly on April 8, 1987, and debate was commenced and concluded on the morning of April 10. There were no hearings.

The amendment moved just as quickly through Parliament. It was introduced in the House of Commons on April 27, 1987, and it was debated and adopted without division on June 23, 1987. There were no hearings. It was introduced in the Senate on June 26 and was debated and adopted on June 30, 1987.

The amendment was proclaimed on December 22, 1987, in the Governor General's study and became the Constitution Amendment, 1987 (Newfoundland Act).

THE CONSTITUTION AMENDMENT, 1993
(NEW BRUNSWICK)

The third amendment by proclamation had a much longer history. New Brunswick adopted a bill which became known as Bill or Law 88 in 1981. It received royal assent on July 17, 1981.

Bill 88 provided for the equality of status and equal rights and privileges for the English and French linguistic communities of New Brunswick and recognized their right to distinct institutions within which cultural, educational and social activities may be carried on. Premier Richard Hatfield, who had supported Prime Minister Trudeau's unilateral patriation package of October 1980, asked whether Bill 88 could be entrenched in the Constitution at the time of patriation. The Prime Minister thought this would complicate matters and suggested it should be held in abeyance for action after patriation had been achieved.

However, following patriation, the Hatfield government's attempts to secure greater equity in practice for the French-speaking community was met with growing opposition by some portions of the English-speaking community and the Premier did not push for a constitutional amendment. The McKenna government, which took office on October 27, 1987, was committed to the constitutional entrenchment of Bill 88.

Premier Frank McKenna subsequently concluded, as had the Government of Canada, that the entrenchment of the principles of Bill 88 would be preferable to entrenching the precise provisions of the bill, some of which might have been potentially ambiguous and could have provoked needless court challenges. It was in this light that the Premier sought agreement with the federal government, in the context of the ratification of the Meech Lake Accord, on a companion bilateral amendment to recognize the role of the legislature and Government of New Brunswick to promote the equality of status and equal rights of the two linguistic communities.

The companion bilateral amendment was developed on the basis of the public hearings undertaken by a select committee of the New Brunswick legislature on the Meech Lake Accord in 1989. The bilateral amendment formed part of a companion resolution to improve the Meech Lake Accord introduced in the Assembly on March 21, 1990, and which was debated for three days. Following the Constitutional Agreement of First Ministers on June 9, 1990, it was withdrawn and a bilateral amendment on the equality of the two linguistic communities agreed upon in Ottawa on June 9 was introduced along with the Meech Lake Accord and a broader companion resolution. The three resolutions were adopted on June 15. However, following the death of the Meech Lake Accord, no further action was taken on New Brunswick's bilateral amendment, the language of which was closely related to the distinct society/linguistic duality clause in the Meech Lake Accord.

Another attempt at a companion bilateral amendment on the issue was made in the context of the Charlottetown Accord negotiations. The text was drafted by the federal Department of Justice after private discussions between federal and New Brunswick officials. The bilateral amendment differed somewhat from the 1990 text. It was attached to the Charlottetown Accord and put to the people in the referendum of October 26, 1992. The referendum passed in New Brunswick with the support of over 61 percent of the vote in the province, although it was not successful nationally.

The Government of New Brunswick decided that it had received a mandate to act on the bilateral amendment, the principle of which had been examined by the New Brunswick Commission on Canadian Federalism (September 10, 1990 to January 14, 1992) and a select committee of the legislature on the Constitution (February 12, 1992, to March 27, 1992). Given the extensive examination of the issue during focus-groups, in-presentations and public hearings over the previous two years and the referendum results, the provincial government decided against further public consultations. The bilateral amendment resolution was introduced on December 4, 1992, and was adopted on December 8, 1992, after two days of debate, by a vote of 37 yeas and 8 nays.

The New Brunswick bilateral amendment resolution was introduced into, debated and adopted by the Senate on December 16, 1992. There were no hearings and the resolution was adopted without division. This was the first (and, to date, the only) amendment resolution leading to a proclamation by the Governor General that was disposed of by the Senate before the House of Commons.

The resolution was introduced in the House of Commons on December 8, 1992, and was debated for one day on December 11, 1992. For technical reasons, it was put to a vote on February 1, 1993. There were no hearings and the resolution was adopted unanimously, on division.

The Constitution Amendment, 1993 (New Brunswick) was proclaimed by the Governor General in the ballroom of Rideau Hall in Ottawa on March 12, 1993.

Prior to proclamation of the New Brunswick amendment, Deborah Coyne, a private citizen resident in Ontario, launched an action in the Federal Court of Canada on February 15, 1993, for a declaration that the Governor General had no jurisdiction to issue the proclamation. She alleged, among other things, that the amendment went beyond the use of English or French within a province and that it was subject to the 7/50 general amending procedure, not the bilateral procedure. Ms. Coyne ultimately concluded that the Federal Court lacked jurisdiction for hearing the case and withdrew her application. The Federal Court passed an order striking out her request for a declaration on July 30, 1993.

THE CONSTITUTION AMENDMENT, 1994 (PRINCE EDWARD ISLAND)

For the better part of a century, there have been advocates of linking Prince Edward Island to the mainland by a bridge or a tunnel and opponents who feared a fixed link would cause the Island to lose its special character, would have a harmful environmental impact and would not necessarily have economic benefits.

It was the decision of whether or not to proceed with a fixed link that deeply divided Islanders. A referendum was held on January 18, 1988, and over 59 percent voted in favour of the fixed link. Once the decision had been taken, there was a technical matter to resolve. The federal government, under the Island's Terms of Union of 1873, had a constitutional obligation to provide and defray all the costs of a steamboat service linking the Island to the mainland. The question arose: could the fixed link replace the federal government's obligation to provide a boat service? In March 1993, the federal court ruled that it could not. The court also raised questions about the constitutionality of levying tolls on a fixed link, given the obligation to defray all costs of the steamboat service.

The federal and provincial governments negotiated the text of an amendment that would clarify that the fixed link is an acceptable substitute for the existing ferry service and that the federal government or a private developer would have the right to charge tolls for use of the fixed link. Again, the federal Department of Justice drafted the text.

The constitutional resolution was introduced into the Prince Edward Island Assembly and adopted unanimously after one day of debate on June 15, 1993. There were no public hearings.

The resolution was subsequently introduced into the House of Commons on February 15, 1994, and debated for one day before it was adopted on February 16, 1994, on a recorded division. There were no public hearings. It was then submitted to the Senate on February 24, 1994, and debated for three days before it was adopted on division on March 21, 1994. There were no public hearings.

The Constitution Amendment, 1994 (Prince Edward Island) was proclaimed at the Governor General's residence in Ottawa, Rideau Hall, on April 15, 1994.

THE PRECEDENTS

All four amendments proclaimed since 1982 resulted from executive level discussions — "executive federalism" in the case of the three bilateral amendments and "extended executive federalism" in the case of the Aboriginal rights amendment.

There were no legislative hearings after introduction of each of the amendment resolutions (except for one day of hearings in Manitoba on the Aboriginal rights amendment).

There was wide public involvement in the broad public policy issue at stake in the case of the Prince Edward Island amendment and the New Brunswick amendment. Once the decision was taken on the fixed link, the policy issue had largely been resolved. The amendment was largely a technical matter.

The substance of the New Brunswick amendment had been debated for over a decade. The English-speaking community was divided on whether or not the equality of the two communities should be entrenched. The French-speaking community was divided in the latter years on whether the language of the amendment should be designed to provide precise justiciable rights or whether it should be more concerned with the principle. The text of the proposed amendment was put before the people during the 1992 referendum. Against this background, no hearings were held on the precise amendment proposal.

All four amendments were essentially one-issue amendments, although the Aboriginal rights amendment had several facets.

The bilateral amendments, obviously, were supported by the provincial governments concerned and no government opposed the 7/50 Aboriginal amendment (although Quebec did not participate in the ratification process). In all cases, the governments had the confidence of the elected House and were able to secure adoption of the constitutional resolutions in a timely fashion.

In all cases, the federal Department of Justice drafted the actual text of the amendment resolution and the federal draft provided the basis for provincial (and, in one case, Aboriginal and territorial) comment.

In the case of the three bilateral amendments, the amendments were initiated by adoption of a resolution by the province concerned. Only subsequently was action undertaken in the Senate and the House of Commons.

Section 47 of the Constitution Act, 1982, which provides the Senate with a six-month suspensive veto over amendments made by proclamation, including bilateral amendments, suggests to some that the House of Commons should pronounce upon an amendment first. The Senate could then determine whether it wished to exercise its veto by rejecting, amending or refusing to take action on the resolution adopted by the House. After six months, the House of Commons could overcome negative action or inaction by the Senate by readopting its initial resolution.

However, section 46 makes clear that the Senate could initiate an amendment on its own and need not wait to respond to action by the House of Commons. Thus, there was no problem in the Senate's adopting the New Brunswick bilateral amendment a month and a half before it was put to a vote in the House of Commons.

6

UNSUCCESSFUL ATTEMPTS AT CONSTITUTIONAL AMENDMENT SINCE 1982

THERE HAVE BEEN more unsuccessful than suc-cessful attempts to amend the Constitution of Canada since 1982. Unsuccessful attempts may be divided into three categories: those pursued by gov-ernments acting in concert; those proposed by gov-ernments acting unilaterally; and non-government initiatives.

GOVERNMENTS ACTING IN CONCERT

There have been six unsuccessful attempts by governments acting in concert to amend the Constitution: the second con-stitutionally mandated Aboriginal rights process; a non-Aboriginal rights constitutional amendment process; the Manitoba lan-guage amendment; the powers of the Senate amendment; the Meech Lake process; and the Charlottetown Accord process.

The Second Aboriginal Rights Process (1983–87)

After agreement was reached on the Constitution Amendment Proclamation, 1983 at the First Ministers' Conference on March 16, 1983, the participants began to prepare for three more first ministers' conferences on Aboriginal rights — one that had been agreed upon in the political accord of March 16 and two that would be required under the terms of the amendment following its eventual proclamation.

Participants were conscious that a high degree of consensus would be required. With Quebec not participating in the ratification process, seven of the other nine provinces representing at least 50 percent of the population would have to support an amendment. In addition, governments wanted significant support from the Aboriginal organizations.

Prior to the 1984 First Ministers' Conference, meetings of officials took place in technical working groups representing the 17 governments or Aboriginal organizations. Four working groups were constituted to deal with: Aboriginal rights; self-government; land and resources; and equality. The working groups allowed all participants to understand the complexity of the issues and encouraged Aboriginal leaders to focus their attention on a few items of particular concern. In the end, it became clear that Aboriginal leaders wished to focus on self-government.

At the 1984 First Ministers' Conference, the federal government introduced a draft amendment to implement self-government through delegated powers; this fell substantially short of the expectations of the Aboriginal peoples. While the proposal did not win the support of the Aboriginal leadership and was supported by only three provinces, it nevertheless brought the concept of self-government to centre stage. Although self-government had been discussed as a concept during parliamentary discussions, and Aboriginal groups had made their own suggestions regarding a self-government amendment, the federal government withheld its draft constitutional amendment until the conference. Other participants reacted negatively to this surprise proposal and the conference ended without agreement.

The process leading to the 1985 First Ministers' Conference focused on constitutional drafts. These drafts recognized self-government rights of the Aboriginal peoples while ensuring that such rights could only be exercised in accordance with agreements negotiated with the federal and provincial governments. The federal draft was circulated in advance and reflected prior multilateral discussions. At least six provinces were prepared to support a version modified by Saskatchewan. However, two of the Aboriginal associations withheld their support.

Subsequent to the 1985 First Ministers' Conference, the federal government put in place a "two-track" strategy: constitutional and non-constitutional. Because some provinces were not prepared to agree to an amendment without more detail on what self-government actually meant, a process of self-government negotiations at the community level (i.e., the non-constitutional track) was initiated. While these self-government discussions were meant to proceed independently of the national debate, they were also intended to demonstrate, in concrete terms, what self-government actually meant. Multilateral meetings of officials and ministers on the constitutional track continued throughout 1986.

Well before the final First Ministers' Conference, it was clear that participants did not want to repeat the experiences of the 1984 and 1985 conferences. From the federal perspective surprises were to be avoided, and all issues were to be addressed by officials — and considered by ministers — prior to the conference. All issues were known and all variables discussed well in advance of the conferences. Yet positions did not change, and indeed became further entrenched. For example, Aboriginal leaders continued to insist that any amendment should confirm the continued existence of their inherent right to self-government. They also insisted that this right should be immediately enforceable in the Constitution, and that provinces should have no role in the constitutional protection of self-government. Some provinces continued to insist that all elements of a self-government amendment should be defined prior to agreeing to an amendment, and that there should be no constitutional commitment to negotiate.

To avoid surprises, several approaches to an amendment were discussed in the months prior to the 1987 First Ministers' Conference. When it became apparent that an agreement would not be reached on the basis of those discussions, several variations of the existing proposals were presented on the eve of the conference. Proposals were developed by provinces which strongly supported an amendment, particularly New Brunswick, Nova Scotia, and Ontario. None was capable of achieving the consensus required.

On the eve of the second day of the conference, the federal government drafted an amendment which tried to capture the views of all participants, in a best effort to reach an agreement. That agreement again failed to achieve the necessary degree of support and the conference ended in failure on March 27, 1987. It was not clear whether, had Quebec been an active participant, the outcome might have been different.

The Non-Aboriginal Constitutional Process (1982–83)

Following patriation of the Constitution, some provinces wished to pursue discussions upon constitutional items that would not be dealt with in the Aboriginal rights process. It was agreed that these matters could be explored tentatively in a separate process. Meetings at the level of officials and ministers on non-Aboriginal rights issues could be held just prior to the scheduled meetings on Aboriginal rights since many (but by no means all) officials would be involved in both processes. Quebec attended the meetings as an observer, but would not participate.

However, to avoid confusion between the two processes and the possibility of paralysing linkages, it was decided that the non-Aboriginal constitutional meetings would be secret and, while held in the same city, at a separate venue. In discussions which began in August 1982, it soon became apparent that:

■ with patriation, the provinces had lost much of their clout in the negotiation process since the federal government did not have its own non-Aboriginal constitutional agenda which might provide the basis for horse-trading; and

■ the federal government was interested in being realistic and practical — which inevitably meant that it would want to whittle down the eight-item agenda proposed by the provinces which included five institutional matters (unified family courts, administrative tribunals, Supreme Court appointments, the Senate and lieutenant-governors), one charter issue (property rights) and two powers items (cablevision/closed circuit television and inland fisheries).

This process carried on until a meeting of ministers in February 1983, at which time the agenda had narrowed to four items (administrative tribunals, unified family courts, lieutenant-governors and property rights). Unanimous agreement by the active participants was reached on only one matter — a technical amendment respecting lieutenant-governors. However, since this was a unanimity item under the amending formula and since Quebec would not move on any amendment until after its own agenda had been addressed, nothing could be accomplished. No further meetings on the non-Aboriginal rights constitutional issues were held.

The Manitoba Language Amendment (1983–84)

On December 13, 1979, the Supreme Court of Canada upheld, in the Forest case, a decision of the Manitoba Court of Appeal to the effect that the 1890 Manitoba statute allowing, among other things, Manitoba statutes to be printed and published in English only was inoperative.

The Government of Manitoba gradually moved to adopt new laws in both languages and to produce regulations in both languages, but it was agreed by the Franco-Manitoban community and the government of Premier Howard Pawley that the provision of certain social services to francophones in areas where they were sufficiently well concentrated to justify the services would be more beneficial to the community than the immediate translation of old laws which, in any event, would not be physically possible.

There was an immediate pressing and practical problem that had to be addressed. The Supreme Court of Canada might declare as a consequence of the Forest decision that all laws adopted in English only since 1890 were null and void — an issue that was raised in the Bilodeau case. If all such laws since 1890 were void, chaos would ensue, because the legislative assembly itself had been elected on the basis of a unilingual English law.

To ensure that Manitoba would be able to meet its constitutional obligations without any threat of chaos in the short term, federal and provincial officials agreed that a constitutional amendment to provide adequate time for the translation, editing and publishing of statutes in French was necessary. In return for agreeing to a period of up to 10 years before the province would have to have completed the task, the Franco-Manitoban community wanted a clear recognition that English and French were the official languages of the province and, under certain circumstances, the public could communicate with certain government offices or agencies and receive services in English or French.

An amendment to achieve these goals was drawn up by federal and Manitoba officials in French and in English and was moved in the legislative assembly on July 4, 1983 (the Constitution Amendment Proclamation, 1983 [Manitoba Act]). There were public hearings in Winnipeg, Thomson, Swan River, Ste. Rose, Brandon, Morden, Arborg and Ste. Anne between September 6 and September 27, 1983, and a large number of witnesses were heard. The proposed amendment roused old passions in Manitoba and grass-roots opposition — as well as grass-roots support — soon dominated the public debate. On January 26, 1984, the legislative assembly was immobilized by a bell-ringing crisis, when the Opposition refused to appear for a vote on a motion to terminate debate on the constitutional resolution.

The impasse continued until February 7, 1984, when the matter was abandoned by the provincial government. On two separate occasions, the House of Commons intervened in the debate:

■ on October 5, 1983, the Prime Minister moved a motion to support the agreement on the amendment that had been reached by the federal and provincial governments with the participation of the Société Franco-Manitobaine and to ask the government and legislative assembly of Manitoba to take action on the issue as expeditiously as possible (under a pre-arranged agreement, the motion was "deemed" to have been adopted following the October 5 debate);

■ on February 24, 1984, the Minister of Transport (Lloyd Axworthy) moved a similar motion which was also "deemed" to have been adopted.

It was all to no avail. Faced with strong opposition, Premier Pawley decided not to pursue the matter. Because of the issues raised in the Bilodeau case, the federal government made a reference to the Supreme Court on the validity of Manitoba laws enacted in English only. The Supreme Court ruled, on June 13, 1985, that all English-only laws were invalid but deemed temporarily valid for the minimum time necessary for their translation and re-enactment in English and French.

Powers of the Senate Amendment (1985)

The Conservative government that came to power in Ottawa in September 1984 was confronted by a Senate that had a Liberal majority. Towards the end of the year, the Senate blocked a government borrowing authority bill and the Government became concerned that its capacity to govern would be severely jeopardized if it could not secure timely passage of key legislation and, in particular, financial bills.

As the impasse carried on into the new year, the Government prepared a constitutional amendment resolution to curb the powers of the Senate along the lines of the United Kingdom Parliament acts of 1911 and 1949 that restricted the powers of the House of Lords. Under the terms of the proposed amendment, the Senate would have a suspensive veto of 30 days on money bills and a 45-day suspensive veto on all other bills. Such a change would be subject to the 7/50 procedure.

The federal government communicated by telephone and by letter with the provinces on its proposed amendment. It was made clear to the provinces that the amendment was not seen by the federal government as a substitute for a more wide-ranging reform of the Senate. Rather, it was a limited change to deal with the pressing partisan challenge by the existing Senate to the Government's authority.

The provincial governments were sympathetic and all agreed to secure adoption of the resolution by their assemblies, except for Quebec and Manitoba. Quebec would take no action on any constitutional amendment pending redress of its own constitutional grievances, but would not oppose the amendment. Manitoba's New Democratic Party government would not approve the amendment since it could only support a proposal to abolish the Senate.

The Minister of Justice, John Crosbie, introduced the Constitution Amendment, *year of proclamation* (Powers of Senate) into the House of Commons on June 7, 1985. Ultimately, it died on the Order Paper for two reasons. First, the new Liberal government of Ontario, sworn in on June 26, 1985, was not disposed to support the amendment and, with the non-participation of Quebec, the 50 percent of the population qualification could not be met for this 7/50 amendment. Second, the Senate had ceased to obstruct the Government and the urgent need for an amendment disappeared.

The Manitoba-Saskatchewan Boundary Amendment (1985)

A portion of the Manitoba-Saskatchewan boundary not then constitutionalized had been surveyed and marked between 1961 and 1972. It was not, however, entrenched in the Constitution through federal legislation with the consent of the legislatures of the two provinces concerned — the pre-patriation method of effecting such a constitutional change.

After April 17, 1982, the new constitutional amendment procedures required an amendment by proclamation by the Governor General authorized by resolutions of the Senate, the House of Commons and the legislative assemblies of the two provinces concerned. The appropriate resolutions were drawn up in 1985, but no action was taken on them. They could be dusted off and brought forward if the federal and two provincial governments concerned were in agreement to proceed.

At the practical level, the border is not in doubt. It has been recorded with the Surveyor General of Canada. The purpose of the amendment would be to give it constitutional protection.

The Alberta-British Columbia Boundary Amendment (1985)

Portions of the Alberta-British Columbia boundary had been based on physical features that may have altered over time. Improved surveying methods provided for clarification of those portions between 1979 and 1981 and the resurveyed border was recorded by the Surveyor General of Canada.

As in the case of the Manitoba-Saskatchewan border, resolutions for an amendment by proclamation by the Governor General authorized by the Senate, the House of Commons and the legislative assemblies of the two provinces concerned were prepared in 1985. The amendment would give constitutional protection to the recorded boundary.

No action was taken on the resolutions, but they could be dusted off and brought forward if the federal and two provincial governments concerned were in agreement to proceed.

Meech Lake (1987–90)

The correspondence between Premier René Lévesque of Quebec and Prime Minister Trudeau following the agreement of November 5, 1981, on patriation and the subsequent proclamation of the Constitution Act, 1982 indicated that the Premier accepted the legality of the patriation package, but not its legitimacy. It also indicated that the Prime Minister was willing, under certain circumstances, to address some of Quebec's constitutional concerns. Nothing concrete transpired, however.

In the 1984 general election, the Leader of the Opposition, Brian Mulroney, held out an olive branch when he said, at Sept-Îles on August 6, 1984:

> There is room in Canada for all identities to be affirmed, for all aspirations to be respected, and for all ideals to be pursued.
>
> I know that many men and women in Quebec will not be satisfied with mere words. We will have to make commitments and take concrete steps to reach the objective that I have set for myself and that I repeat here: to convince the Quebec National Assembly to

give its consent to the new Canadian Constitution with honour and enthusiasm.

I am prepared to study with the provinces possible changes to the amending formula.

But the olive branch was conditional. In the Sept-Îles speech, he added:

But, knowing the importance and the complexity of federal-provincial issues, I will not undertake a constitutional path with ambiguity and improvisation. To proceed otherwise would risk making things much worse rather than better. Before putting gestures which risk engaging us, one more time, in an impasse, it is necessary to have precise terms and ground rules and to meet the minimal conditions of success.

The necessary dialogue will open at an opportune moment, and will proceed within the framework of Canadian federalism, with the legitimate government elected by Quebec.

Following the election, the new Prime Minister and Premier Lévesque met on a number of occasions, but there was no indication that they would reopen the constitutional file. The Liberal Party of Quebec — the Official Opposition in Quebec — adopted on March 3, 1985, a political platform called *Maîtriser l'avenir*. It included five conditions for resolving Quebec's constitutional boycott. For its part, the Parti Québécois government unveiled its *Projet d'accord constitutionnel* on May 17, 1985, which contained 22 constitutional demands, including the virtual removal of Quebec from the application of the Canadian Charter of Rights and Freedoms.

On December 2, 1985, Robert Bourassa's Liberals were elected as the new Government of Quebec. Nothing transpired on the constitutional front until Gil Rémillard enunciated Quebec's conditions for accepting the Constitution Act, 1982 in a speech at Mont Gabriel on May 9, 1986. The conditions were essentially the same at those set out in *Maîtriser l'avenir*. The Mont Gabriel speech set in motion a discreet process aimed at determining whether successful negotiations could be conducted on the Quebec conditions. Those conditions related to constitutional recognition of Quebec's distinct society; a constitutional veto for

Quebec or the equivalent; provincial participation in the nomination of Supreme Court judges; constraints on the spending power of Parliament; and a strengthening of provincial powers over immigration.

At their annual meeting, the premiers issued the Edmonton Declaration of August 12, 1986, which identified as their top constitutional priority the launching of a federal-provincial process, using Quebec's five proposals as a basis for discussion, to bring about Quebec's "full and active participation in the Canadian federation." Subsequently, further constitutional discussions could be pursued on matters such as Senate reform, fisheries and property rights.

In adopting this position, the premiers essentially called for a "Quebec round" before pursuing other constitutional issues. The Prime Minister formally endorsed this position at the November 1986 First Ministers' Conference.

Agreement on the terms of patriation was reached in November 1981 through an exercise of executive federalism. It is not surprising that political actors assumed Quebec's reintegration into the constitutional family could be achieved through executive federalism. However, *the process of executive federalism they adopted was new:* there were no multilateral mechanisms put in place, such as the Continuing Committee of Ministers on the Constitution or the Continuing Committee of Officials on the Constitution, and there were no deadlines set in advance.

Rather, there was a double process of bilateralism established for the "vérification des préalables": formal negotiations would not be launched unless the minimal conditions for success had been met. Gil Rémillard, the Quebec minister, met each of his provincial counterparts individually and, after each meeting, he briefed Senator Lowell Murray, the federal minister. Senator Murray met with each of the provincial ministers individually and briefed Gil Rémillard after each meeting to ensure that there were no misunderstandings or misinterpretations.

Only when this *double process of bilateral executive federalism* produced a reasonable assurance that the political will to reach an accommodation with Quebec had emerged was a multilateral meeting of officials convened

in Ottawa on March 5–6, 1987. This led to a first ministers' conference at a secluded retreat at Meech Lake in the
Gatineau Hills, just north of Ottawa, on April 30. Agreement
in principle was reached. Quebec held public hearings on
the agreement in principle while federal and provincial officials refined a legal draft that had been prepared by the
federal Department of Justice. First ministers met again
in the Langevin Building in Ottawa on June 2–3, 1987,
and unanimous agreement on the legal text of a constitutional amendment resolution was reached.

The Meech Lake Accord would have changed the amending formula in two respects (see Appendix 19):

■ it would have extended obligatory reasonable compensation to all cases where a province opts out of
   an amendment transferring provincial legislative
   powers to Parliament (as Premier Lévesque had
   asked in 1981–82); and

■ it would have expanded the list of items subject to
   unanimous consent for amendment by adding Senate
   reform, all aspects of the Supreme Court, the principle of proportionate representation of the provinces
   in the House of Commons and the creation of new
   provinces and the extension of existing provinces
   into the territories (giving Quebec — and all provinces,
   in order to respect the principle of the equality of the
   provinces — a veto over institutional matters where
   opting out was not applicable).

Initial broad public support greeted the signing of the
Meech Lake Accord. Quebec moved quickly to approve the
constitutional resolution on June 23, 1987, thereby initiating the ratification process. Because Quebec said that
all five of its conditions had to be addressed to end its constitutional isolation, the constitutional resolution was
drafted as an unseverable whole. Since the resolution contained amendments requiring unanimous legislative
approval, for which there was no time limit for ratification, and amendments requiring the consent of Parliament
and two-thirds of the legislative assemblies representing
at least 50 percent of the population, for which a three-
year time limit existed, it was determined that:

■   the resolution would have to be adopted by all legislative assemblies and Parliament; and

■   unanimous ratification would have to be achieved
within three years.

Parliamentary hearings were held on the resolution, but
no amendments to it would be contemplated by the federal government unless there was an egregious error: any
change would have to be renegotiated with the provinces
and would invalidate the resolutions already adopted.
Gradually, various voices started to express concerns: in
particular, certain women's organizations, multicultural
groups, Aboriginal peoples and the territories said their
interests had been ignored or would be jeopardized or
harmed by the proposed changes. Canadians, particularly in Western Canada, felt the new unanimity rule for
Senate reform would make eventual reform impossible.
What had been conceived of by governments as the Quebec
Round, and would open the door to subsequent constitutional changes, was perceived by many as an exclusion of
the interests of others.

To growing popular dissatisfaction was added another factor that made ratification problematic. In October 1987,
the Government of New Brunswick was defeated by an opposition that had clearly stated it would not ratify Meech Lake
unless it was amended. Subsequently, the governments of
Manitoba and Newfoundland fell: this meant that three
of the premiers were not signatories of the Meech Lake
Accord, which was a political agreement, and not legally
binding.

During the ratification process (see Appendixes 21 and 22),
public hearings on the resolution were not held in
Saskatchewan, Alberta, Nova Scotia, British Columbia or
Newfoundland, nor in Quebec (where hearings had been
held on the agreement in principle, but not on the legal
text). Hearings that did not produce changes to the legal
text were held by the House of Commons (jointly with the
Senate on one occasion, separately on another), Prince
Edward Island and Ontario. Hearings in New Brunswick
suggested the desirability of changes, perhaps through a
companion (or supplementary resolution), and hearings in
Manitoba also suggested changes — notably the adoption
of a "Canada clause" to embrace all of the basic charac-

teristics of Canada, and not just Quebec's distinct society. Separate hearings by the Senate resulted in changes to the resolution by the Senate: this required a second resolution by the House of Commons to override the Senate.

It became clear in the course of public hearings that the proclamation of the Charter of Rights and Freedoms in 1982 had a profound effect on Canadian society: it had created a sense of empowerment under the Charter, particularly among minorities, and a sense of ownership of the Constitution. Furthermore, the Charter gave Canadians a fundamental legal tool to challenge federal and provincial government action.

New Brunswick proposed a companion resolution to address the concerns of those who felt excluded from the Quebec Round. The House of Commons held hearings on New Brunswick's companion resolution and responded affirmatively in the Charest Report of May 17, 1990.

By the beginning of June 1990, with the June 23 deadline for ratification only a few weeks away, two provinces (New Brunswick and Manitoba) had not ratified Meech Lake and one (Newfoundland) had rescinded its earlier approval. From June 3 to June 9, first ministers met in another exercise of executive federalism, in private. On June 9, they issued a communiqué that seemed to provide the basis for the successful ratification of the Meech Lake Accord, but that did not transpire.

New Brunswick adopted three resolutions on June 15 — one on the Meech Lake Accord, one on a companion resolution that would supplement the Meech Lake Accord and one on a bilateral amendment on the equality of the two linguistic communities in New Brunswick. The Government of Manitoba, with the support of the two opposition parties, sought to introduce, from June 12 to the expiry of the ratification period, the Meech Lake constitutional resolution, but one New Democratic Party member, Elijah Harper, refused the unanimous consent necessary to proceed.

In Newfoundland, there was a question of political will to resolve. Under the terms of the June 9 constitutional agreement, the Premier of Newfoundland agreed to "undertake to submit the *Constitution Amendment, 1987* for appropriate legislative or public consideration and to use every possible effort to achieve decision prior to June 23, 1990." As the deadline for ratification drew near, it was apparent that Manitoba would not be able to meet it for procedural reasons. If Manitoba could not ratify the resolution within the three-year time limit, was the amendment dead? In the circumstances, why would the House of Assembly in Newfoundland have to pronounce one way or the other?

The federal government, seeking a way out of what appeared to be an impasse because of the procedural problem in Manitoba, thought that if Newfoundland demonstrated its political will by adopting the amendment before the deadline, a reference could be made to the Supreme Court of Canada on whether the second resolution assenting to the amendment — by Saskatchewan, on September 23, 1987 — could be deemed the resolution that initiated the Meech Lake ratification process. If so, Manitoba would have up to three months to resolve its procedural problems and, of course, Quebec would have to adopt the resolution again.

If, however, Newfoundland had not demonstrated its political will to resolve the issue by adopting the resolution, the Court would have to pronounce on a situation where there were technical difficulties in one province and no demonstration of a firm commitment to action in another. The Government of Canada felt that only the technical issue in Manitoba should be outstanding when the Court was asked to pronounce.

This proposition was put to Premier Clyde Wells on June 22 by Senator Murray. Premier Wells thought that an immediate vote in Newfoundland would result in rejection of the amendment and he felt the Court should pronounce on legalities, not political commitment, even if the resolution had not been adopted by Newfoundland. Senator Murray disagreed. When the Manitoba and Newfoundland assemblies adjourned on June 22 without having brought the matter to a vote, the Meech Lake Accord was deemed to be dead.

The failure of Meech was therefore attributed in large measure to three factors: *process, substance* and *political will.* On the question of process, it was clear that not involving the public in hearings until every legal detail had been locked in was unsatisfactory. On the question of process, also, it was felt that the indivisible character of the constitutional resolution subject to the double constraints of unanimity and three years might be at issue and, indeed, perhaps the amending formula itself might need to be reexamined. On the question of substance, it was also clear that there was not broad public understanding and support outside Quebec for a limited Quebec Round: rather, there was a desire to be comprehensive and inclusive. On the question of political will, the lack of a vote in Newfoundland meant that the federal government could not make an extraordinary reference to the Supreme Court arising out of purely procedural difficulties.

The Charlottetown Accord (1990–92)

After the failure of Meech, it might have been preferable to take a pause, to reflect and to await a more opportune time to return to constitutional issues. That could not be.

Meech died on the eve of *La St-Jean Baptiste,* the *fête nationale,* or national holiday, of Quebecers. June 24 is a public holiday in Quebec and the streets of Montreal seethed with blue and white provincial flags as nationalist sentiment ran high. Polls suggested that over 60 percent of Quebecers would have supported sovereignty if a referendum were held at that time. Sovereignists, indeed, called for an immediate referendum.

Throughout the rest of Canada, feelings were also running high. In some quarters, there was a call for Quebec to become a province like all the others or to depart — and not necessarily on the most generous terms. There was anger also among those who had felt excluded from the Quebec Round and who wanted to see their constitutional goals realized.

During the summer of 1990, a crisis occurred when Mohawks at Oka, Quebec, put up barricades in the course of a dispute with the townspeople and the Quebec Provincial Police. Matters escalated and a Quebec Provincial Police officer was killed. A settlement was eventually reached, but not until after the Canadian Armed Forces had been drawn in. One effect of the Oka crisis was to highlight the need for governments to address long-standing Aboriginal constitutional concerns, including the issue of Aboriginal self-government.

The atmosphere was volatile and it was imperative to buy time until cooler heads and more rational analysis could prevail.

It was in Quebec that the situation was most acute. To the perception of the "betrayal" of Quebec by the rest of Canada on November 5, 1981, was added the perception of "rejection" of Quebec by the rest of Canada on June 23, 1990.

The Quebec Liberal Party, during the last period of the Meech Lake ratification process, reaffirmed its support for the Meech Lake Accord in February 1990 and established an internal commission, under the chairmanship of Jean Allaire, to develop a constitutional position for the subsequent round of negotiations that would follow the proclamation of Meech. The Allaire Report, published on January 28, 1991 — after the demise of Meech — represented a radical departure from the five conditions that had led to the Accord.

The Meech Lake Accord had been high on symbolism and affirming the right of Quebec to be an active participant in Canada's future constitutional development. It would have recognized Quebec as a distinct society within Canada, entrenched the existing statutory requirement that three of the nine Supreme Court judges come from the Quebec civil law bar, provided a veto for Quebec — and all other provinces — over the reform of national institutions and the creation of new provinces, established a constraint on the exercise of the spending power of Parliament and expanded the jurisdiction of Quebec over immigration (an area of joint jurisdiction, but with federal primacy, under the Constitution).

The Allaire Report — which was adopted by the Quebec Liberal Party — rejected this approach and focused squarely on a new distribution of powers that would have expanded considerably the jurisdiction of Quebec at the expense of the federal Parliament. It recommended a new Canadian political structure that would reinforce the Canadian economic union, while providing political autonomy for the Quebec state, principally by establishing exclusive Quebec legislative jurisdiction over 22 areas, ranging from matters such as social affairs, culture, health, family policy and manpower policy to communications, the environment, agriculture and public security.

The report also recommended that a Quebec referendum be held before the end of the fall of 1992, either on a Quebec–Canada proposal for reform or on the accession of Quebec to sovereignty.

The Allaire Report was an expression of the high level of nationalist sentiment in Quebec in the wake of the failure of Meech, but many interests in the rest of the country rejected it as unrealistic.

On September 4, 1990, the Quebec National Assembly established an "extended" legislative commission, composed of 36 persons, including 17 who were not elected politicians and who represented municipalities, unions, cooperatives, the cultural milieu, business and education. The elected politicians on the commission included three Quebec MPs from the federal Parliament. It was co-chaired by Michel Bélanger and Jean Campeau.

The commission's mandate was to examine the political and constitutional status of Quebec and to make recommendations to the National Assembly. The commission's composition was designed to foster as broad a consensus as possible among Quebecers. The commission held public televised hearings in eleven cities and towns in Quebec, received 607 briefs and heard 237 groups or individuals.

The Bélanger-Campeau Commission concluded in its report on March 27, 1991, that there were two possible solutions to bring to an end the impasse between Quebec and the rest of Canada:

- a profoundly altered federal system; or

- Quebec sovereignty.

The commission recommended that the National Assembly:

- adopt a referendum law that would require a referendum on sovereignty as early as June 8, 1992, and no later than October 26, 1992; and

- establish two legislative commissions, one to examine the question of Quebec's accession to sovereignty and one to examine any offer of renewed federalism that the Government of Canada and the other provinces might bring forward.

Three consequences flowed from the acceptance of these recommendations by the National Assembly:

■ the constitutional debate could not be avoided;

■ there would be a timetable for resolving the issue; and

■ Quebec would not join multilateral discussions in which the governments of Canada and the other provinces might seek agreement on renewed federalism: but the Allaire Report, which had been adopted by the Quebec Liberal Party, gave a clear indication of the sort of renewed federalism the Government of Quebec envisaged.

All other provinces and territories took initiatives to examine the constitutional question, although not at the same time and not through the same means. However, one thing was common to them all: they sought to get a clearer understanding of the views of the people within each province or territory on the Constitution.

■ *Yukon* set up a select committee on constitutional development on May 14, 1990, and hearings were held before it submitted its report in May 1991;

■ *Prince Edward Island* established a special committee in the summer of 1990 which held hearings and reported in September 1991;

■ *New Brunswick* created a legislative commission on Canadian federalism in September 1990: it held no public hearings, but it did receive briefs and organized round-tables and in camera sessions before reporting in March 1992;

■ *Ontario* appointed a select committee in December 1990 which held public hearings before reporting in February 1992;

■ *Manitoba* established a legislative constitutional task force in December 1990 which held public hearings and reported in October 1991;

■ *Alberta's* Select Special Committee on Constitutional Reform was created in March 1991: it held public hearings and reported in March 1992;

- in *Nova Scotia,* a non-legislative working group was set up in June 1991 and held hearings before tabling its report in November 1991;

- *Saskatchewan* set up a task force on Saskatchewan's future in Confederation in August 1991: it held hearings and reported in February 1992;

- *Newfoundland* established a constitutional committee in September 1991: it was formed by seven members of the House of Assembly and seven persons from outside the Assembly and held hearings, but its report to the Premier was not made public;

- the *Northwest Territories* appointed a special committee of the assembly on constitutional reform in December 1991, but it did not make a substantive report; and

- *British Columbia's* Select Special Committee on Constitutional Reform originated in January 1992 and reported in April of that year, following public hearings.

On November 1, 1990, the Government of Canada announced the creation of a commission to promote dialogue among all Canadians and encourage the development of a new consensus about Canada and its future. The Prime Minister stated that much of the consensus Canadians had developed on what constituted Canada and where the country should go had dissipated, and Canada was running the risk of fracturing along linguistic and regional fault lines. The commission, under the chairmanship of Keith Spicer, was to be "an initiative for the people and of the people," the Prime Minister said, and it was to be "informal and easily accessible."

The mandate was broad and the Spicer Commission moved into largely uncharted waters, not without considerable organizational and other difficulties. It had to cope with widespread cynicism towards politicians and the political process, and a public mood described by a former premier of Ontario as "cranky."

In its report, tabled on June 27, 1991, the Spicer Commission concluded that Canadians were disenchanted with elected politicians and that politicians of all parties should consider using new techniques to increase greatly grass-

roots consultations in developing ideas, policies and programs and in solving problems which affect citizens directly. In short, it called for *new processes,* without recommending
the substance that should orient Canada's future constitutional development.

The Government of Canada also moved on a second front:
a special joint committee, the Beaudoin-Edwards Committee,
was established on December 17, 1990, to examine the amending formula and the process for achieving constitutional
change. The committee received over 500 briefs, and heard
209 groups or individuals while travelling to every province
and territory before delivering its report on June 20, 1991.

The principal recommendation of the Beaudoin-Edwards
Committee was that amendments now subject to the 7/50
formula revert, in essence, to the so-called Victoria formula of 1971 which would have given individual vetoes to
both Ontario and Quebec, but to no other province acting
alone. This was roundly denounced by three provinces,
which defended the principle of the equality of the
provinces. Since changes to the amending formula require
unanimous consent, it was clear that this recommendation would not provide a solution for a key question of
process.

The Beaudoin-Edwards Report did propose that federal legislation be adopted to enable the federal government, at
its discretion, to hold a consultative referendum on a constitutional proposal, either to confirm the existence of a
national consensus or to facilitate the adoption of the
required resolutions to ratify an amendment. Indeed, this
was not incompatible with government policy revealed a
month earlier.

In the speech from the throne of May 13, 1991, the federal government announced that Parliament would "be called
upon to enact legislation permitting the men and women
of Canada to participate more fully in the process of constitutional change." Two days later, on May 15, 1991, the
Quebec government tabled Bill 150, which required a
provincial referendum on Quebec sovereignty in June or
October 1992, as proposed by the Bélanger-Campeau
Commission. The bill was passed on June 20, 1991.

On May 15, 1992, the federal government tabled its own legislation providing for referendums on the Constitution. It would permit a Canada-wide referendum or a referendum in one or more provinces. Bill C-81 was adopted on June 22, 1992.

Quebec was not the only province that made provision for a constitutional referendum. British Columbia adopted the Constitutional Amendment Approval Act in July 1990. In Alberta, the Constitutional Referendum Act was passed in June 1992. Newfoundland amended its Election Act in June 1992 to allow a plebiscite on constitutional matters "in conjunction with a plebiscite or referendum held by the Government of Canada."

On the issue of *substance,* the federal government began to take important steps in early 1991. On April 21, 1991, Joe Clark was appointed Minister Responsible for Constitutional Affairs and Chairman of the Cabinet Committee on Canadian Unity (CCCU). The CCCU began to meet on a weekly basis and to hold meetings in various centres across Canada, with the avowed purpose of developing federal constitutional proposals for consideration by the people of Canada.

On September 28, 1991, the federal government published *Shaping Canada's Future Together,* its proposals for constitutional change. They were broad and far-reaching. They dealt with, among other things:

- the Canadian identity;

- Quebec's distinctiveness;

- the Aboriginal peoples;

- the reform of national institutions;

- the economic union;

- clarifying the distribution of powers, including the spending power, to serve Canadians better; and

- streamlining government.

The federal government also published a series of background papers on constitutional issues to facilitate public debate.

If the proposals were broad and far-reaching, there was one respect in which they were not: only 7/50 matters were actively proposed. While the federal government indicated a willingness to contemplate action on certain unanimity matters, this would depend on a consensus emerging both on the substance of the amendment and the desirability of proceeding with such an amendment in the final package. If only 7/50 matters were in the package, and if the elements in the ultimate constitutional resolution were severable, there would be greater flexibility: one need not have the same 7/50 combination on every matter and the danger of paralysing linkages would be reduced.

Thus, while the federal government continued to support the Meech Lake amending formula proposal, it would only be prepared to proceed with it under the following conditions:

- a consensus on the proposal would have to develop;

- the accession of existing territories to provincehood would have to proceed on the basis of the current procedure (7/50) and not unanimity, as under the Meech Lake Accord; and

- there would have to be agreement on the desirability of proceeding on unanimity matters in the final package.

Parliament had established a special joint committee on a renewed Canada on June 21, 1991, mandated "to enquire into and make recommendations to Parliament on the Government of Canada's proposals for a renewed Canada contained in the documents to be referred to it by the Government." The September proposals were duly submitted to the committee — eventually known as the Beaudoin-Dobbie Committee.

By November, for a number of reasons, including logistics, the committee's work was in question and — with a February 28, 1992, reporting deadline — tensions mounted. It was not clear whether the committee would be able to complete its work successfully and in a timely fashion.

In this context, the Government decided on an initiative that would assist the committee and, if a report were not ultimately possible, that would provide an acceptable alternative. Five three-day national conferences would be organized under the arms-length auspices of independent organizations or institutes:

- on January 17–19, the Atlantic Provinces Economic Council held a conference on the distribution of powers in Halifax;

- on January 24–26, the Canada West Foundation organized a conference in Calgary on national institutions;

- from January 31 to February 2, the C. D. Howe Institute and the Institute for Research on Public Policy sponsored a conference on the economic union in Montreal;

- the Niagara Institute was responsible for a conference in Toronto on the distinct society, the Canada clause and the charter on February 7–9; and

- the five independent agencies and the federal government shared responsibility for the closing conference on February 14–16 in Vancouver.

There were between 200 and 260 participants in each conference. The members of the Beaudoin-Dobbie Committee were invited to all (the conferences were held from Friday to Sunday). The conference organizers were instructed to provide a balanced representation of regions, the two official languages and the two genders when selecting participants from among experts and interest groups. The federal, provincial and territorial governments, as well as the Aboriginal peoples, had a number of places each.

However, there was a major innovation. "Ordinary" citizens were invited to participate in a lottery for about 50 places reserved for the general public at each conference. Applications were classed by preferred conference and by province: names were then drawn by chance (with a regional balance) and the successful candidate would be invited to attend at no cost to the individual.

The conferences operated on the basis of working groups of 15 to 20 persons which would debate and then report back to plenary sessions, with a final wrap-up session. There was national television coverage of the conferences.

The conferences were a clear success from the organizational and logistical point of view and helped restore credibility to the federal government after the initial tribulations of the Beaudoin-Dobbie Committee. They raised the profile of the constitutional debate and provided good public coverage of often complex issues. However, the final conference produced what was deemed a "fragile" consensus, which included support for recognition of Quebec's distinct society.

The Government of Canada had agreed in the fall of 1991 to fund a parallel process by the four national Aboriginal associations. Each association held hearings or consultations on constitutional issues among its membership and provided input into the Beaudoin-Dobbie Committee. Furthermore, the Aboriginal associations and the federal government organized a sixth national conference in Ottawa on Aboriginal issues, but it took place on March 13–15, after the Beaudoin-Dobbie Committee had reported.

Notwithstanding its early difficulties, the Beaudoin-Dobbie Committee received over 3,000 briefs and heard 700 witnesses. The committee experienced some high drama as it tried to reach unanimity on a report by its deadline. In the end, the report was unanimous and the committee respected its deadline by a whisker's breadth.

By this point, every province had concluded or was nearing conclusion of consultations with the public on constitutional renewal. The federal government had conducted three consultations: the Spicer Commission, the Beaudoin-Edwards Committee and the Beaudoin-Dobbie Committee. Five national conferences had been held. The Aboriginal peoples of Canada had conducted four consultations with their constituents and were soon to hold a national conference. The two territorial governments also had consulted their constituents.

In brief, from the demise of Meech on June 23, 1990, to the spring of 1992, all governments and the Aboriginal peoples engaged in consultations, but no intergovernmental negotiations were held.

As noted earlier, the precedents established before Meech provided no clear rules for the successful negotiation of a constitutional agreement. Meech itself provided lessons, but not prescriptions.

It was in this context that Joe Clark launched a new multilateral process on March 12, 1992. It proved to be, in one respect, the most broadly based exercise in *extended executive federalism,* because the territories and the Aboriginal peoples were included as full participants in a comprehensive Canada Round. Yet it was also truncated, because Quebec — representing over 25 percent of the Canadian population — was not at the table. There were 16 delegations at the table, but a seventeenth — Quebec — was absent.

The Multilateral Meetings on the Constitution (MMC), comprising federal, provincial and territorial ministers and the representatives of the Aboriginal peoples, were chaired by Mr. Clark. Collectively, the members of the MMC were referred to as the Principals.

Although it constituted an exercise in *extended executive federalism,* the MMC did provide full and frank briefings at the end of each day of its work to the press: each of the 16 members would make a brief presentation and answer questions. In this way, it was hoped to open up a closed process and to keep the people of Canada abreast of the issues.

The MMC was supported by the Continuing Committee on the Constitution (CCC), comprising federal, provincial and territorial deputy ministers and the representatives of the four national Aboriginal associations. Four working groups of officials were established:

- Working Group 1 examined the Canada Clause — the definition of the fundamental characteristics of Canada — and the amending formula. It was co-chaired by a federal and a provincial official;

- Working Group 2 dealt with institutions, notably with the contentious issue of whether a new elected Senate should have equitable or equal provincial representation. It was chaired by a federal official.

- Working Group 3 concentrated on Aboriginal peoples and their inherent and treaty rights. It was co-chaired by a federal, a provincial and an Aboriginal official.

■ Working Group 4, which turned its attention to the distribution of powers, the spending power, the economic union and a social charter, was co-chaired by a federal and a provincial official.

Reports from the working groups were cleared by the CCC before they were submitted to the MMC.

The multilateral process was to conclude its work by the end of May in order to set out to Quebec proposals upon which a referendum on renewed federalism, rather than sovereignty, could be held. Progress was slow and difficulties emerged. In particular, Quebec's known demand for a constitutional veto over institutional reform was challenged by governments that claimed an equal Senate had to be part of a constitutional agreement. The federal government's September 1991 proposal of a 7/50 package had to give way to a unanimity proposal, with a number of linkages among the items.

The MMC concluded its work on June 11, 1992, without resolving some outstanding issues, including the Senate representation question. At a July 7 meetings of the premiers, with Mr. Clark, the territories and Aboriginal representatives in attendance, agreement was reached on a package which included the inherent right to Aboriginal self-government, recognition of Quebec's distinct society, a Canada clause, an equal Senate, a veto for all provinces over subsequent institutional reform, except the creation of new provinces in the territories and strengthened legislative jurisdiction for the provinces.

The Premier of Quebec and the Prime Minister of Canada were not present at the July 7 meeting and the agreement remained tentative. However, after some bilateral enquiries, Premier Robert Bourassa concluded that the "essence" of the Meech Lake Accord was covered by the July 7 consensus report and he agreed to join the other first ministers at the Prime Minister's summer residence on August 4 and again on August 10 for informal discussions. Territorial and Aboriginal representatives were not present at these discussions, but they were full participants at two further meetings of first ministers in Ottawa and Charlottetown, where unanimous agreement was reached on a consensus report on August 28, 1992.

One major new element in the Charlottetown Accord was an agreement to readjust representation in the House of Commons to better reflect representation by population to respond to pressures from populous Ontario and fast-growing British Columbia. This constituted a trade-off for equal representation in the Senate. Furthermore, Quebec was given a guarantee in perpetuity of at least 25 percent of the seats in the House of Commons.

With respect to the amending formula (see Appendix 23), the Charlottetown Accord would have provided for obligatory reasonable compensation in all cases of opting out of transfers of provincial jurisdiction to Parliament, as agreed upon in the Meech Lake Accord.

It would also have placed the institutional matters in section 42 (the 7/50 procedure, with no opting out) under section 41 (the unanimity rule), as agreed upon in the Meech Lake Accord, with the following differences:

■ the method of selecting judges of the Supreme Court of Canada would remain under section 42;

■ the unanimity rule would also apply to the procedure in the Constitution Act, 1871 governing the creation of new provinces in the territories or the extension of existing provinces into the territories (but new provinces so created would not have a role in authorizing amendments to the Constitution);

■ the unanimity rule would further apply to the "Senate floor" for House of Commons representation contained in section 51A of the 1867 act; and

■ the unanimity rule would extend, tentatively, to the number and qualifications of Aboriginal senators (although this matter would have to be pursued in the autumn of 1992).

A special procedure was added to the amending formula which would have required the "substantial consent" of the Aboriginal peoples referred to in an amendment directly referring to or amending a provision of the Constitution that directly referred to one or more of the Aboriginal peoples of Canada or their governments. Furthermore, any of the Aboriginal peoples of Canada could initiate such an amendment.

The scope of the amending procedure requiring the substantial consent of the Aboriginal peoples was precise and narrow: only amendments *directly referring* to the Aboriginal peoples — and not amendments *affecting* them — were covered. On the other hand, the term "substantial consent" was less precise and it was not clear how and by whom it would be expressed.

The proposed changes to the amending formula represented a special victory for the territories. Under the Constitution Act, 1871, Saskatchewan and Alberta were carved out of the territories and made provinces by act of the federal Parliament. Under the Constitution Act, 1982, the creation of new provinces in the territories was made subject to the 7/50 procedure. The Meech Lake Accord would have made the rule even more difficult by requiring unanimous consent.

Under the Charlottetown Accord, the creation of new provinces in the territories would revert to the 1871 rule which did not require the consent of any of the existing provinces. However, the addition of new provinces could change the operation of the amending formula. At present, at least one Atlantic province must consent to a 7/50 amendment, but if there were 12 or 13 provinces, such an amendment could be achieved notwithstanding the unanimous opposition of the Atlantic provinces.

Since changes to the amending formula are subject to the unanimity rule, it was agreed that provinces created in the territories by Parliament with no requirement of consent from the existing provinces would have no role to play in authorizing 7/50 and unanimity amendments. The new provinces could only gain a role in the amending procedure through a subsequent constitutional amendment, which would require unanimous consent.

First ministers also agreed at Charlottetown to hold two referendums on October 26: one in all of Canada, except Quebec, under federal auspices and one in Quebec under that province's jurisdiction. Through negotiations among all governments, it was agreed to put the following question to the people in both referendums:

> Do you agree that the Constitution of Canada should be renewed on the basis of the agreement reached on August 28, 1992?

In British Columbia and Newfoundland, no legislation was necessary to allow the federal referendum to supplant the provincial one. In Alberta, the Constitutional Referendum Act was amended on September 22 by Bill 54, which allowed federal legislation to displace provincial legislation for the purposes of the October 26 referendum (or any future federal referendum the assembly might agree to allow to displace the requirement for a provincial referendum). In Quebec, Bill 36 had been introduced on May 14, 1992, and adopted on June 19 to allow the provincial government to delay until September 9 a vote on the question to be put in the referendum. Bill 44, introduced on September 3 and adopted on September 8, provided for the question on the Charlottetown Accord, and not sovereignty, in the provincial referendum.

As a political matter, it was agreed among leaders that the referendum would have to be supported in all provinces in order to pass, although this was not legally required.

Notwithstanding the unanimous agreement of eleven first ministers, two government leaders and four Aboriginal leaders, the referendum campaign did not go well for proponents of the Accord.

To facilitate debate and understanding, the text of the Charlottetown Accord was sent to every household in the country, and when the legal drafts to give effect to the Accord were agreed upon on October 9, copies of the drafts were made available to the public at Post Offices throughout the country.

There is no clear answer to explain why the people of Canada did not approve the Charlottetown Accord in the referendum. There are, however, some indicators.

The "yes" committees were poorly organized at the outset. The Accord was sold largely as an honourable compromise that would avoid the unhappy consequences of failure, rather than as a stirring vision of the future. The "no" committees attacked specific elements of a large and complex agreement, often arguing that the whole deal should be rejected because of one element that was deemed unacceptable. The sense of popular empowerment and ownership engendered by the proclamation of the Charter of Rights and Freedoms in 1982 probably reinforced the desire to seek full satisfaction on specific items and perhaps lessened interest in the broader picture and the ultimate need for compromise.

In some quarters, the 25 percent guarantee of Commons seats for Quebec offended democratic sensibilities. In others, it fed anti-Quebec sentiment. Some people called for a clearer understanding of exactly what Aboriginal self-government would entail. Others maintained that the equal and elected Senate had been bought at the cost of ineffectiveness. Some women's groups felt that gender equality issues had not be adequately addressed. Aboriginal leaders said that there was insufficient time for them to study the legal drafts and to arrive at a proper assessment.

Preston Manning, Leader of the Reform Party, played upon the disenchantment of electors with politicians and presented the agreement negotiated by 17 parties as "the Mulroney deal."

In Quebec, there was hard-core sovereignist opposition in the order of 30 percent to begin with. Early in the campaign, tapes of a private telephone conversation between two of Premier Robert Bourassa's top advisors were leaked: they portrayed the Premier as weak in the final negotiations and as having settled for too little to satisfy Quebec's interests. Later in the campaign, secret Quebec documents reinforcing these perceptions were leaked and published in a Quebec bi-monthly news magazine, *L'actualité*.

The political requirement of unanimous provincial consent compelled leaders in each province to prove that the province was a "winner" — and this was often done by trying to score off the interests of other provinces.

The people of Quebec and British Columbia remained opposed to the Accord throughout the campaign. One polling expert believes that the first week of October was decisive: following the October 1 attack on the Accord by former Prime Minister Trudeau and polling results that indicated Quebec would not vote in favour of the Accord, many Canadians, he claimed, felt liberated from the obligation to vote yes in the name of national unity: there was a dramatic drop in support of 20 percent after the first week in October and the loss proved irreversible.

On October 26, the Accord was rejected by a majority of Canadians in a majority of provinces, including a majority of Quebecers and a majority of Indians living on reserves. 54 percent of Quebecers rejected the Accord. 62 percent of Indians living on reserves said "no." In Ontario, the "yes" option won narrowly by 49.8 percent to 49.6 percent: there were 29,000 rejected ballots that made up the balance.

It should be noted, however, that almost 4,500,000 Canadians outside Quebec, or over 45 percent of those voting, said "yes" and 1,700,000 Quebecers, or over 43 percent of those voting, also said "yes." Over 37 percent of Indians living on reserves voted for the Accord.

Voter turnout was not as high as had been anticipated: the average turnout outside Quebec was 72 percent and ranged from a high of 76 percent in British Columbia to a low of 54 percent in Newfoundland. The turnout in Quebec was high: 82.8 percent.

A desirable outcome for governments would have been an affirmative vote in all provinces. Failing such a result, the results obtained were probably the next most desirable: Quebecers had not been rejected by the rest of Canada, the rest of Canada had not been rejected by Quebec, Aboriginal peoples had not been rejected by non-Aboriginal peoples. This led to a generalized calm following the referendum — unlike the failure to ratify the Meech Lake Accord.

What can be said of the process? The period from June 23, 1990, to March 12, 1992, was marked by the most extensive and multiple *consultations* of the Canadian people ever undertaken. The *extended executive federalism* process that began on March 12, 1992, was complemented by *public briefings* by all participants throughout the process. A major weakness was the *absence of Quebec* from most of the negotiation process, which meant that Quebec did not participate in shaping the Accord. It also meant that accommodations arrived at in August to bring Quebec onside were highlighted at a very late stage in the process. Furthermore, the *slippage in time* in reaching an agreement (originally the multilateral process was to have ended in May) meant that the time to explain the deal and dialogue with Canadians was limited: October 26 was a *fixed deadline* and there was no flexibility. The *referendum* expanded the process of constitutional change to the broadest level of public participation ever in Canadian history. Has the *precedent of a referendum* added a new element to the amending process in Canada and, if so, under what circumstances and at what stage in negotiations should future referendums be contemplated?

One thing is clear: while lessons can be drawn from the Charlottetown exercise, it does not provide infallible rules for ensuring the success of future constitutional amendment exercises.

GOVERNMENTS ACTING UNILATERALLY

The Government of Canada undertook one major unilateral constitutional initiative following patriation — on Senate reform — and several governments undertook unilateral initiatives on entrenched property rights in the Constitution.

The Federal Senate Reform Initiative (1982–84)

Senate reform was an issue ardently pursued by some provinces during the constitutional negotiations in 1978–79 and 1980, particularly in British Columbia and, subsequently, Alberta. Because of strong feelings of alienation in Western Canada and the nearly total lack of MPs on the government benches from Western Canada and the territories (there were only two Liberal MPs elected in Manitoba), the federal government was interested in Senate reform as a possible antidote.

On December 20, 1982, the Senate adopted a motion establishing a special joint committee to consider ways by which the Senate could be "reformed in order to strengthen its role in representing people from all regions of Canada and to enhance the authority of Parliament to speak and act on behalf of Canadians in all parts of the country." The House of Commons adopted an identical motion on December 22, 1982.

The special joint committee, co-chaired by Senator Gildas Molgat and Roy MacLaren (subsequently, by Paul Cosgrove) held hearings in all provincial and territorial capitals, as well as in Ottawa. It heard 119 witnesses and received 280 briefs.

The federal government submitted a discussion paper, *Reform of the Senate,* to assist the special joint committee in its work. The committee's report was published in January 1984 and the Minister of Justice, Mark MacGuigan, held a series of bilateral meetings with provincial counterparts on Senate reform, but a new Prime Minister was sworn in June 1984 and elections were held in September 1984 that resulted in a change in government. The initiative was not pursued and an amendment resolution was not submitted to Parliament.

Property Rights

The question of entrenching property rights in the Constitution was raised during the parliamentary hearings on the Canadian Charter of Rights and Freedoms in 1980–81. The federal government had no objection in principle: Prime Minister John Diefenbaker's 1960 Canadian Bill of Rights had provided for the right of individuals to the "enjoyment of property, and the right not to be deprived thereof except by due process of law." The Bill of Rights, which only applied in areas of federal jurisdiction, had operated without difficulty in the area of property rights for over 20 years.

However, the New Democratic Party, which supported the unilateral patriation package, including the Charter, 1980, opposed entrenched property rights because such rights might make more difficult the enactment of laws related to zoning and land use, environmental protection, rent control and other programs that impinge upon the individual's enjoyment of property. Of course, programs that affected property rights through the due process of law would probably be sustained by the courts in the longer term, but there could be costly litigation and delays in the short term if the laws were challenged.

Following the proclamation of the Constitution Act, 1982, which includes the Canadian Charter of Rights and Freedoms, opposition to entrenched property rights spread to new quarters. Women's groups feared that such rights could jeopardize the rights of women in property settlements after marriage breakdown, for example. Aboriginal leaders thought that it might make land claims more difficult to resolve.

On the other hand, the concept of property rights was particularly popular in Western Canada, and the Canadian Real Estate Association lobbied throughout the country for entrenchment.

On September 21, 1982, the legislative assembly of British Columbia unanimously passed a resolution proposed by the provincial government to amend the Constitution and to provide the right to the enjoyment of property and the right not to be deprived thereof "except in accordance with the principles of fundamental justice." The text of the resolution was in English only, and the form was criticized by some (there was no citation clause, for example). It contained an exhortation to Parliament and the other provinces to follow suit. Although the resolution was adopted unanimously, it is not clear whether a majority of the membership of the whole House was present at the vote: since the amendment would derogate from the rights, powers and privileges of the government and legislature of the province, a simple majority of those present would not be sufficient to authorize proclamation of the amendment.

The British Columbia constitutional resolution was the first adopted following patriation of the Constitution.

The federal government decided to present a constitutional amendment resolution to Parliament. On April 18, 1983, the Prime Minister offered to the Official Opposition to introduce a constitutional resolution on property rights for adoption during the session if there was agreement on the text of the resolution and on a one-day debate. He shared the Government's proposed text with the Official Opposition: it was drafted in English and in French and contained a citation clause (Constitution Amendment Proclamation, 1984 [property rights]). However, the basis for protecting property rights ("principles of fundamental justice") was the same as in the British Columbia resolution.

On April 29, the Official Opposition used the opportunity afforded by an opposition day to present the government's own resolution in the form of a *no-confidence motion*. The government could therefore not support it, and the motion was defeated on May 2 by a vote of 126 to 88. Both the Official Opposition and the New Democratic Party voted in favour of the motion. It was not clear whether the New Democratic Party voted for the resolution because it was a question of no confidence or because of support for property rights.

In New Brunswick, a non-governmental initiative was, through an amendment proposed by the Premier, turned into a government position.

Douglas Young, an opposition member in the New Brunswick legislative assembly, moved a resolution on April 29, 1983, that would entrench property rights and the right not to be deprived thereof "except in accordance with principles of fundamental justice." The Premier moved an amendment to provide the right not to be deprived thereof "except by due process of law." The resolution was debated for three days and adopted, in the amended form, on June 28, 1983. The vote was not recorded. Since the amendment derogated from the existing rights, powers and privileges of the government and legislature, it would have to be adopted by a majority of the membership of the House and not merely a majority of those present.

The Premier's amendment meant that the resolutions adopted in British Columbia and New Brunswick were incompatible.

NON-GOVERNMENT INITIATIVES

There have been a large number of proposals for constitutional amendment proposed in Parliament — not always in the form deemed appropriate by the federal Department of Justice — and a small number in the provincial legislative assemblies.

Property Rights

As noted above, a property rights amendment resolution was initiated by a backbench member in the New Brunswick legislative assembly, but it was subsequently amended by the Premier.

On November 27, 1986, a backbench member of the Ontario legislative assembly, Herbert Arnold Epp, moved a constitutional resolution to entrench property rights on the same basis as proposed in British Columbia and the federal resolution. The form of the resolution resembled that of British Columbia and concluded with an exhortation to Parliament and the other provinces to follow suit. It was adopted in English only. The vote was recorded and the resolution carried by 44 to 20. However, 44 was not a majority of the membership of the legislative assembly and therefore the resolution was invalid for the purposes of authorizing the proclamation of an amendment that would derogate from the rights, powers and privileges of the provincial governments and legislatures.

Resolutions to entrench property rights in the Constitution were proposed in the House of Commons by Jake Epp through a supply motion on April 29, 1983 (defeated by 126 to 88); by Doug Lewis under private members' business on May 26, 1983 (not debated); by Robert Wenman, under private members' business on January 21, 1983 (not debated); by Don Blenkarn under private members' business on December 6, 1984 (died on the Order Paper); by Blaine Thacker under private members' business on February 1, 1985 (died on the Order Paper); and by John Reimer under private members' business on May 17, 1985 (died on the Order Paper) and again on October 15, 1987 (adopted in an amended form on May 2, 1988, by 108 to 16). The last resolution was adopted by less than a majority of the membership of the House of Commons and was, therefore, invalid for the purposes of authorizing a proclamation.

Other Issues

Only on the issue of property rights was a non-government constitutional amendment resolution carried but, as noted, the majority was insufficient for the purposes of proclamation.

Approximately 90 non-government proposals for constitutional amendment were brought forward in the House of Commons between April 17, 1982, and December 31, 1993. Almost all were introduced under private members' business, although on a few occasions they were raised under supply motions.

The most popular issue was the Senate: there were 23 resolutions proposing reform or abolition. Ten proposals dealt with Aboriginal rights, six with language rights and five with the territories. The substantial majority of these proposals were not debated or put to a vote.

In fact, only two non-government amendment resolutions were put to a vote: the property rights amendment referred to above and an amendment resolution to include the rights of the unborn in the Charter of Rights and Freedoms. The resolution on the rights of the unborn was introduced on November 21, 1986, by Gus Mitges. It was debated on four separate occasions and put to a vote on June 2, 1987. It was defeated by 89 to 62.

7

FROM THE RATIFICATION OF AN AMENDMENT TO ITS PROCLAMATION

THE MECHANICS

T HE CONSTITUTION ACT, 1982 says very little about how to proceed once the appropriate number of legislative bodies have ratified or authorized the proclamation of a constitutional amendment, whether it be a bilateral, a multilateral, a 7/50 or a unanimity amendment.

Section 48 of the Constitution Act, 1982 stipulates that the Queen's Privy Council for Canada shall advise the Governor General to issue a proclamation forthwith on the adoption of the resolutions required for an amendment made by proclamation. Before advising the Governor General, the Queen's Privy Council (that is, the federal Cabinet) must be satisfied that the necessary conditions have been met. This involves a number of considerations.

- Is the text of the amendment adopted by the appropriate number of legislative bodies identical? The earlier examination of attempts to entrench property rights in the Constitution demonstrates that resolutions aimed at a general objective may be technically incompatible.

- Where the text of the Constitution is equally authoritative in both English and French, does the resolution amend the text in both languages?

- Have the time-frames for the issuance of a proclamation been respected? As noted earlier, proclamation of a 7/50 amendment is subject to time-frames. Such an amendment cannot be proclaimed until one year has elapsed from the date of the adoption of the first resolution initiating the amendment procedure, unless the Senate, the House of Commons, and the legislative assemblies of all provinces have adopted a resolution authorizing the amendment or dissenting from it in less than a year's time. Furthermore, the amendment cannot be proclaimed if the necessary conditions have not been met within three years of the date of the adoption of the first resolution initiating the amendment procedure. Such time-frames do not exist for bilateral, multilateral and unanimity amendments.

- In the case of a 7/50 amendment which derogates from the legislative powers, the proprietary replies or any other rights or privileges of the legislature or government of a province, it is necessary to determine whether the Senate, the House of Commons and the legislative assemblies have expressed assent or dissent by the required majority. A resolution of assent or dissent (allowing for opting out) must be supported by a majority of the members of the legislative body concerned and not merely by a majority of those present at the time of the vote. Similarly, the revocation of the resolution of dissent must be supported by a majority of all the members of the legislative assembly concerned.

- If the Senate exercises its six-month suspensive veto, has the House of Commons overridden the Senate veto and, in the case of a 7/50 amendment, within the three-year time-frame?

COMMUNICATIONS

In Canada, the debates of the Senate, the House of Commons and the legislative assemblies of the provinces are public and the journals of those bodies record the text of resolutions adopted. Federal officials, acting on behalf of the Queen's Privy Council for Canada, need only examine the journals to determine the state of play on any amendment.

However, following agreement among the Government of Canada and nine provinces on the Constitution Amendment Proclamation, 1983, which dealt with the rights of the Aboriginal peoples of Canada. federal officials suggested in August 1983 that the speaker of each legislative body should send a certified copy of the amendment resolution, once adopted, to the Governor General.

This suggestion was based on the parliamentary principle that the Speaker communicates resolutions and messages on behalf of the House, and on the desirability of having a central record of the resolutions adopted. However, as noted above, all that is legally required to authorize an amendment is the adoption of the required resolutions. The communication of those resolutions is a matter of convenience, not a legal requirement.

As it transpired, the lines of communication were sometimes confused and not always timely. In many cases, the speakers sent a certified copy of the resolution to the Governor General. However, the Clerk of the Legislative Assembly in Prince Edward Island sent the resolution to the Secretary of the Governor General. The Clerk of the Legislative Assembly of Alberta transmitted the resolution to the Governor General. The Minister of Intergovernmental Relations in British Columbia sent a certified copy of the resolution to the Governor General. The Lieutenant-Governor of Manitoba sent the resolution to the Secretary of State and the federal Deputy Minister of Justice, and then forwarded it to the Secretary of the Governor General. The Attorney General of Saskatchewan transmitted the resolution to the federal Minister of Justice, and the federal Deputy Minister of Justice then forwarded it to the Secretary of the Governor General, at which time the Speaker also sent the resolution to the Governor General.

The territorial assemblies do not have a legal role to play in the authorization of amendments. However, the agreement on the Constitution Amendment Proclamation, 1983 was signed by the Yukon government as a participant and the resolution was submitted to the Yukon assembly. The Speaker sent a copy of the resolution, once adopted, to the Governor General and another to the Prime Minister.

Certified copies of resolutions, once adopted, were not always transmitted in a timely fashion. Six months or more elapsed between adoption and communication in the case of the Senate, the House of Commons, Nova Scotia and Prince Edward Island, for example.

In all cases, the resolution was adopted in both English and French (although, in the case of Alberta, the French text was adopted as an appendix to the English text).

The Aboriginal rights amendment did not derogate or take away from any of the powers, rights or privileges of the provinces. Nonetheless, the Speaker of the legislative assembly of Saskatchewan provided the results of the vote (54 yeas, 0 nays and 10 members absent). If the amendment had derogated from provincial powers, it would have been necessary to certify that a majority of members of the assembly, and not merely a majority of those present at the vote, had approved the amendment.

Although federal officials had initially suggested that speakers should communicate the resolutions to the Governor General, it was clear that it was the Queen's Privy Council for Canada (and not the Governor General) that would have to determine when the conditions had been met to authorize the issuance of a proclamation. Accordingly, the Secretary to the Governor General, upon receipt of a resolution sent to the Governor General, immediately forwarded a copy to the official in the Privy Council Office responsible for liaison between the Governor General and the Government. The Privy Council Office official in turn sent it to the Department of Justice: the Minister of Justice and Attorney General of Canada is the legal advisor of the Government of Canada and must advise the Queen's Privy Council for Canada whether the conditions for authorizing the amendment have been met.

All in all, the whole exercise of communications proved to be cumbersome. Furthermore, it could have led to confusion about the role of the Governor General, who does not determine whether the conditions for proclaiming an amendment have been met, but rather acts on the advice of the Queen's Privy Council for Canada.

Accordingly, federal officials suggested a new procedure for communications after agreement had been reached on the Constitution Amendment, 1987 (popularly known as the Meech Lake Accord) on June 3, 1987. It was proposed that the speakers of the Senate, the House of Commons and the legislative assemblies should send the certified copies of the resolutions to the Clerk of the Privy Council, who has custody of the documents of the Queen's Privy Council.

Once again, there was a problem of timeliness in the receipt of certified copies of resolutions. The Secretary to the Cabinet for Federal-Provincial Relations, Norman Spector, wrote to his provincial counterparts on June 20, 1988, to suggest that the speaker would be the appropriate person to communicate the fact that a proclamation amending the Constitution in both official languages had been authorized by the assembly. A certified copy of the resolution, signed by the Clerk of the legislative assembly, should be attached to the Speaker's letter which should be addressed to the Clerk of the Privy Council. The same proposal was transmitted to the Clerks of the Senate and of the House of Commons by an official of the Federal-Provincial Relations Office.

This appeared to be an acceptable approach for the provinces, although Quebec did not, prior to the expiry of the time-frame for the ratification of the Meech Lake Accord, send such a letter. However, the Quebec resolution, which was adopted on June 23, 1987, and which initiated the amendment process, was a matter of public record and there had been ample opportunity to examine it.

An official on the staff of the House of Commons advised the Clerk of the House that the Speaker was on an equal footing with ministers of the Crown and thus, for protocol reasons, he should not write to a federal official. Accordingly, the Clerk of the House of Commons wrote to the Clerk of the Privy Council on behalf of the Speaker, following the adoption of the bilateral amendment with Newfoundland on the denominational school rights of the Pentecostal Assemblies of Newfoundland — the Constitution Amendment, 1987 (Newfoundland Act) — and this procedure was followed in the case of the Meech Lake Accord.

In all other cases where a resolution was adopted on the Meech Lake Accord, the Speaker communicated with the Clerk of the Privy Council.

It would probably be useful for the Speaker to include the results of the vote in the Senate, House or legislative assembly on a constitutional resolution as a matter of course in his or her communication to the Clerk of the Privy Council since, in the event of a resolution that takes away from provincial powers, rights or privileges, it is essential to know whether a majority of the members of the legislative body, and not just a majority of those present, supported the amendment. It would also be useful for the Speaker to send copies of his communication to all other provinces to keep them abreast of the ratification process.

ASCERTAINING THE FACTS

As noted, the Minister of Justice and Attorney General for Canada is the legal advisor to the Government of Canada. The Minister must advise the Cabinet when the conditions for proclaiming an amendment have been met.

In this, the Minister is aided by Department of Justice officials who scrutinize the texts of the resolutions carefully to ensure that they are identical, in English and in French. They must also determine whether the amendment takes away from provincial powers and, if so, whether a majority of all members has supported it.

If time-frames apply, Justice officials must ensure that they have been met. For example, the 1983 amendment on Aboriginal rights was initiated by the adoption of a resolution by Nova Scotia on May 31, 1983. The requirements for a 7/50 amendment had been met by November 1983. However, a 7/50 amendment cannot be proclaimed until after a year has elapsed from the time of initiation unless every provincial assembly has adopted a resolution of assent or dissent in less than a year's time. Since Quebec took no action one way or the other on that amendment, proclamation could not occur until after May 31, 1984.

Clearly, in determining whether the necessary conditions have been met, Justice officials must determine which amending procedure or procedures will apply to the resolution in question. Obviously, this task is facilitated if the preamble to the constitutional resolution identifies the appropriate amendment procedure or procedures under which the amendment is to be made.

Once the conditions for an amendment have been met, the Minister of Justice submits a memorandum to the Governor General in Council — that is, the federal Cabinet — to recommend that the Queen's Privy Council for Canada advise the Governor General to issue a proclamation amending the Constitution.

THE ROLE OF THE QUEEN'S PRIVY COUNCIL FOR CANADA

Following acceptance of the recommendation of the Minister of Justice, the Prime Minister submits a report to a special committee of Council (i.e., the Cabinet) proposing that the Queen's Privy Council for Canada advise the Governor General to issue a proclamation under the Great Seal of Canada amending the Constitution as authorized by the constitutional resolutions.

Acceptance of the Prime Minister's report by the special committee of Council triggers the proclamation by the Governor General. The Government of Canada thus assumes full responsibility for the decision. There is no substantive role for the Governor General in determining whether the conditions have been met and whether the proclamation should be issued. Nor does the Constitution suggest that there is any reserve power of the Crown to accept or reject the advice tendered by the Queen's Privy Council for Canada.

This is designed to protect the Governor General from involvement in the politics of constitutional amendment and possible court challenges. The Governor General's role is limited to participation in decisions on the protocol and ceremony (if any) surrounding the actual proclamation and, even in this area, the role of the Government is predominant.

THE PROCLAMATION DOCUMENT

Canada's first experience with a proclamation document occurred at the time of the patriation of the Constitution in 1982.

At that time, special high-quality paper was produced for the document. The proclamation proper was produced by hand on the high-quality paper by a professional calligrapher: the Coat of Arms of Canada was produced in full colour and the text was printed in Gothic script, partially in red letters and partially in black letters. This was a costly and time-consuming procedure. Space was left for the Queen to sign under the Coat of Arms and provision was made for signatures by the Attorney General and the Registrar General of Canada as witnesses (or by their delegates) as required by Order in Council for the issuance of proclamations.

Given the importance of the occasion, the Prime Minister made clear that he wished to sign the document also. Furthermore, because constitutional amendment proclamations would be extraordinary following patriation, he felt that the Prime Minister should continue to be a witness to such proclamations.

Consequently, the Order in Council was altered to require that the Prime Minister, as well as the Attorney General and the Registrar General, witness the patriation proclamation and all subsequent constitutional amendment proclamations.

Space was provided in the lower left hand corner for impressing the Great Seal of Canada on the document.

The text of the proclamation proper was fairly short and written in rather sober if not, indeed, technical language. The Constitution Act, 1982 was not part of the large one-page proclamation proper, but rather was appended as a schedule to it.

Furthermore, the rather lengthy Constitution Act, 1982 was not drawn up by hand by a professional calligrapher. Rather it was mechanically printed in Gothic script on fine quality paper.

These, then, were the relevant precedents when the Government of Canada had to decide how to handle the first amendment following patriation, the Constitution Amendment Proclamation, 1983.

The Government ultimately chose to follow the precedents quite closely. Once again the proclamation document would be one large page of fine quality paper. Advances in technology allowed for an excellent high-quality reproduction of the Coat of Arms in full colour, so the full document was mechanically produced rather than being drawn up by a professional calligrapher. This also allowed for the production of a number of "original" proclamation documents. The text of the actual amendment would be set out in a schedule appended to the proclamation.

The Order in Council respecting constitutional proclamations already set out the offices of the three ministers of the Crown who would have to witness future proclamations, and provision would have to be made for impressing the Great Seal of Canada on the document.

The major departure from the patriation proclamation, aside from the mechanical production of the text, was the office and name of the person issuing the proclamation. Section 58 of the Constitution Act, 1982 provided that it (the Constitution Act, 1982) would come into force on a day to be fixed by proclamation issued by the Queen or the Governor General under the Great Seal of Canada. As it transpired, it was the Queen who issued the proclamation on April 17, 1982, and the text began with the following words: "Elizabeth the Second by the Grace of God of the United Kingdom, Canada and her other realms and territories Queen, Head of the Commonwealth, Defender of the Faith."

Following patriation, only one other amendment to be made by proclamation could be issued by either the Queen or the Governor General. Section 59 of the Constitution Act, 1982 provided that, where authorized by the legislative assembly or government of Quebec, paragraph 23(1)(a) of the Charter of Rights and Freedoms (respecting minority official language education rights) could come into force in respect of Quebec on a day to be fixed by proclamation issued by the Queen or the Governor General under the Great Seal of Canada.

All other amendments to be made by proclamation would have to be issued by the Governor General. A delegate of the Governor General (such as the Chief Justice of the Supreme Court of Canada) could sign the proclamation on behalf of the Governor General in the event of his or her absence, illness or other inability. But the power is clearly vested in the Governor General and, unlike most powers of the Governor General, is not exercised through delegation from the Queen, in her name or on her behalf.

Monarchy Canada (Vol. 12, No. 2 [Summer 1984]) argued that "the executive act of amending the Constitution is an exercise of the Queen's authority which the Governor General is implicitly carrying out on behalf and in the name of the Queen..." and claimed that the Constitution Amendment Proclamation, 1983 should have been issued under the Queen's name. This is not, in fact, the case. The power is explicitly vested in the Governor General, as it would have been under the Victoria formula of 1971.

Accordingly, the text of the Constitution Amendment Proclamation, 1983 began with the following words: "By Her Excellency the Right Honourable Jeanne Sauvé, Governor General and Commander in Chief of Canada."

The text of the proclamation was drawn up by the Department of Justice, in consultation with the Federal-Provincial Relations Office. The State Ceremonial directorate of the Department of the Secretary of State was responsible for ordering the fine quality paper for the proclamation document and overseeing the printing of the document, in collaboration with the Department of Justice, which was responsible for proofreading the printed text.

In a letter to Benoît Bouchard, Secretary of State, on April 22, 1986, Prime Minister Mulroney said that all future amendment proclamations should be produced mechanically on fine quality paper in the same manner as the document produced for the Constitution Amendment Proclamation, 1983. In this way, no invidious distinctions could be made between first and second class documents. He further stated that if the amendment had special importance, the sponsoring minister could have extra copies produced at his expense.

THE "ORIGINAL" PROCLAMATION

In principle, the Governor General and the ministerial witnesses need only sign one document to effect an amendment and that document is the "original."

However, at the time of patriation, the Queen was to sign the proclamation of the Constitution Act, 1982 in the open air in front of the Parliament buildings. There was concern that, in the event of inclement weather or misadventure, the documents might be damaged, so two proclamation documents were prepared by hand by a professional calligrapher.

There was a shower of rain during the proclamation ceremony and the document was very slightly damaged by water. Following the proclamation, the Queen proceeded to the East Block of the

Parliament Buildings, which had been restored and which she was to inaugurate. The second copy of the proclamation document was awaiting her in a private room where she went for a brief rest and she was asked to sign it, which she did.

It was the second copy, and not the damaged original, which was displayed in the Hall of Honour of the Parliament Buildings on April 17, 1983, to mark the first anniversary of patriation. However, when the second copy was returned to the National Archives, a student asked to see it. When the unprotected document was shown to him, he threw red ink on it to protest the defence policy of the Government of Canada. Both hand-produced documents, damaged and unrepaired, remain in the custody of the National Archives. However, State Ceremonial had a large number of very fine copies of the second document produced mechanically before it was stained with ink.

A third copy of the patriation proclamation was drawn up by hand by a professional calligrapher in early 1983. The British government had decided to give Canada photo reproductions on fine parchment of five British documents that provided important steps in Canada's constitutional development to mark the first anniversary of patriation: The Royal Proclamation of 1763, The Quebec Act of 1774, The Constitutional Act of 1791, The Act of Union of 1840 and The British North America Act, 1867. Canada, in turn, would present the United Kingdom with the third "original" copy of the patriation document. It was duly signed by the Prime Minister, the Attorney General and the Registrar General but the Queen declined to sign it, since she had already signed the original which effected patriation on April 17, 1982. The third document, without the Queen's signature, was duly presented to the Government of the United Kingdom, which now has the only undamaged hand-produced copy of the patriation proclamation — albeit without the Queen's signature.

Since it had been decided to produce the proclamation respecting the Constitution Amendment Proclamation, 1983 mechanically, there would be no significant extra costs in producing more than one "original." It was decided to give an "original" copy to each of the four Aboriginal national organizations and to have a fifth copy, duly signed in public, that would be preserved in the National Archives.

On June 21, 1984, the Governor General, the Prime Minister, the Attorney General and the Registrar General signed four copies of the proclamation in private prior to the public signing ceremony. Legally, the Constitution Amendment Proclamation, 1983 came into force when the first document was signed. However, it is not clear which of the four copies presented to the leaders of the four national Aboriginal organizations was signed first.

The Constitution Amendment, 1987 (Newfoundland Act), a bilateral amendment respecting the denominational school rights of the Pentecostal Assemblies in Newfoundland, was proclaimed on December 22, 1987. Two copies were signed and the second was given to the Attorney General, John Crosbie, who was the sponsoring minister and a Newfoundlander.

The Constitution Amendment, 1993 (New Brunswick), a bilateral amendment respecting the equality of the English-speaking and French-speaking communities of New Brunswick, was proclaimed on March 12, 1993. Two copies were produced. One was signed by the ministerial witnesses prior to proclamation, but not by the Governor General. The second copy was signed by the Governor General and the three ministerial witnesses, thus becoming the "original." Following proclamation, the Governor General signed the first copy, which was given to the Premier of New Brunswick.

The Constitution Amendment, 1994 (Prince Edward Island), a bilateral amendment respecting a fixed link with the mainland, was proclaimed on April 13, 1994. Two copies were produced. The Governor General signed both, and then the ministerial witnesses signed both. The second copy was presented forthwith to the Premier of Prince Edward Island.

WHAT CONSTITUTES "FORTHWITH"?

Section 48 of the Constitution Act, 1982 states that the Queen's Privy Council for Canada shall advise the Governor General to issue a proclamation "forthwith" when the conditions for an amendment by proclamation have been met. This requires timely action, but the maximum length of time elapsing between fulfilling the conditions for an amendment and the proclamation is not spelled out. Only three weeks elapsed in the case of the Constitution Amendment Proclamation, 1983. However, six months elapsed in the case of Constitution Amendment, 1987 (Newfoundland Act).

While six months begins to test the limits of what might constitute timely action, it does provide a precedent for allowing a certain flexibility in proclaiming future amendments.

WHERE AND IN WHAT CIRCUMSTANCES DOES PROCLAMATION OCCUR?

The legal requirements for a proclamation are the signature of the Governor General and the ministerial witnesses (or their legal delegates) on the proclamation document. There is no requirement that it be done in Ottawa, for example, nor that there be a ceremony to mark the event.

The patriation proclamation was held in front of the Peace Tower on Parliament Hill in Ottawa. It was open to the public and was televised.

The Constitution Amendment Proclamation, 1983 was proclaimed at a ceremony in the grounds of Rideau Hall (the Governor General's residence) in Ottawa. It was attended by Aboriginal representatives and other invited guests, but was not open to the public. After the document was signed, the Under-Secretary of State read the proclamation. The Governor General, the Prime Minister and Aboriginal leaders then made brief statements. A reception was held in the gardens afterwards for all guests.

The Constitution Amendment, 1987 (Newfoundland Act) was proclaimed privately in the Governor General's study at Rideau Hall. There was no ceremony and no reception.

The Constitution Amendment, 1993 (New Brunswick) was proclaimed in the ballroom of Rideau Hall. Invited guests were in attendance and the press was present. After the document was signed, the Under-Secretary of State read the proclamation.

The Governor General, the Prime Minister and the Premier of New Brunswick made brief statements. A reception for the invited guests followed the ceremony.

The Constitution Amendment, 1994 (Prince Edward Island) was proclaimed in the ballroom of Rideau Hall. A small number of invited guests were in attendance and the press was present. After the document was signed, the Under-Secretary of State read the proclamation. The Governor General, the Prime Minister and the Premier of Prince Edward Island made brief statements. A reception for the invited guests followed the ceremony.

THE ROLE OF EXECUTIVE FEDERALISM, POPULAR PARTICIPATION AND OTHER OPERATIONAL QUESTIONS

WHILE WE CAN TRACE the steps from ratification — or authorization — of an amendment to its ultimate proclamation, it is more difficult to determine how one should proceed from the initial proposal of an amendment to the required resolutions by the Senate, the House of Commons and the requisite number of legislative assemblies.

THE ROLE OF EXECUTIVE FEDERALISM

All four amendments achieved to date have involved the exercise of what is called executive federalism — that is, negotiations between governments or executives. In the case of the Aboriginal rights amendment, it was what might be called extended executive federalism, including not only the federal and provincial governments, but the territorial governments and representatives of the Aboriginal peoples seeking to establish an Aboriginal order of government.

However, of the four amendments, one — the Constitution Amendment, 1987 (Newfoundland Act) — was a classic case of executive federalism with no broader involvement. The Newfoundland and federal governments negotiated the amendment to entrench the denominational school rights of the Pentecostal Assemblies in that province. There was one day of debate in the Newfoundland legislative assembly and no public hearings before adoption of the constitutional resolution. The resolution was adopted by the House of Commons and the Senate, without hearings.

The Constitution Amendment, 1994 (Prince Edward Island) was adopted with similar despatch. It was a "technical" amendment to clarify that a fixed link to the mainland would be an acceptable substitute for the existing ferry service and that tolls could be charged for use of the fixed link. The real policy issue which sharply divided the Island's population was whether there should be a fixed link. A referendum on the issue was held in Prince Edward Island on January 18, 1988, by the provincial government. Over 59 percent of those voting supported the fixed link. Hence, it could be argued that the population had been consulted directly on the substance of the amendment and that the actual drafting and adoption of the amendment was a technical matter arising from the popular decision.

The Constitution Amendment, 1993 (New Brunswick) was adopted by the legislative assembly in Fredericton after only two days of debate and by the Senate and House of Commons with only one day of debate in each. The provincial government argued that the principle of the amendment — the equality of the two language communities in New Brunswick — had been extensively debated since 1989 and had been supported by the provincial population when it approved the Charlottetown Accord in the 1992 referendum.

The Constitution Amendment Proclamation, 1983 on Aboriginal rights was the result of an exercise of extended executive federalism and some of the deliberations leading to agreement among the participants were public.

If all four amendments were negotiated through executive federalism, there are several reasons to explain why this was so.

Firstly, in Canada's parliamentary system of government, the federal and provincial governments are normally in a majority position in the House of Commons and the legislative assemblies. This usually means that a measure opposed by the government will fail to pass. If an amendment is to be authorized, it is important to ensure that the requisite number of governments will be supportive. Hence, as a practical matter, it has been useful to involve governments in the development of constitutional amendment proposals.

Secondly, the better argument is that each legislative body has to adopt identical texts in French and in English to authorize an amendment — and the practice to date in Canada has confirmed this view. Once an amendment has been initiated by a legislative body, the other legislative bodies have to adopt it without change to achieve an amendment. If a legislative body alters or amends the initial resolution, it is, in effect, introducing a new constitutional resolution rather than ratifying the initial one. Hence the desirability, as a practical matter, of coordinating efforts *before* initiating an amendment. Executive federalism has played a useful role in ensuring such coordination.

Clearly, however, reaching agreement on an amendment among governments is not a guarantee that an amendment, once initiated, will be successfully ratified. Meech Lake is proof of the contrary. The fate of the Constitution Amendment Proclamation, 1983 (Manitoba Act) is perhaps even more telling. The amendment was designed to provide the Manitoba legislature with time to meet its obligations to translate, edit and publish its laws in French, in return recognizing English and French as the official languages of the province and providing, under certain circumstances, certain public services in French. The amendment was negotiated by the federal and provincial governments, with the participation of representatives of the Franco-Manitoban community. However, procedural obstruction in the legislature and strong grass-roots opposition in the province led Premier Howard Pawley to abandon the amendment.

So, while executive federalism may be useful in reaching agreement on the text of an amendment, it does not necessarily guarantee success. The question arises: in what circumstances and in what way should the public participate in the amendment process?

PUBLIC PARTICIPATION

It is by no means certain that the public has to be involved in every constitutional amendment. Common sense and a clear evaluation of the significance of the amendment might rule out the need for public involvement in certain well-defined cases.

For example, during the non-Aboriginal constitutional process in 1982–83, unanimous agreement was reached by the active participants (all governments except Quebec) on a technical amendment respecting the office of lieutenant-governor (a unanimity matter under the amending formula). The federal government can appoint an administrator to execute the office of lieutenant-governor during his absence, illness or other inability, but not in the case of his death. Five lieutenant-governors had died in office between 1966 and 1978, and the provincial constitution in each case was frozen until a successor was found and sworn into office. The solution would be to amend the Constitution to allow for the appointment of an administrator in the case of the death of a lieutenant-governor. It is not clear that broad public debate and participation would be necessary before adopting such a technical amendment. The pending technical amendment respecting certain portions of the Alberta–British Columbia border is another example.

Where, however, amendments are proposed that would require major policy decisions affecting the Charter, the distribution of powers or national institutions, the question of public involvement is more germane. Two issues are of interest:

- at what stage — or stages — in the development of the amendment should the public be involved?

- in what manner should the public be involved?

The earliest stage at which people could be involved is at the development of the constitutional amendment, perhaps in a constituent assembly or a variant thereof. However, Patrick Fafard and Darrel R. Reid found, in *Constituent Assemblies: A Comparative Survey,* that constituent assemblies are most successful in two sets of circumstances: in the aftermath of a significant break with the past, such as revolution or civil war, on the one hand, or where a group of independent states or former colonies have come together in a new union, on the other. Constituent assemblies have been much less successful in attempts to revise existing constitutions, either partially or totally.

Furthermore, the legitimacy of the constitutional assembly would depend in large measure on public acceptance or support for the method of selection of the delegates and the distribution of seats. Should they be selected directly or indirectly and, if the latter, by whom? Should the provinces be represented on the basis of population, on the basis of equality, or by region (four or five)? Should Quebec delegates — or those of any other province or region — have a veto on all matters or some and, if the latter, which? Should Aboriginal peoples have a veto on some matters and, if so, which? Should official language minorities, certain denominations which enjoy entrenched education guarantees, or other groups or minorities be guaranteed a place at the table and a veto over the matters that affect them directly?

It took Canada 56 years — from 1926 to 1982 — to resolve the issue of an amending formula: essentially, the issue of who decides how to amend the Constitution. And the solution in 1982 left perceived wounds in one part of the country — Quebec. Subsequent attempts to resolve Quebec's concerns revealed other concerns in the territories and among the representatives of Aboriginal peoples.

In short, determining the composition and voting procedures for a constituent assembly would prove almost as daunting as reaching agreement on substantive amendments.

The next stage might be to ask the public to react to broad proposals by governments or a government prior to developing legislative texts. This is the approach the Government of Canada adopted when it published its constitutional proposals in September 1991 and asked a special joint committee of the Senate and the House of Commons to hold hearings on them. The Government also organized a series of national conferences to debate the proposals.

However, after listening, governments, including the territories and representatives of Aboriginal organizations, then engaged in a new exercise of extended executive federalism behind closed doors. When they reached agreement at Charlottetown on August 28, 1992, new elements which had not been raised in the earlier public consultations had entered into the Accord, such as the guarantee of 25 percent of the seats in the House of Commons in perpetuity for Quebec in return for that province's acceptance of equality of provincial representation in the Senate.

In the six weeks leading to the referendum, the public was asked to assess the fruits of extended executive federalism and to pronounce in favour or against the entire proposal. There was no chance for further public input. In the absence of general agreement, the result — generalized rejection — meant that no one group or region had rejected another. The result diffused possible anger, but it did not provide a useful road-map for future attempts at constitutional renewal.

Quebec offered an interesting alternative in 1987. After agreement in principle was reached by governments at Meech Lake on April 30, Quebec held public legislative hearings on the "principles" (some of which were, in effect, legislative drafts). Those hearings were largely ignored by the rest of the country. When Quebec entered the final phase of negotiations on legal texts in the Langevin Building on June 2–3, 1982, it had a clear idea of its manoeuvrability. No other government had yet "tested the waters" through public consultation.

When Quebec adopted the Meech Lake Accord on June 23, 1987, it launched the ratification process. The legal text was effectively locked in: any alteration to the text by another legislative body would, in effect, initiate a separate amendment. If all twelve legislative bodies concerned (the Senate, the House of Commons and the ten legislative assemblies) each adopted slightly different amendment resolutions, twelve different amendments would have been initiated and there would be no chance of ratification.

Hence, the approach adopted by governments in 1987: the amendment, once initiated, was a "seamless web." Hearings were designed to elicit views about future possible amendments, but the amendment under review could only be amended if an "egregious error" were identified.

As the debate dragged on, the initial public enthusiasm at the unanimous agreement reached by eleven first ministers declined. People looked at the fine print and suggested that changes might be in order. They were rebuffed by political leaders, and opposition grew.

An alternative approach might have been to turn to the people nationally after an agreement in principle, as Quebec had done provincially, to consult before meeting again to agree on legal texts.

John Holtby, a former Clerk Assistant of the Ontario legislature, proposed in 1987 to the Special Joint Committee on the Constitutional Accord the establishment of a national joint committee on constitutional amendments. It would be composed of members representing each party in the Senate, the House of Commons and the ten legislative assemblies.

The proposal was interesting: government and opposition parties would be able to dialogue with each other and with their provincial counterparts. Federal members would be sensitized, during hearings across the country, to regional concerns, and provincial members would gain a greater national perspective. The public and elected members of all political stripes could air their views, dialogue and seek common ground before trying to lock in a legal text.

The idea was brought forward too late to be of use in the Meech Lake process. And, clearly, trans-Canada hearings by a national joint committee would be cumbersome and costly. But on a high-profile amendment of great moment, it might be worth the effort to develop a national consensus on the principles underlying an amendment before locking in the legal text for ratification. And it would be less costly than a referendum.

Alternatively, a joint committee of the Senate and House of Commons could tour the country to hold hearings on the agreement in principle. It could, in each province, ask government and opposition MLAs to sit with the joint committee during its hearings in the province in question as locally participating, but non-voting, members of the committee.

The disadvantage of this alternative would be the lack of cross-fertilization between MLAs from all the provinces that would occur in a national joint committee. Furthermore, the joint committee, in drawing up its report, would probably be controlled by the federal government of the day, which would probably ensure passage by Parliament, but could also introduce a partisan element into the debate which could make passage more problematic in some provincial assemblies.

The next stage for public participation would be that of hearings on the first resolution initiating the amendment or a referendum on the legal text before submitting it to legislative bodies for ratification. If an amendment were to be initiated after the national hearings process, it would be advisable to initiate it in Parliament, where it could be fine-tuned and adjusted, if need be, in a national forum. Once adopted by Parliament, of course, it would be "locked in" and hearings by provincial assemblies, if any, would largely be pro forma. In the case of bilateral amendments, the process could be reversed: the amendment could be introduced in the provincial assembly where adjustments might occur, if necessary, before being sent to Ottawa for largely pro forma ratification.

If a national referendum were held by the federal government alone or by the government in collaboration with one or more provinces (as in the case of Charlottetown) on a legal text, the need for hearings on the amendment resolution would diminish dramatically. Perhaps hearings to ensure there was no egregious error in the text would be useful, but the policy issues would be settled by the people in the referendum.

One issue that will have to be addressed each time the option of a national referendum is raised is the degree of support required to pass. As a political matter, it was agreed among leaders that the Charlottetown Accord would have to be supported in all provinces in order to pass. Was this too high a threshold? Yet is a simple majority at the national level sufficient to protect regional interests? Would national unity be strengthened if a proposal for Senate reform (a 7/50 matter) were opposed by the three Maritime provinces or the three Prairie provinces or Quebec, but passed elsewhere?

There is no clear answer. It depends in part on the nature of the amendment. Senate reform touches the very fabric of the national decision-making process and so the threshold for consent should perhaps be high for such an amendment. However, in the event of an amendment to transfer jurisdiction over a provincial power to the Parliament of Canada — health care, for example — dissenting provinces could opt out of the amendment, so the argument for a high threshold is not as strong. If the amendment transferred jurisdiction over post-secondary education to Ottawa, the argument is weaker still, for not only could a dissenting province opt out of the amendment, it would also be guaranteed reasonable compensation.

Another question which arises is whether an omnibus constitutional proposal should be put to the people as a take-it-or-leave-it proposition, as in the case of the Charlottetown Accord, or whether electors should be able to accept or reject discrete items within the Accord. The second approach seems appealing in the perspective of pure majoritarian democracy. However, it could be argued that such an approach ignores the inevitable trade-offs that are necessary to reach a broadly-based consensus in a complex society spanning a continent, and that it puts minority interests and rights at the whim of the majority.

In any event, until such time as changes are made to the current amending formula, referendums must remain a subordinate adjunct to the amendment process. Referendums can dissuade legislative bodies from action or they can encourage them to take positive steps. They cannot, however, supplant the role of legislative bodies in authorizing amendments.

In this context, it is useful to recall that the House of Commons — and the House of Commons alone — has a veto over *all* amendments made by proclamation.

Not all amendments in future will necessarily generate the heat and passion that marked the later stages of the Meech Lake debate, the Charlottetown Accord referendum or the Manitoba language amendment of 1983–84, and there is much to be said for analysing each proposal on its own merits and using common sense in determining if, to what degree and how the public should be involved in ratifying specific amendments.

LOCKING IN OPERATIONAL PROCEDURES

Manitoba was the first province to "lock in" an operational procedure respecting the ratification of a constitutional amendment.

It will be recalled that the Manitoba language amendment of 1983–84 stirred up such strong passions in the province that the Premier ultimately abandoned the attempt to adopt the amendment resolution.

Two years later, the Standing Committee on the Rules of the House in Manitoba recommended adoption of a new standing order 36.1 respecting constitutional amendment motions which would provide that a government motion proposing an amendment to the Constitution of Canada (and amendments to the motion) would take precedence over all other House business for ten sitting days (unless debate had been concluded earlier). Prior to the sixth day of debate on the motion, it would be referred to a standing or special committee to receive submissions from the public and report back to the House. The proposed standing order was adopted on August 20, 1986.

This standing order has introduced a certain rigidity into the amendment process. The standing order does not require that debate on the motion (that is, the constitutional resolution) last for the full 10 days, but it does require referral to a committee to receive submissions from the public. The inability of the Manitoba legislative assembly to adopt the Meech Lake Accord and the Companion Accord in June 1990 was, in part, due to procedural mistakes. Proper notice of the resolutions was not given prior to the June 12 sitting of the House and, with further procedural mistakes and in the absence of unanimous consent to waive the normal requirements, debate did not begin until June 20. By June 23 it was clear that referral to a committee for public submissions and reporting back to the House could not be completed before midnight on that day, which was the deadline for ratification. Approximately 3,700 individuals had registered to appear during the committee stage.

It is interesting to note that the same strictures (10 days of debate, interrupted by committee hearings) do not apply to constitutional resolutions moved by government backbenchers or opposition MLAs. But then again, debate on their motions would not take precedence over all other business in the House.

British Columbia was next to lock in a special procedure. In the wake of Meech Lake, the Referendum Act was adopted and given assent on July 27, 1990. The Constitutional Amendment Approval Act was subsequently adopted and given assent on March 22, 1991: it obliges the provincial government to hold a referendum on the subject matter of a proposed amendment before introducing a resolution in the legislative assembly to authorize an amendment.

Alberta adopted the Constitutional Referendum Act in 1992 and it received assent on June 26, 1992. It requires that a referendum be held before a resolution authorizing an amendment to the Constitution of Canada is voted upon by the legislative assembly (but the resolution can be introduced in the legislative assembly before the referendum is held). The Constitutional Referendum Amendment Act, 1992 amended the earlier act and allowed the legislative assembly, under certain conditions, to substitute a federal referendum under Canada's Referendum Act; the federal referendum would have to precede a vote in the assembly on the amendment. This act received assent on September 22, 1992.

No other jurisdiction has an operational procedure that requires a referendum (or any other mandatory exercise) before adoption of a constitutional amendment resolution. Three, however, have referendum procedures in place which may be invoked if that is thought desirable: Canada (the Referendum Act, 1992), Quebec (Loi sur la consultation populaire, 1978) and Newfoundland (the Election Act as amended in 1975 and 1992).

None of the procedures that have been "locked in" by some provinces are irreversible: Alberta revised its referendum procedure prior to the 1992 Charlottetown referendum by a subsequent act of the legislature. However, until such time as constitutional amendment in Canada becomes a more mundane activity, legislative bodies that have locked in supplementary procedures may wish to make those procedures optional.

SINGLE-ISSUE AMENDMENTS, MULTIPLE-ISSUE AMENDMENTS AND SEPARATE TRACKS

In an ideal world, it would appear best to pursue each proposal for constitutional amendment independently on its own merits. But we do not live in an ideal world and, in Canada, a lot of constitutional baggage has accumulated over the past quarter century.

Since the 1968–71 constitutional review exercise, there has been a tendency to pursue a multiple-issue agenda (1978–79, 1980, 1981, 1982–83, 1992). Prime Minister Trudeau sought to narrow the agenda to one item — patriation with amending formula — in 1975, but the agenda expanded before the exercise was terminated in 1977. In 1986, the premiers agreed at their meeting in Edmonton on a narrow focus — Quebec's five conditions — but the focus expanded somewhat during the Meech Lake exercise to include, for example, a new interim procedure for appointing senators and entrenchment of a future constitutional agenda. Meech Lake ultimately failed because, among other reasons, many felt the agenda was too narrow or not sufficiently inclusive of other interests.

No one could claim that the Charlottetown Accord was too narrow in focus. Indeed, its complexity may have contributed to its defeat in the 1992 referendum: people who may have been willing to support some aspects might have rejected it because of their objections to others. But, as noted earlier, a pick-and-choose approach might have been, ultimately, highly divisive instead of unifying.

Bilateral amendments are, almost by definition, narrow in scope and tend to be single-issue matters. That has been the case with the three adopted since 1982. The Aboriginal rights amendment agreed upon in 1983 was narrow in focus and restricted to a few matters. It also was proclaimed. The Senate powers amendment proposal in 1985 was single-issue and narrow in focus. It failed to pass because of a change of government in Ontario, coupled with decreased confrontation in the Senate itself.

The second Aboriginal rights process, focusing on self-government, was more complex and ultimately failed in 1987 to garner sufficient provincial support to result in an amendment. The separate track on non-Aboriginal matters was essentially an exercise in whittling down expectations and it died, largely because of a lack of will on the part of the federal government to proceed and, on one item requiring unanimity (appointment of an administrator in the event of the death of a lieutenant-governor), because Quebec would not take action until after its own issues had been addressed. The separate track approach was abandoned in the course of the exercise that led to Charlottetown in 1992. That exercise also failed.

The single issue amendment proposals respecting boundaries between Manitoba and Saskatchewan, and between Alberta and British Columbia, have "failed" through lack of follow-up; they could always be dusted off and brought forward for ratification.

The single-issue amendment on language in Manitoba in 1983–84 failed because of strong public opposition and procedural tactics by the opposition in the legislature.

After 13 years of experience with the amending formula, what can be said? The four successful amendment exercises to date were narrow in scope and, essentially, single-issue matters. Three resulted from an exercise in bilateral executive federation although, in the case of two (in New Brunswick and Prince Edward Island), there was prior public consultation on the policy issue. The fourth amendment was a result of extended multilateral executive federalism. But a narrow focus on a single item is not enough to ensure success: witness the failure of the Senate powers amendment of 1985 or the Manitoba language amendment of 1983–84.

On the other hand, all multiple-item amendment proposals have been unsuccessful.

Is there a lesson to be learned? Should all attempts at multiple-item amendments be avoided? Should various amendments or groups of amendments be pursued on separate tracks and with independent deadlines? Should there be deadlines for reaching agreement? Should there be shorter deadlines for ratification by legislative bodies? Is executive federalism or extended executive federalism the culprit? Is the amending formula itself the problem? There is no easy answer to these questions. The one thing that is certain is that we must live with the amending formula we have until, through the operation of that formula itself, it is altered or replaced.

IS THE FORMULA THE PROBLEM?

Following the failure of the Meech Lake Accord, the federal government published a discussion paper in December 1990 called *Amending the Constitution of Canada* and referred the issue to the Beaudoin-Edwards Special Joint Committee of the Senate and House of Commons. Among other things, the paper asked whether the ratification period for 7/50 amendments (three years) was too long because the lack of early action by legislative bodies might allow the initial consensus to unravel: elections can and will occur, governments may change, partisan politics will continue, and extraneous issues and events may occur which, while legally unrelated to the amendment proposal, could affect attitudes and derail the ratification process. There is nothing to prevent governments from reaching agreement on a much shorter ratification period than that specified in the Constitution. They could, for example, agree to bring the matter to a vote within six months. But they would be foolish to do so if they had not ascertained beforehand that there was a broad public consensus supporting the amendment.

Executive federalism (and, indeed, extended executive federalism) has been identified as a possible culprit in the amending process. The discussion paper raised the possibility of "popularizing" the amendment process by resort to a constituent assembly or the use of referendums. Perhaps both suggestions were overly dramatic reactions to one failed amendment exercise. For, in the last analysis, Meech failed because governments had not succeeded in developing a popular consensus on the need for the amendment and on the principles it sought to incorporate in the Constitution, nor on the desirability of proceeding successively on different sets of constitutional issues, rather than seeking to resolve all outstanding issues at once.

It is difficult to see, as a practical matter, how amendments may be successfully ratified without the operation of executive federalism (or in certain cases, extended executive federalism). In the denunciation of executive federalism in 1990 — "eleven men wheeling and dealing behind closed doors" — people perhaps forgot that the many benefits Canadians enjoy from the concerted efforts of governments — including Medicare — are the fruits of executive federalism.

In a post-patriation Canada where the charter has infused many Canadians with a sense of proprietary interest in their constitution, governments may have to look more carefully at how to build a popular consensus before ratifying legal texts for an amendment by proclamation. Consensus building, depending upon the nature and profile of the amendment, may involve:

- seeking to convince the public on the desirability of giving priority to one issue or a limited set of issues;

- seeking, under certain circumstances, to enlist public support for proceeding on separate issues (or groups of issues) on separate tracks with different timetables;

- involving the public (depending on the profile of the issue or issues) in an examination of the detailed principles or draft legal texts of the proposed constitutional amendment or amendments before proceeding to ratification, perhaps through national parliamentary hearings;

- ensuring, once a public consensus emerges, that major new elements are not introduced into the resolution through a subsequent exercise in executive federalism;

- providing, if deemed necessary by the nature or profile of an amendment, an opportunity for the public to express its views through a referendum;

- proceeding, through a political agreement, in a timely fashion (perhaps within six months or a year) on ratification while the consensus holds.

Governments should avoid to the degree possible:

- seeking to reach agreement prematurely on issues where the public is strongly divided and where the short-term development of a public consensus is highly doubtful, if not impossible;

- involving the public in the discussion of one set of proposals and then presenting it with a new set negotiated through a subsequent exercise as a fait accompli;

- overloading the agenda in any one constitutional exercise: the more discrete elements in a package, the more targets for attack by various dissidents; and

- believing that the resolution of all public policy disputes has to be locked into the Constitution through an amendment.

While Canada has engaged in some high-profile constitutional battles in the last quarter-century and particularly in the past seven years, failure to secure certain broad amendments is due to a variety of complex factors. The 1982 amending formula itself was clearly a factor in the failure of the Meech Lake Accord, but not in that of the Charlottetown Accord.

It is premature to say that the amending formula is the problem or that the formula is unworkable. But clearly, broad consensus building is the prerequisite for any new attempt to secure an important multilateral constitutional amendment.

acidu...

our Majesty's loyal subjects, the Hon

s of Canada in Parliament assemb

approach Your Majesty, requesting

graciously be pleased to cause to be

Parliament of the United Kingd

containing the recitals and

ter set forth :

An Act to give effect to a request by t
and House of Commons of C

Whereas Canada has requested a
the enactment of an Act of the Par
United Kingdom to give effect to
alter set forth and the Senate ar
nada in Parliament
Majest

CONCLUSION

THE LONG PATRIATION DEBATE ended with the proclamation of the Constitution Act, 1982 on Parliament Hill in Ottawa on April 17, 1982.

The occasion was solemn, but muted. After the expenditure of so much time and resources, both human and financial, on the patriation issue, political actors had decided in November 1981 that a chapter had to come to an end. Most players had to settle for a compromise and to accept something other than their ideal solution.

Ontario (as well as Quebec) lost the veto that all previous proposals since 1960 would have provided. Prime Minister Trudeau had to accept the opting-out formula he had so vigorously attacked. To assuage the feelings of Quebecers, he agreed that the full range of minority language education rights in the rest of the country would not apply in Quebec, and that reasonable compensation would be provided to a province that opted out of an amendment transferring provincial legislative jurisdiction over education or other cultural matters to Parliament. He also accepted a "notwithstanding" clause that would allow legislative bodies to override many rights and freedoms in the Charter, including fundamental freedoms and equality rights. And, of course, the Government of Quebec was not a signatory to the agreement, although public opinion polls indicated that a majority of Quebecers supported the various rights and freedoms in the Charter, including minority language education rights.

After searching for perfection and unanimous agreement for over 50 years, governments compromised and settled for less on November 5, 1981. It was not the desired outcome, but it was liveable and opened the doors to future constitutional development in Canada without reference to a foreign power.

Perhaps one lesson to be learned from the patriation debate is that while there is no harm in aiming at the stars, aiming a bit closer to earth is more likely to produce results. The results may not be as uplifting, but they will be tangible and practical.

And perhaps another lesson to be drawn from attempts to amend the Constitution since 1982 is that governments should not get too far ahead of public opinion or overload the agenda before seeking amendments. The development of a broad consensus on the desirability and nature of amendments may be the necessary prelude to any further attempt to amend the Constitution of Canada. On the other hand, governments should not lag too far behind public opinion, as some provinces opposed to a charter of rights discovered in 1980–81.

Finally, Canadians should realize that constitutions change — often in fundamental ways — without formal constitutional amendment. Judicial interpretation and changing conventions are part of the picture. But so too is the exercise — or non-exercise — of powers under the Constitution. Intergovernmental agreements and new forms of collaboration permit federal societies to evolve dramatically without formal constitutional amendment.

In the United States, over 9,100 amendments have been proposed since 1789. Only 33 have made it through the brokers in Congress to be put to the states over the past 200 years. Only 26 were ratified (and two of those, prohibition and its repeal, cancelled each other out). Yet few would say that the United States is stagnant, caught in the doldrums of a constitutional status quo.

Perhaps we Canadians have become captivated by the quest for formal constitutional amendments. Perhaps we have become too concerned with perfection and have forgotten that less than perfect compromises are the basis for civilized life.

Federal societies are, by their nature, dynamic and the exercise of powers under the constitution adapts to changing circumstances. The constitutional and political situation of the federal government and the provinces today bears little resemblance to what it was 35 years ago, in 1960.

In short, the myth of the constitutional status quo is simply that: a myth.

ADDENDUM

A NEWFOUNDLAND BILATERAL
CONSTITUTIONAL AMENDMENT RESOLUTION

FOLLOWING TWO YEARS of unsuccessful discussions between the provincial government and the seven religious denominations that have the constitutional right to control and manage their own schools under Term 17 of Newfoundland's Terms of Union with Canada, the Government of Newfoundland produced a draft bilateral constitutional amendment resolution to reduce the education rights of the seven denominations. (Bilateral amendments under the terms of section 43 of the Constitution Act, 1982 are discussed in chapters 4, 5 and 6.)

The denominations and the Government of Canada were provided an opportunity to comment on the draft resolution, but it was made clear that substantive changes to it would not be made. Two denominations were strongly opposed to the resolution (the Catholics and the Pentecostal Assemblies).

A referendum was held on the Government of Newfoundland's proposal on September 5, 1995. Approximately 52 percent of the electorate participated in the vote. Of those voting, 54 percent supported the Government's proposal and 46 percent opposed it.

The Government of Newfoundland introduced the constitutional resolution into the House of Assembly on October 16, 1995. There were seven days of debate and the House adopted the resolution on October 31, 1995, by a vote of 31 to 20. On November 2, 1995, the Speaker of the House of Assembly sent a copy of the resolution to the Clerk of the Privy Council/Secretary to the Cabinet in Ottawa for consideration by the Government of Canada.

The resolution was introduced in the House of Commons on May 31, 1996. There were two days of debate. A proposed amendment to the resolution was defeated on division: 182 opposed and 27 in favour. The resolution was adopted by the House of Commons in a free vote on June 3, 1996: 170 in favour, 46 opposed.

The resolution was introduced in the Senate on June 6, 1996. A Senate committee was to hold hearings over seven days in Ottawa and St. John's and to report by July 17, 1996.

A FEDERAL REGIONAL VETO BILL

On October 24, 1995, towards the end of the Quebec referendum campaign on sovereignty, Prime Minister Jean Chrétien promised not to proceed with any constitutional change that affects Quebec without Quebecers' consent.

Any change to the amending formula to accommodate a Quebec "veto" would require the unanimous consent of the provinces (see section 41 of the Constitution Act, 1982). Rather than seek an amendment to the Constitution requiring provincial consent, the Prime Minister decided to honour his promise by providing a legislative limit on the Government's capacity to introduce a constitutional amendment resolution into Parliament. On November 29, 1995, the Prime Minister introduced Bill C-110 into the House of Commons.

The bill provided that no cabinet minister shall present a constitutional amendment resolution in Parliament unless the amendment has first been consented to by a majority of provinces, including:

- Ontario,

- Quebec,

- two or more Atlantic provinces representing at least 50 percent of the population of that region, and

- two or more Western provinces representing at least 50 percent of the population of that region.

On December 12, 1995, the Government introduced an amendment to recognize British Columbia as a fifth region on the same basis as Ontario and Quebec. The provision respecting the Western provinces was also amended to require the consent of at least two of the Prairie provinces representing at least 50 percent of that region. Since Alberta has over 50 percent of the population of the Prairie provinces, this amendment would effectively give a veto to Alberta.

Bill C-110 did not stipulate by what means the consent of a province was to be expressed.

Three categories of amendment were exempted from the procedure: matters subject to the unanimity procedure (section 41 of the Constitution Act, 1982) already were protected by a veto for all provinces; the bilateral amending procedure (section 43) provided a veto any province to which such an amendment related; and the opting out procedure (section 38[3]) already allowed a dissenting province to express its dissent and to remove itself from the application of the amendment (this is what has sometimes been called a negative veto). (The amending procedures adopted in the Constitution Act, 1982 are examined in chapter 4.)

While Bill C-110 would not change the amending procedures contained in Canada's Constitution, it would establish a test to be met before the Government would introduce a constitutional amendment resolution in Parliament (in British Columbia and Alberta, amendments must be approved in a referendum before a constitutional amendment resolution may be introduced [in British Columbia] or adopted [in Alberta]). Since the House of Commons is the only legislative body in Canada which has a veto over all amendments made by proclamation of the Governor General, it was said that the Government would be "lending" the federal veto power to five regions of Canada under Bill C-110.

Bill C-110 was adopted by the House of Commons on December 13, 1995, by a vote of 150 to 101. Bill C-110 was introduced in the Senate on December 14, 1995 and debated for two days before being referred to a Special Committee. The Special Committee sat for seven days and received 18 briefs and heard from 51 witnesses. The Special Committee reported on February 1 and proposed three amendments to the bill. They were debated and defeated by a vote of 48 opposed and 36 in favour on

February 2, 1996. Subsequently, on the same day the bill was adopted on division with no recorded vote, and royal assent was given forthwith.

THE SECTION 49 FIRST MINISTERS' CONFERENCE TO REVIEW THE AMENDING FORMULA

Section 49 of the Constitution Act, 1982 required the Prime Minister to convene a First Ministers' Conference to review the amending formula before April 17, 1997. That obligation was discharged when the Prime Minister convened First Ministers to a meeting explicitly for that purpose on June 21, 1996. The government leaders of the territories were also invited to attend. The private meeting was of very short duration and there was no decision on how best to pursue further discussions on this matter.

APPENDIXES

In order to facilitate the reading of the documents that follow, their layouts have been standardized without affecting the contents of the originals.

our Majesty's loyal subjects, the Hou
s of Canada in Parliament assembl
approach Your Majesty, requesting
graciously be pleased to cause to be
Parliament of the United Kingd
containing the recitals and
ter set forth :

An Act to give effect to a request by t
and House of Commons of C

Whereas Canada has requested a
the enactment of an Act of the Parl
United Kingdom to give effect to
lter set forth and the Senate an
nada in Parliament
Majesty

AMENDMENTS TO THE
BRITISH NORTH AMERICA ACT*

In most respects, the British North America Act of 1867 did not provide for its amendment by any legislative authority in Canada. It therefore could be amended only by further Acts passed by the Parliament of the United Kingdom.

Since 1867, many amendments have, in fact, been made by the United Kingdom Parliament. The following is a brief account of these amendments:

(1) *The Rupert's Land Act, 1868* authorized the acceptance by Canada of the rights of the Hudson's Bay Company over Rupert's Land and the North-Western Territory. It also provided that, on Address from the Houses of Parliament of Canada, the Crown could declare this territory part of Canada and the Parliament of Canada could make laws for its peace, order and good government.

(2) *The British North America Act of 1871* ratified the Manitoba Act passed by the Parliament of Canada in 1870, creating the province of Manitoba and giving it a provincial constitution similar to those of the other provinces. The British North America Act of 1871 also empowered the Parliament of Canada to establish new provinces out of any Canadian territory not then included in a province; to alter the boundaries of any province (with the consent of its legislature), and to provide for the administration, peace, order and good government of any territory not included in a province.

(3) *The Parliament of Canada Act of 1875* amended section 18 of the British North America Act, 1867, which set forth the privileges, immunities and powers of each of the Houses of Parliament.

(4) *The British North America Act of 1886* authorized the Parliament of Canada to provide for the representation in the Senate and the House of Commons of any territories not included in any province.

(5) *The Statute Law Revision Act, 1893* repealed some obsolete provisions of the British North America Act of 1867.

(6) *The Canadian Speaker (Appointment of Deputy) Act, 1895* confirmed an Act of the Parliament of Canada which provided for the appointment of a Deputy-Speaker for the Senate.

(7) *The British North America Act, 1907* established a new scale of financial subsidies to the provinces in lieu of those set forth in section 118 of the British North America Act of 1867. While not expressly repealing the original section, it made its provisions obsolete.

(8) *The British North America Act, 1915* re-defined the Senatorial Divisions of Canada to take into account the provinces of Manitoba, British Columbia, Saskatchewan and Alberta. Although this statute did not expressly amend the text of the original section 22, it did alter its effect.

(9) *The British North America Act, 1916* provided for the extension of the life of the current Parliament of Canada beyond the normal period of five years.

---

* Guy Favreau, *The Amendment of the Constitution of Canada* (Ottawa: Queen's Printer, 1965).

(10) *The Statute Law Revision Act, 1927* repealed additional spent or obsolete provisions in the United Kingdom statutes, including two provisions of the British North America Acts.

(11) *The British North America Act, 1930* confirmed the natural resources agreements between the Government of Canada and the Governments of Manitoba, British Columbia, Alberta and Saskatchewan, giving the agreements the force of law notwithstanding anything in the British North America Acts.

(12) *The Statute of Westminster, 1931* while not directly amending the British North America Acts, did alter some of their provisions. Thus, the Parliament of Canada was given the power to make laws having extraterritorial effect. Also, Parliament and the provincial legislatures were given the authority, within their powers under the British North America Acts, to repeal any United Kingdom statute that formed part of the law of Canada. This authority, however, expressly excluded the British North America Act itself.

(13) *The British North America Act, 1940* gave the Parliament of Canada the exclusive jurisdiction to make laws in relation to Unemployment Insurance.

(14) *The British North America Act, 1943* provided for the postponement of redistribution of the seats in the House of Commons until the first session of Parliament after the cessation of hostilities.

(15) *The British North America Act, 1946* replaced section 51 of the British North America Act, 1867, and altered the provisions for the readjustment of representation in the House of Commons.

(16) *The British North America Act, 1949* confirmed the Terms of Union between Canada and Newfoundland.

(17) *The British North America Act (No. 2), 1949* gave the Parliament of Canada authority to amend the Constitution of Canada with certain exceptions.

(18) *The Statute Law Revision Act, 1950* repealed an obsolete section of the British North America Act, 1867.

(19) *The British North America Act, 1951* gave the Parliament of Canada concurrent jurisdiction with the provinces to make laws in relation to Old Age Pensions.

(20) *The British North America Act, 1960* amended section 99 and altered the tenure of office of superior court judges.

(21) *The British North America Act, 1964* amended the authority conferred upon the Parliament of Canada by the British North America Act, 1951, in relation to benefits supplementary to Old Age Pensions.

(22) *Amendment by Order in Council*

Section 146 of the British North America Act, 1867 provided for the admission of other British North American territories by Order in Council and stipulated that the provisions of any such Order in Council would have the same effect as if enacted by the Parliament of the United Kingdom. Under this section, Rupert's Land and the North-Western Territory were admitted by Order in Council on June 23rd, 1870; British Columbia by Order in Council on May 16th, 1871; Prince Edward Island by Order in Council on June 26, 1873. Because all these Orders in Council contained provisions of a constitutional character — adapting the provisions of the British North America Act to the new provinces, but with some modifications in each case — they may therefore be regarded as constitutional amendments.

SCHEDULE
to the
CONSTITUTION ACT, 1982
MODERNIZATION OF THE CONSTITUTION

Item	Column I Act Affected		Column II Amendment	Column III New Name
1	British North America Act, 1867, 30-31 Vict., c. 3 (U.K.)	(1)	Section 1 is repealed and the following substituted therefor: "1. This Act may be cited as the *Constitution Act, 1867.*"	Constitution Act, 1867
		(2)	Section 20 is repealed.	
		(3)	Class 1 of section 91 is repealed.	
		(4)	Class 1 of section 92 is repealed.	
2	An Act to amend and continue the Act 32-33 Victoria chapter 3; and to establish and provide for the Government of the Province of Manitoba, 1870, 33 Vict., c. 3 (Can.)	(1)	The long title is repealed and the following substituted therefor: "*Manitoba Act, 1870.*"	Manitoba Act, 1870
		(2)	Section 20 is repealed	
3	Order of Her Majesty in Council admitting Rupert's Land and the North-Western Territory into the union, dated the 23rd day of June, 1870			Rupert's Land and North-Western Territory Order

Item	Column I Act Affected	Column II Amendment	Column III New Name
4	Order of Her Majesty in Council admitting British Columbia into the Union, dated the 16th day of May, 1871		British Columbia Terms of Union
5	British North America Act, 1871, 34-35 Vict., c. 28 (U.K.)	Section 1 is repealed and the following substituted therefor: "1. This Act may be cited as the *Constitution Act, 1871.*"	Constitution Act, 1871
6	Order of Her Majesty in Council admitting Prince Edward Island into the Union, dated the 26th day of June, 1873		Prince Edward Island Terms of Union
7	Parliament of Canada Act, 1875, 38-39 Vict., c. 38 (U.K.)		Parliament of Canada Act, 1875
8	Order of Her Majesty in Council admitting all British possessions and Territories in North America and islands adjacent thereto into the Union, dated the 31st day of July, 1880		Adjacent Territories Order

Item	Column I Act Affected	Column II Amendment	Column III New Name
9	British North America Act, 1886, 49-50 Vict., c. 35 (U.K.)	Section 3 is repealed and the following substituted therefor: "3. This Act may be cited as the *Constitution Act, 1886*."	Constitution Act, 1886
10	Canada (Ontario Boundary) Act, 1889, 52-53 Vict., c. 28 (U.K.)		Canada (Ontario Boundary) Act, 1889
11	Canadian Speaker (Appointment of Deputy) Act, 1895, 2nd Sess., 59 Vict., c. 3 (U.K.)	The Act is repealed.	
12	The Alberta Act, 1905, 4-5 Edw. VII, c. 3 (Can.)		Alberta Act
13	The Saskatchewan Act, 1905, 4-5 Edw. VII, c. 42 (Can.)		Saskatchewan Act

Item	Column I Act Affected	Column II Amendment	Column III New Name
14	British North America Act, 1907, 7 Edw. VII, c. 11 (U.K.)	Section 2 is repealed and the following substituted therefor: "2. This Act may be cited as the *Constitution Act, 1907*."	Constitution Act, 1907
15	British North America Act, 1915, 5-6 Geo. V, c. 45 (U.K.)	Section 3 is repealed and the following substituted therefor: "3. This Act may be cited as the *Constitution Act, 1915*."	Constitution Act, 1915
16	British North America Act, 1930, 20-21 Geo. V, c. 26 (U.K.)	Section 3 is repealed and the following substituted therefor: "3. This Act may be cited as the *Constitution Act, 1930*."	Constitution Act, 1930
17	Statute of Westminster, 1931, 22 Geo. V, c. 4 (U.K.)	In so far as they apply to Canada, (a) section 4 is repealed; and (b) subsection 7(1) is repealed.	Statute of Westminster, 1931
18	British North America Act, 1940, 3-4 Geo. VI, c. 36 (U.K.)	Section 2 is repealed and the following substituted therefor: "2. This Act may be cited as the *Constitution Act, 1940*."	Constitution Act, 1940

Item	Column I Act Affected	Column II Amendment	Column III New Name
19	British North America Act, 1943, 6-7 Geo. VI, c. 30 (U.K.)	The Act is repealed.	
20	British North America Act, 1946, 9-10 Geo. VI, c. 63 (U.K.)	The Act is repealed.	
21	British North America Act, 1949, 12-13 Geo. VI, c. 22 (U.K.)	Section 3 is repealed and the following substituted therefor: "3. This Act may be cited as the *Newfoundland Act*."	Newfoundland Act
22	British North America (No. 2) Act, 1949, 13 Geo. VI, c. 81 (U.K.)	The Act is repealed.	
23	British North America Act, 1951, 14-15 Geo. VI, c. 32 (U.K.)	The Act is repealed.	
24	British North America Act, 1952, I Eliz. II, c. 15 (Can.)	The Act is repealed.	
25	British North America Act, 1960, 9 Eliz. II, c. 2 (U.K.)	Section 2 is repealed and the following substituted therefor: "2. This Act may be cited as the *Constitution Act, 1960*."	Constitution Act, 1960

Item	Column I Act Affected	Column II Amendment	Column III New Name
26	British North America Act, 1964, 12-13 Eliz. II, c. 73 (U.K.)	Section 2 is repealed and the following substituted therefor: "2. This Act may be cited as the *Constitution Act, 1964.*"	Constitution Act, 1964
27	British North America Act, 1965, 14 Eliz. II, c. 4, Part I (Can.)	Section 2 is repealed and the following substituted therefor: "2. This Part may be cited as the *Constitution Act, 1965.*"	Constitution Act, 1965
28	British North America Act, 1974, 23 Eliz. II, c. 13, Part I (Can.)	Section 3, as amended by 25-26 Eliz. II, c. 28 s. 38(1) (Can.), is repealed and the following substituted therefor: "3. This Part may be cited as the *Constitution Act, 1974.*"	Constitution Act, 1974
29	British North America Act, 1975, 23-24 Eliz. II, c. 28, Part I (Can.)	Section 3, as amended by 25-26 Eliz. II, c. 28, s. 31 (Can.), is repealed and the following substituted therefor: "3. This Part may be cited as the *Constitution Act (No. 1), 1975.*"	Constitution Act (No. 1), 1975

Item	Column I Act Affected	Column II Amendment	Column III New Name
30	British North America Act (No. 2), 1975, 23-24 Eliz. II, c. 53 (Can.)	Section 3 is repealed and the following substituted therefor: "3. This Act may be cited as the *Constitution Act (No. 2), 1975.*"	Constitution Act (No. 2), 1975

our Majesty's loyal subjects, the Hou
s of Canada in Parliament assembl
approach Your Majesty, requesting
graciously be pleased to cause to be
Parliament of the United Kingdo
containing the recitals and c
er set forth :

An Act to give effect to a request by th
and House of Commons of C

Whereas Canada has requested an
the enactment of an Act of the Parl
nited Kingdom to give effect to t
in after set forth and the Senate an
anada in Parliament
er Majesty

THE FULTON-FAVREAU FORMULA

AN ACT TO PROVIDE FOR THE AMENDMENT IN CANADA
OF THE CONSTITUTION OF CANADA*

(Preamble)

WHEREAS Canada has requested, and consented to, the enactment of an Act of Parliament of the United Kingdom in the terms hereinafter set forth, and the Senate and House of Commons of Canada in Parliament assembled have submitted Addresses to Her Majesty praying that Her Majesty may graciously be pleased to cause a Bill to be laid before the Parliament of the United Kingdom for that purpose:

Be it therefore enacted by the Queen's most Excellent Majesty by and with the advice and consent of the Lords Spiritual and Temporal, and Commons, in this present Parliament assembled, and by the authority of the same, as follows:

PART I
POWER TO AMEND THE CONSTITUTION OF CANADA

1. Subject to this Part, the Parliament of Canada may make laws repealing or re-enacting any provision of the Constitution of Canada.

2. No law made under the authority of this Part affecting any provision of this Act or section 51A of the British North America Act, 1867, or affecting any provision of the Constitution of Canada relating to

    (a)   the powers of the legislature of a province to make laws,
    (b)   the rights or privileges granted or secured by the Constitution of Canada to the legislature or the government of a province,
    (c)   the assets or property of a province, or
    (d)   the use of the English or French language,

    shall come into force unless it is concurred in by the legislatures of all the provinces.

3. (1)   No law made under the authority of this Part affecting any provision of the Constitution of Canada that refers to one or more, but not all, of the provinces, shall come into force unless it is concurred in by the legislature of every province to which the provision refers.

    (2)   Section 2 of this Act does not extend to any provision of the Constitution of Canada referred to in subsection (1) of this section.

4. (1)   No law made under the authority of this Part affecting any provision of the Constitution of Canada relating to education in any province other than Newfoundland shall come into force unless it is concurred in by the legislatures of all the provinces other than Newfoundland.

---

* Guy Favreau, *The Amendment of the Constitution of Canada* (Ottawa: Queen's Printer, 1965).

(2) No law made under the authority of this Part affecting any provision of the Constitution of Canada relating to education in the province of Newfoundland shall come into force unless it is concurred in by the legislature of the province of Newfoundland.

(3) Sections 2 and 3 of this Act do not extend to any provision of the Constitution of Canada referred to in subsections (1) and (2) of this section.

5. No law made under the authority of this Part affecting any provision of the Constitution of Canada not coming within section 2, 3 or 4 of this Act shall come into force unless it is concurred in by the legislatures of at least two-thirds of the provinces representing at least fifty per cent of the population of Canada according to the latest general census.

6. Notwithstanding anything in the Constitution of Canada, the Parliament of Canada may exclusively make laws from time to time amending the Constitution of Canada in relation to the executive Government of Canada, and the Senate and House of Commons, except as regards

(a) the functions of the Queen and the Governor General in relation to the Parliament or Government of Canada;

(b) the requirements of the Constitution of Canada respecting a yearly session of Parliament;

(c) the maximum period fixed by the Constitution of Canada for the duration of the House of Commons, except that the Parliament of Canada may, in time of real or apprehended war, invasion or insurrection, continue a House of Commons beyond such maximum period, if such continuation is not opposed by the votes of more than one-third of the members of such House;

(d) the number of members by which a province is entitled to be represented in the Senate;

(e) the residence qualifications of Senators and the requirements of the Constitution of Canada for the summoning of persons to the Senate by the Governor General in the Queen's name;

(f) the right of a province to a number of members in the House of Commons not less than the number of Senators representing such province;

(g) the principles of proportionate representation of the provinces in the House of Commons prescribed by the Constitution of Canada; and

(h) the use of English or French language.

7. Notwithstanding anything in the Constitution of Canada, in each province the legislature may exclusively make laws in relation to the amendment from time to time of the Constitution of the province, except as regards the office of Lieutenant-Governor.

8. Any law to repeal, amend or re-enact any provision of the Constitution of Canada that is not authorized to be made either by the Parliament of Canada under the authority of section 6 of this Act or by the legislature of a province under the authority of section 7 of this Act is subject to the provisions of sections 1 to 5 of this Act.

9. Nothing in this Part diminishes any power of the Parliament of Canada or of the legislature of a province existing at the coming into force of this Act, to make laws in relation to any matter.

10.   No Act of the Parliament of the United Kingdom passed after the coming into force of this Act shall extend or be deemed to extend to Canada or to any province or territory of Canada as part of the law thereof.

11.   Without limiting the meaning of the expression "Constitution of Canada", in this Part that expression includes the following enactments and any order, rule or regulation thereunder, namely,

    (a)   the British North America Acts, 1867 to 1964;
    (b)   the Manitoba Act, 1870;
    (c)   the Parliament of Canada Act, 1875;
    (d)   the Canadian Speaker (Appointment of Deputy) Act, 1895, Session 2;
    (e)   the Alberta Act;
    (f)   the Saskatchewan Act;
    (g)   the Statute of Westminster, 1931, in so far as it is part of the law of Canada; and
    (h)   this Act.

PART II

BRITISH NORTH AMERICA ACT, 1867, AMENDED

12.   Class 1 of section 91 of the British North America Act, 1867, as enacted by the British North America (No. 2) Act, 1949, and class 1 of section 92 of the British North America Act, 1867, are repealed.

13.   The British North America Act, 1867, is amended by renumbering section 94A thereof as 94B and by adding thereto, immediately after section 94 thereof, the following heading and section:

Delegation of Legislative Authority

"94A. (1)   Notwithstanding anything in this or in any other Act, the Parliament of Canada may make laws in relation to any matters coming within the classes of subjects enumerated in classes (6), (10), (13) and (16) of section 92 of this Act, but no statute enacted under the authority of this subsection shall have effect in any province unless the legislature of that province has consented to the operation of such a statute in that province.

    (2)   The Parliament of Canada shall not have authority to enact a statute under subsection (1) of this section unless

        (a)   prior to the enactment thereof the legislatures of at least four of the provinces have consented to the operation of such a statute as provided in that subsection, or

        (b)   it is declared by the Parliament of Canada that the Government of Canada has consulted with the governments of all the provinces, and that the enactment of the statute is of concern to fewer than four of the provinces so declared to be concerned have under the authority of their legislatures consented to the enactment of such a statute.

    (3)   Notwithstanding anything in this or in any other Act, the legislature of a province may make laws in the province in relation to any matter coming within the legislative jurisdiction of the Parliament of Canada.

(4) No statute enacted by a province under the authority of sub-section (3) of this section shall have effect unless

(a) prior to the enactment thereof the Parliament of Canada has consented to the enactment of such a statute by the legislature of that province, and

(b) a similar statute has under the authority of sub-section (3) of this section been enacted by the legislatures of at least three other provinces.

(5) The Parliament of Canada or the legislature of a province may make laws for the imposition of punishment by fine, penalty or imprisonment for enforcing any law made by it under the authority of this section.

(6) A consent given under this section may at any time be revoked, and

(a) if a consent given under subsection (1) or (2) of this section is revoked, any law made by the Parliament of Canada to which such consent relates that is operative in the province in which the consent is revoked shall thereupon cease to have effect in that province, but the revocation of the consent does not affect the operation of that law in any other province, and

(b) if a consent given under subsection (4) of this section is revoked, any law made by the legislature of a province to which the consent relates shall thereupon cease to have effect.

(7) The Parliament of Canada may repeal any law made by it under the authority of this section, in so far as it is part of the law of one or more provinces, but if any repeal under the authority of this subsection does not relate to all of the provinces in which that law is operative, the repeal does not affect the operation of that law in any province to which the repeal does not relate.

(8) The legislature of a province may repeal any law made by it under the authority of this section, but the repeal under the authority of this subsection of any law does not affect the operation in any other province of any law enacted by that province under the authority of this section."

PART III

FRENCH VERSION

14. The French version of this Act set forth in the Schedule shall form part of this Act.

PART IV

CITATION AND COMMENCEMENT

15. This Act may be cited as the Constitution of Canada Amendment Act.

16. This Act shall come into force on . . . day of . . . .

Appendix 4

APPENDIX 4

THE VICTORIA FORMULA

PART IX*
AMENDMENTS TO THE CONSTITUTION

Art. 49.   Amendments to the Constitution of Canada may from time to time be made by proclamation issued by the Governor General under the Great Seal of Canada when so authorized by resolutions of the Senate and House of Commons and of the Legislative Assemblies of at least a majority of the Provinces that includes

(1)   every Province that at any time before the issue of such proclamation had, according to any previous general census, a population of at least twenty-five per cent of the population of Canada;

(2)   at least two of the Atlantic Provinces;

(3)   at least two of the Western Provinces that have, according to the then latest general census, combined populations of at least fifty per cent of the population of all the Western Provinces.

Art. 50.   Amendments to the Constitution of Canada in relation to any provision that applies to one or more, but not all, of the Provinces may from time to time be made by proclamation issued by the Governor General under the Great Seal of Canada when so authorized by resolutions of the Senate and House of Commons and of the Legislative Assembly of each Province to which an amendment applies.

Art. 51.   An amendment may be made by proclamation under Article 49 or 50 without a resolution of the Senate authorizing the issue of the proclamation if within ninety days of the passage of a resolution by the House of Commons authorizing its issue the Senate has not passed such a resolution and at any time after the expiration of the ninety days the House of Commons again passes the resolution, but any period when Parliament is prorogued or dissolved shall not be counted in computing the ninety days.

Art. 52.   The following rules apply to the procedures for amendment described in Articles 49 and 50:

(1)   either of these procedures may be initiated by the Senate or the House of Commons or the Legislative Assembly of a Province;

(2)   a resolution made for the purpose of this Part may be revoked at any time before the issue of a proclamation authorized by it.

Art. 53.   The Parliament of Canada may exclusively make laws from time to time amending the Constitution of Canada, in relation to the executive Government of Canada and the Senate and House of Commons.

Art. 54.   In each Province the Legislature may exclusively make laws in relation to the amendment from time to time of the Constitution of the Province.

---

*Canadian Intergovernmental Conference Secretariat, *Constitutional Review, 1968–1971: Secretary's Report*
(Ottawa: Information Canada, 1974), pp.389-391.

Art. 55. Notwithstanding Articles 53 and 54, the following matters may be amended only in accordance with the procedure in Article 49:

(1) the office of the Queen, of the Governor General and of the Lieutenant-Governor;

(2) the requirements of the Constitution of Canada respecting yearly sessions of the Parliament of Canada and the Legislatures;

(3) the maximum period fixed by the Constitution of Canada for the duration of the House of Commons and the Legislative Assemblies;

(4) the powers of the Senate;

(5) the number of members by which a Province is entitled to be represented in the Senate, and the residence qualifications of Senators;

(6) the right of a Province to a number of members in the House of Commons not less than the number of Senators representing the Province;

(7) the principles of proportionate representation of the Provinces in the House of Commons prescribed by the Constitution of Canada; and

(8) except as provided in Article 16, the requirements of this Charter respecting the use of the English or French language.

Art. 56. The procedure prescribed in Article 49 may not be used to make an amendment when there is another provision for making such amendment in the Constitution of Canada, but that procedure may nonetheless be used to amend any provision for amending the Constitution, including this Article, or in making a general consolidation and revision of the Constitution.

Art. 57. In this Part, "Atlantic Provinces" means the Provinces of Nova Scotia, New Brunswick, Prince Edward Island and Newfoundland, and "Western Provinces" means the Provinces of Manitoba, British Columbia, Saskatchewan and Alberta.

LETTER FROM PRIME MINISTER TRUDEAU
TO PREMIERS

CONFIDENTIAL

March 31, 1976

My dear Premier:

I had been hoping to be in touch with you well before this to advise you about progress in the exercise we started last April, with our discussion at 7 Rideau Gate, for "patriation" of the B.N.A. Act. Since then, all of you, with the exception of Premier Bennett, have received Mr. Gordon Robertson who has discussed the project with you on my behalf. Those discussions took place between May and mid-July of 1975. Premier Barrett was unable to arrange a meeting prior to the election in British Columbia but Mr. Robertson will be meeting Premier Bennett in early April. Discussions with Quebec have taken a good deal of time and it was not until March 5th that I had the opportunity of reviewing the question with the Premier of Quebec. I thought it essential to know his attitude before proceeding to further action.

You will recall that we started with agreement in principle on the desirability of "patriating" the B.N.A. Act and, at the same time, establishing as law the amending procedure that had been agreed to in Victoria in 1971. We also agreed that we would not, in the present "patriation" exercise, consider substantive changes to the B.N.A. Act itself since any entry on that course would, as the discussions from 1968 to 1971 had shown, make early action impossible. Mr. Bourassa indicated, however, that it would be difficult for his government to agree to this, unless the action also included "constitutional guarantees" for the French language and culture. We agreed that our general acceptance of the plan, in principle, would be subject to more precise exploration and definition, and this was the purpose of the discussions Mr. Robertson had with you on my behalf. I should first report on what developed in the course of those discussions, although the Premiers Mr. Robertson saw later will be generally aware of the way in which our original proposal grew.

It quickly became apparent in Mr. Robertson's discussions that the action for "patriation" and establishment of the amending procedure would be more meaningful for, and more acceptable to, a number of provinces if certain other alterations in our constitutional situation could be established at the same time. Most of these alterations, with the exception of Mr. Bourassa's "constitutional guarantees", were among the things that had been included in the Victoria Charter. They included the provision for consultation with the provinces about appointments to the Supreme Court of Canada and the special handling of cases arising from the civil law of Quebec. They included also the provision concerning the reduction of regional disparities. Certain of the western provinces wanted to have the amending procedure itself modified so that the requirement with regard to consent from the four western provinces would be the same as that for the four eastern provinces. This would mean deletion of the population provision respecting the western provinces that was inserted at Victoria.

The main problem was the definition of the "constitutional guarantees" to which Mr. Bourassa had referred at the outset. Mr. Robertson found that the Premiers he spoke to after the initial discussions with Mr. Bourassa in May had no objection in principle to "constitutional guarantees", although all made it clear that they would want to consider them in detail once they had been worked out with Quebec and reduced to writing.

I will not go into all the difficulties that are presented by the concept of "constitutional guarantees"; they are many and complex. Discussions with Mr. Bourassa's representatives finally led to a formulation that was included in a document sent to him in November, 1975. I am enclosing a copy of the full document herewith. I would draw your attention especially to Parts IV and VI. The formulation of the principal "constitutional guarantee" is Part IV (Article 38). It is buttressed by Part VI (Article 40) and also by the provisions concerning language in Part III.

As I have mentioned, the "constitutional guarantee" was a concept raised by Mr. Bourassa and stated by him to be essential. Articles 38 and 40 attempt to cover the points made by his representatives. Mr. Bourassa knows that my colleagues and I share some concern about the Articles, and he understands that it will fall to him to explain them to his fellow Premiers, in the light of the facts relating to the position of the French language and culture in Canada.

I should emphasize that the document, while it is styled a "Draft Proclamation", was put in this form simply to show with maximum clarity what the result would be if all the proposals, as they had emerged in the course of Mr. Robertson's consultations, were found acceptable by all governments. It should not be regarded as a specific proposal or draft to which anyone is committed at this stage, since there has not been agreement to the totality of it by anyone. It is rather in the nature of a report on the various ideas, including Mr. Bourassa's "constitutional guarantee", as they developed in the course of the informal discussions from April to November 1975.

As I stated earlier, most of the "Draft Proclamation" consists of provisions of the Victoria Charter which various Premiers have asked to have included in any action we take. In some cases there are adjustments of the Victoria provisions in order to take into account altered circumstances since 1971 and to benefit by some hind-sight. The new parts of this "report" are the Parts IV and VI to which I have already referred. For ease of reference the main elements are:

(a)   A Preamble. This is entirely new and is simply an idea of the way a total presentation might look.

(b)   Part I is the amending formula contained in the Victoria Charter made applicable to those parts of the Constitution now amendable in Canada. Thus Articles 49, 50, 51, 52, 56 and 57 of Part IX of the Victoria Charter are included, while Articles 53, 54 and 55, which were designed to replace Articles 91(1) and 92(1) of the British North America Act, are not. The amending formula has not been modified to take account of the views expressed by certain Western Premiers concerning the population qualification for agreement by the Western provinces. I suggest that this might be a matter that, in the first instance, the four Western Premiers might attempt to solve among themselves.

(c)   Part II, which is Part IV of the Victoria Charter concerning the Supreme Court, with a final Article (included in another Part of the Victoria Charter) to protect the status of Judges already appointed.

(d)   Part III, which is a modified version of Part II of the Victoria Charter concerning language rights. It would entrench the constitutional status of the English and French languages federally. It would not affect the provinces, but it would permit a province, under Article 35, to entrench its own provision if it so wished.

(e)   Part IV, which is the "guarantee" designed to protect the French Language and culture against adverse action by the Parliament and Government of Canada.

(f)   Part V, which is essentially Part VII of the Victoria Charter on Regional Disparities. The presentation has been slightly altered but there is no change in substance whatever.

(g)   Part VI, which is a new Article designed to indicate the spirit in which Governments may enter into agreements. In two of the three areas specifically mentioned, major agreements with Quebec have been concluded over the past two years (family allowances and consultation on immigration).

Mr. Bourassa advised me in our conversation on March 5th that the things he considers to be necessary might well go beyond what we, in the federal government, have understood to be involved in the present exercise. In part they might relate to the distribution of powers. I advised him that the Government of Canada, for its part, feels that it can go no further as part of this exercise than the constitutional guarantees that are embodied in the document and that indeed even they might find difficulty of acceptance in their present form. To go further would involve entry upon the distribution of powers, with the consequences to which I have referred. We must, then, consider three alternatives that are open to us in these circumstances.

Let us begin with the simplest alternative. The Government of Canada remains firmly of the view that we should as a minimum, achieve "patriation" of the B.N.A. Act. It is not prepared to contemplate the continuation of the anomalous situation in which the British Parliament retains the power to legislate with respect to essential parts of the constitution of Canada. Such "patriation" could be achieved by means of an Address of the two Houses of the Canadian Parliament to the Queen, requesting appropriate legislation by the British Parliament to end its capacity to legislate in any way with respect to Canada. Whereas unanimity of the federal government and the provinces would be desirable even for so limited a measure, we are satisfied that such action by the Parliament of Canada does not require the consent of the provinces and would be entirely proper since it would not affect in any way the distribution of powers. In other words, the termination of the British capacity to legislate for Canada would not in any way alter the position as between Parliament and the provincial legislatures whether in respect of jurisdictions flowing from Sections 91 and 92 or otherwise.

However, simple "patriation" would not equip us with an amending procedure for those parts of our constitution that do not come under either Section 91(1) or Section 92(1) of the B.N.A. Act. To meet this deficiency, one could provide in the Address to the Queen that amendment of those parts of the constitution not now amendable in Canada could be made on unanimous consent of Parliament and the legislature until a permanent formula is found and established. In theory this approach would introduce a rigidity which does not now exist, since at present it is the federal Parliament alone which goes to Westminster, and the degree of consultation of or consent by the provinces is a matter only of convention about which there can be differences of view. In practice, of course, the federal government has in the past sought the unanimous consent of the provinces before seeking amendments that have affected the distribution of powers.

A second and perhaps preferable alternative would be to include in the action a provision that could lead to the establishment of a permanent and more flexible amending procedure. That could be done by detailing such a procedure in our Joint Address and having it included in the British legislation as an enabling provision that would come into effect when and only when it had received the formal approval of the legislatures of all the provinces. The obvious amending procedure to set forth would be the one agreed to at Victoria in application to those parts of our constitution not now amendable in Canada. (Part I of the attached "Draft Proclamation".) This could be with or without modification respecting the four western provinces. (On this last point, the federal government would be quite prepared to accept the proposed modification and it is my understanding that the other provinces would equally agree if the western provinces can arrive at agreement.)

If we took the above step, we would achieve forthwith half of our objective of last April — "patriation" — and we would establish a process by which the other half — the amending procedure — would become effective as and when the provincial legislatures individually signify their agreement. Over a period of time, which I hope would not be long, we would establish the total capacity to amend our constitution under what is clearly the best and most acceptable procedure that has been worked out in nearly fifty years of effort, since the original federal-provincial conference on this subject in 1927. Until full agreement and implementation had been achieved, any constitutional changes that might be needed, and which did not come under Section 91(1) or Section 92(1) or which could not otherwise be effected in Canada could be made subject to unanimous consent. This would impose an interim rigidity for such very rare requirements for amendment, but, as I have said, the practice has, in any event, been to secure unanimous consent before making amendments that have affected the distribution of powers.

A third and more extensive possibility still, would be to include, in the "patriation" action, the entirety of the "Draft Proclamation" I am enclosing. In other words the British Parliament, in terminating its capacity to legislate for Canada, could provide that all of the substance of Parts I to VI would come into effect in Canada and would have full legal force when, and only when, the entirety of those Parts had been approved by the legislatures of all the provinces. At that point, we would have, not only "patriation" and the amending procedure, but also the other provisions that have developed out of the discussions thus far. Here again, of course, until all the Provinces had approved the entire Draft Proclamation, any constitutional change which did not come under Section 91(1) or Section 92(1) would be subject to unanimous consent.

As you can see, there are several possibilities as to the course of action now to take. So far as the federal government is concerned, our much preferred course would be to act in unison with all the provinces. "Patriation" is such a historic milestone that it would be ideal if all Premiers would associate themselves with it.

But if unanimity does not appear possible, the federal government will have to decide whether it will recommend to Parliament that a Joint Address be passed seeking "patriation" of the B.N.A. Act. A question for decision then will be what to add to that action. We are inclined to think that it should, at the minimum, be the amending procedure agreed to at Victoria by all the provinces, with or without modification respecting the western provinces, and subject to the condition about coming into force only when approved by the legislatures of all the provinces as explained above.

The implications of the different possibilities are complex, and you will undoubtedly want to consider them with care. To facilitate consideration, Mr. Robertson would be glad to come to see you, at a convenient time, for such discussions as you might wish to have. When opportunity offers at an early meeting, we might also discuss the matter together.

I would welcome your comments. Mr. Robertson will be in touch with your office to see if you would wish to have a meeting with him and, if so, what time would suit.

Prior to my meeting with Mr. Bourassa, I did not feel that I was in a position to place any documents before Parliament, but I now feel it proper to do so. I would like to table copies of this letter, as well as of the "Draft Proclamation" that is enclosed. If you have any objection, could you please advise me forthwith. If I do not hear to the contrary, I shall plan to table on April 9th. Should you wish to do the same in your legislature, I would of course, have no objection.

Sincerely,

[Signed P E Trudeau]

November 10, 1975

FORM FOR A PROCLAMATION

OF THE GOVERNOR GENERAL

WHEREAS it is fitting that it should be possible to amend the Constitution of Canada in all respects by action of the appropriate instrumentalities of government in Canada acting separately or in concert as may best suit the matter in question;

AND WHEREAS it is desirable to make more specific provision respecting the constitutional status of the English and French languages in Canada and to ensure that changes in the Constitution, interpretation of its provisions or action by the Parliament or Government of Canada should not endanger the continuation and full development of the French language and the culture based thereon;

AND WHEREAS it is desirable that the Parliament and Government of Canada and the Legislatures and Governments of the Provinces act effectively to promote equality of opportunity and an acceptable level of public services among the different regions of Canada;

THEREFORE it is desirable to establish among other things:

(a)   A method for the amendment in Canada of those parts of the Constitution of general interest and concern that cannot now be amended in Canada in which the consent will be required of the Legislatures of Provinces representative of both the official language groups of Canada as well as of the Legislatures of Provinces in all of the geographical regions of Canada;

(b)   means by which Provinces can participate in the selection of persons to be appointed to the Supreme Court of Canada; and

(c)   principles to guide the Parliament of Canada in the exercise of powers allotted to it under the Constitution of Canada and to guide the Government of Canada in the exercise of powers conferred upon it by the Constitution of Canada and by laws enacted by the Parliament of Canada;

NOW THEREFORE We .... do proclaim as follows:

PART I

AMENDMENTS TO THE CONSTITUTION

Art. 1 Amendments to the Constitution of Canada may from time to time be made by Proclamation issued by the Governor General under the Great Seal of Canada when so authorized by resolutions of the Senate and the House of Commons and of the Legislative Assemblies of at least a majority of the Provinces that includes:

(1)   every Province that at any time before the issue of such Proclamation had, according to any previous general census, a population of at least twenty-five per cent of the population of Canada;

(2)   at least two of the Atlantic Provinces;

(3)   at least two of the Western provinces that have, according to the then latest general census, combined populations of at least fifty per cent of the population of all the Western Provinces.

Art. 2 Amendments to the Constitution of Canada in relation to any provision that applies to one or more, but not all, of the Provinces may from time to time be made by Proclamation issued by the Governor General under the Great Seal of Canada when so authorized by resolutions of the Senate and House of Commons and of the Legislative Assembly of each Province to which an amendment applies.

Art. 3 An amendment may be made by Proclamation under Articles 1 or 2 without a resolution of the Senate authorizing the issue of the Proclamation if within ninety days of the passage of a resolution by the House of Commons authorizing its issue the Senate has not passed such a resolution and at any time after the expiration of the ninety days the House of Commons again passes the resolution, but any period when Parliament is prorogued or dissolved shall not be counted in computing the ninety days.

Art. 4 The following rules apply to the procedures for amendment described in Articles 1 and 2:

(1)   either of these procedures may be initiated by the Senate or the House of Commons or the Legislative Assembly of a Province;

(2)   a resolution made for the purposes of this Part may be revoked at any time before the issue of a Proclamation authorized by it.

Art. 5 The procedures prescribed in Articles 1 and 2 may not be used to make an amendment when there is another provision for making such amendment in the Constitution of Canada, but the procedure in Article 1 may nonetheless be used to amend any provision for amending the Constitution, including this Article, or in making a general consolidation and revision of the Constitution.

Art. 6 In this Part "Atlantic Provinces" means the Provinces of Nova Scotia, New Brunswick, Prince Edward Island and Newfoundland, and "Western Provinces" means the Provinces of Manitoba, British Columbia, Saskatchewan and Alberta.

Art. 7 The enactments set out in the Schedule shall continue as law in Canada and as such shall, together with this Proclamation and any Proclamation subsequently issued under this Part, collectively be known as the Constitution of Canada, and amendments thereto shall henceforth be made only according to the authority contained therein.

PART II

SUPREME COURT OF CANADA

Art. 8 There shall be a general court of appeal for Canada to be known as the Supreme Court of Canada.

Art. 9 The Supreme Court of Canada shall consist of a chief justice to be called the Chief Justice of Canada, and eight other judges, who shall, subject to this Part, be appointed by the Governor General in Council by letters patent under the Great Seal of Canada.

Art. 10 Any person may be appointed a judge of the Supreme Court of Canada who, after having been admitted to the Bar of any Province, has, for a total period of at least ten years, been a judge of any court in Canada or a barrister or advocate at the Bar of any Province.

Art. 11 At least three of the judges of the Supreme Court of Canada shall be appointed from among persons who, after having been admitted to the Bar of the Province of Quebec, have, for a total period of at least ten years, been judges of any court of that Province or of a court established by the Parliament of Canada or barristers or advocates at that Bar.

Art. 12 Where a vacancy arises in the Supreme Court of Canada and the Attorney General of Canada is considering a person for appointment to fill the vacancy, he shall inform the Attorney General of the appropriate Province.

Art. 13 When an appointment is one falling within Article II or the Attorney General of Canada has determined that the appointment shall be made from among persons who have been admitted to the Bar of a specific Province, he shall make all reasonable efforts to reach agreement, with the Attorney General of the appropriate Province, before a person is appointed to the Court.

Art. 14 No person shall be appointed to the Supreme Court of Canada unless the Attorney General of Canada and the Attorney General of the appropriate Province agree to the appointment, or such person has been recommended for appointment to the Court by a nominating council described in Article 16, or has been selected by the Attorney General of Canada under Article 16.

Art. 15 Where after the lapse of ninety days from the day a vacancy arises in the Supreme Court of Canada, the Attorney General of Canada and the Attorney General of a Province have not reached agreement on a person to be appointed to fill the vacancy, the Attorney General of Canada may inform the Attorney General of the appropriate Province in writing that he proposes to convene a nominating council to recommend an appointment.

Art. 16 Within thirty days of the day when the Attorney General of Canada has written the Attorney General of the Province that he proposes to convene a nominating council, the Attorney General of the Province may inform the Attorney General of Canada in writing that he selects either of the following types of nominating councils:

(1)   a nominating council consisting of the following members: the Attorney General of Canada or his nominee and the Attorneys General of the Provinces or their nominees;

(2)   a nominating council consisting of the following members: the Attorney General of Canada or his nominee, the Attorney General of the appropriate Province or his nominee and a Chairman to be selected by the two Attorneys General, and if within six months from the expiration of the thirty days they cannot agree on a Chairman, then the Chief Justice of the appropriate Province, or if he is unable to act, the next senior Judge of his court, shall name a Chairman;

and if the Attorney General of the Province fails to make a selection within the thirty days above referred to, the Attorney General of Canada may select the person to be appointed.

Art. 17 When a nominating council has been created, the Attorney General of Canada shall submit the names of not less than three qualified persons to it about whom he has sought the agreement of the Attorney General of the appropriate Province to the appointment, and the nominating council shall recommend therefrom a person for appointment to the Supreme Court of Canada; a majority of the members of a council constitutes a quorum, and a recommendation of a majority of the members at a meeting constitutes a recommendation of the council.

Art. 18 For the purpose of Articles 12 to 17 "appropriate Province" means, in the case of a person being considered for appointment to the Supreme Court of Canada in compliance with Article 11, the Province of Quebec, and in the case of any other person being so considered, the Province to the Bar of which such a person was admitted, and if a person was admitted to the Bar of more than one Province, the Province with the Bar of which the person has, in the opinion of the Attorney General of Canada, the closest connection.

Art. 19 Articles 12 to 18 do not apply to the appointment of the Chief Justice of Canada when such appointment is made from among the judges of the Supreme Court of Canada.

Art. 20 The judges of the Supreme Court of Canada hold office during good behaviour until attaining the age of seventy years, but are removable by the Governor General on address of the Senate and House of Commons.

Art. 21 The Supreme Court of Canada has jurisdiction to hear and determine appeals on any constitutional question from any judgement of any court in Canada and from any decision on any constitutional question by any such court in determining any question referred to it, but except as regards appeals from the highest court of final resort in a Province, the Supreme Court of Canada may prescribe such exceptions and conditions to the exercise of such jurisdiction as may be authorized by the Parliament of Canada.

Art. 22 Subject to this Part, the Supreme Court of Canada shall have such further appellate jurisdiction as the Parliament of Canada may prescribe.

Art. 23 The Parliament of Canada may make laws conferring original jurisdiction on the Supreme Court of Canada in respect of such matters in relation of the laws of Canada as may be prescribed by the Parliament of Canada, and authorizing the reference of questions of law or fact to the court and requiring the court to hear and determine the questions.

Art. 24 Subject to this Part, the judgment of the Supreme Court of Canada in all cases is final and conclusive.

Art. 25 Where a case before the Supreme Court of Canada involves questions of law relating to the civil law of the Province of Quebec, and involves no other question of law, it shall be heard by a panel of five judges, or with the consent of the parties, four judges, at least three of whom have the qualifications described in Article 11, and if for any reason three judges of the court who have such qualifications are not available, the court may name such ad hoc judges as may be necessary to hear the case from among the judges who have such qualifications serving on a superior court of record established by the law of Canada or of a superior court of appeal of the Province of Quebec.

Art. 26 Nothing in this Part shall be construed as restricting the power existing at the commencement of this Proclamation of a Provincial Legislature to provide for or limit appeals pursuant to its power to legislate in relation to the administration of justice in the Province.

Art. 27 The salaries, allowances and pension of the judges of the Supreme Court of Canada shall be fixed and provided by the Parliament of Canada.

Art. 28 Subject to this Part, the Parliament of Canada may make laws to provide for the organization and maintenance of the Supreme Court of Canada, including the establishment of a quorum for particular purposes.

Art. 29 The court existing on the day of the coming into force of this Proclamation under the name of the Supreme Court of Canada shall continue as the Supreme Court of Canada, and the judges thereof shall continue in office as though appointed under this Part except that they shall hold office during good behaviour until attaining the age of seventy-five years, and until otherwise provided pursuant to the provisions of this Part, all laws pertaining to the court in force on that day shall continue, subject to the provisions of this Proclamation.

PART III
LANGUAGE RIGHTS

Art. 30 English and French are the official languages of Canada, but no provision in this Part shall derogate from any right, privilege, or obligation existing under any other provision of the Constitution.

Art. 31 A person has the right to use English and French in the debates of the Parliament of Canada.

Art. 32 The statutes and the records and journals of the Parliament of Canada shall be printed and published in English and French; and both versions of such statutes are authoritative.

Art. 33 A person has the right to use English and French in giving evidence before, or in any pleading or process in the Supreme Court of Canada and any courts established by the Parliament of Canada, and to require that all documents and judgments issuing from such courts be in English or French.

Art. 34 An individual has the right to the use of the official language of his choice in communications between him and the head or central office of every department and agency of the Government of Canada.

Art. 35 A provincial Legislative Assembly may, by resolution, declare that provisions similar to those of any part of Articles 32, 33 and 34 shall apply to the Legislative Assembly, and to any of the provincial courts and offices of the provincial departments and agencies according to the terms of the resolution, and thereafter such parts apply to the Legislative Assembly, courts and offices specified according to the terms of the resolution; and any right conferred under this Article may be abrogated or diminished only in accordance with the procedure prescribed in Article 2.

Art. 36 A person has the right to the use of the official language of his choice in communications between him and every principal office of the department and agencies of the Government of Canada that are located in an area where a substantial proportion of the population has the official language of his choice as its mother tongue, but the Parliament of Canada may define the limits of such areas and what constitutes a substantial proportion of the population for the purposes of this Article.

Art. 37 In addition to the rights provided by this Part, the Parliament of Canada may, within its legislative jurisdiction, provide for more extensive use of English and French.

PART IV
PROTECTION OF THE FRENCH
LANGUAGE AND CULTURE

Art. 38 The Parliament of Canada, in the exercise of powers allotted to it under the Constitution of Canada, and the Government of Canada, in the exercise of powers conferred upon by the Constitution of Canada and by laws enacted by the Parliament of Canada, shall be guided by, among other considerations for the welfare and advantage of the people of Canada, the knowledge that a fundamental purpose underlying the federation of Canada is to ensure the preservation and the full development of the French language and the culture based on it and neither the Parliament nor the Government of Canada, in the exercise of their respective powers, shall act in a manner that will adversely affect the preservation and development of the French language and the culture based on it.

PART V
REGIONAL DISPARITIES

Art. 39 Without altering the distribution of powers and without compelling the Parliament of Canada or the Legislatures of the Provinces to exercise their legislative powers, the Parliament of Canada and the Legislatures of the Provinces, together with the Government of Canada and the Governments of the Provinces, are committed to:

(a)   the promotion of equality of opportunity and well-being for all individuals in Canada;

(b)   the assurance, as nearly as possible, that essential public services of reasonable quality are available to all individuals in Canada; and

(c)   the promotion of economic development to reduce disparities in the social and economic opportunities for all individuals in Canada wherever they may live.

PART VI
FEDERAL-PROVINCIAL AGREEMENTS

Art. 40   (1) In order to ensure a greater harmony of action by governments, and especially in order to reduce the possibility of action that could adversely affect the preservation and development in Canada of the French language and the culture based on it, the Government of Canada and the Governments of the Provinces or of any one or more of the Provinces may, within the limits of the powers otherwise accorded to each of them respectively by law, enter into agreements with one another concerning the manner of exercise of such powers, particularly in the fields of immigration, communications and social policy.

(2) Nothing in this Article shall be held to limit or restrict any authority conferred either before or after the coming into force of this Proclamation upon the Government of Canada or the Government of a Province to enter into agreements within the limits of the powers otherwise accorded to it by law.

SCHEDULE
This Schedule is NOT final, subject to confirmation.

Enactments

British North America Act, 1867, 30-31 Vict., c. 3 (U.K.).

An Act to amend and continue the Act 32 and 33 Victoria chapter 3; and to establish and provide for the Government of the Province of Manitoba, 1870, 33 Vict., c. 3 (Can.).

Order of Her Majesty in Council admitting British Columbia into the Union, dated the 16th day of May 1871.

British North America Act, 1871, 34-35 Vict., c. 28 (U.K.), and all acts enacted under section 3 thereof.

Order of Her Majesty in Council admitting Prince Edward Island into the Union, dated the 26th day of June, 1873.

Parliament of Canada Act, 1875, 38-39 Vict., c. 38 (U.K.).

Order of Her Majesty in Council admitting all British possessions and Territories in North America and islands adjacent thereto into the Union, dated the 31st day of July, 1880.

British North America Act, 1886, 49-50 Vict., c. 35 (U.K.)

Canada (Ontario Boundary) Act, 1889, 52-53 Vict., c. 28 (U.K.).

Canadian Speaker (Appointment of Deputy) Act, 1895, Session 2, 59 Vict., c. 3 (U.K.).

Alberta Act, 1905, 4-5 Edw. VII, c. 42 (Can.).

Saskatchewan Act, 1905, 4-5 Edw. VII, c. 42 (Can.).

British North America Act, 1907, 7 Edw. VII, c. 11 (U.K.).

British North America Act, 1915, 5-6 Edw. V, c. 45 (U.K.).

British North America Act, 1930, 20-21 Geo. V, c. 26 (U.K.).

Statute of Westminster, 1931, 22 Geo. V, c. 4 (U.K.) in so far as it applies to Canada.

British North America Act, 1940, 3-4 Geo. VI, c. 36 (U.K.).

British North America Act, 1943, 7 Geo. VI, c. 30 (U.K.).

British North America Act, 1946, 10 Geo. VI, c. 63 (U.K.)

British North America Act, 1949, 12 and 13 Geo. VI, c. 22 (U.K.).

British North America (No. 2) Act, 1949, 13 Geo. VI, c. 81 (U.K.).

British North America Act, R.S.C., 1952, c. 304 (Can.).

British North America Act, 1960, 9 Eliz. II, c. 2 (U.K.).

British North America Act, 1964, 12 and 13, Eliz. II, c. 73 (U.K.).

British North America Act, 1965, 14 Eliz. II, c. 4, Part I, (Can.).

APPENDIX 6

REPORT TO CABINET ON CONSTITUTIONAL DISCUSSIONS, SUMMER 1980, AND THE OUTLOOK FOR THE FIRST MINISTERS' CONFERENCE AND BEYOND

(Excerpt)

(Kirby Memorandum)

August 30, 1980

Patriation, including Amending Formula

11.   Federal and Provincial Positions

(a)   Patriation

At the August 26th to 29th meetings, provinces challenged the federal government on the constitutionality of patriating the Constitution with an amending formula without provincial consent. The government was firm in asserting that it was completely confident that it would be legal for the two Houses of the Canadian Parliament to adopt a Joint Address to the Queen and for the U.K. Parliament to act upon it whether or not there had been prior provincial consent. Saskatchewan agreed that such action would be legal, but Ontario announced that it had a legal opinion to the contrary. A few provinces have indicated that they would challenge the constitutionality of such action.

(b)   The Amending Formula

All of the provinces agreed in principle that they would be willing to adopt the Alberta proposal for an amending formula, subject to examination of a legal draft. The Alberta proposal provides for general amendments to be made with the assent of Parliament and 2/3 of the provinces with at least 50% of the population. However, if the amendment so approved by seven provinces is one affecting —

(i)   the powers of the legislature of a province to make laws,

(ii)   the rights and privileges granted or secured by the Constitution to the legislature or government of a province,

(iii) the assets or property of a province, or

(iv)   the natural resources of a province,

it would not apply to any other province that had expressly dissented from it. (This procedure has been termed "opting-out".) However, the general CCMC view was that opting-out would not be available on matters of universal applicability such as those affecting the Supreme Court, the Upper House, a Charter of Rights or the use of English and French.

The advantages, from the federal viewpoint, of agreeing to the Alberta proposal would be:

- there is a possibility of full agreement on a formula which could be included in the patriation action;

- it would be an important "victory" for Alberta and for the West in general since it would not provide a general veto for Ontario and Quebec;

- no amendment could be made without the consent of Parliament, so there would be a federal check on any checkerboard effect that might be brought about by "opting-out": that is, Parliament or the government could decline to proceed with an amendment where the provinces did not all agree.

The disadvantages of the Alberta proposal would be:

- if Parliament were to be opposed <u>at all times</u> to "opting-out" by any one province, the formula could in practice require unanimous consent for amendments;

- there would be no special protection for Quebec on matters of special concern to it (proportion of civil law judges on the Supreme Court, the use of English and French at the federal level);

- the possibility of "opting-out" would remove the pressure on provinces to reach agreement on matters of constitutional change after patriation — each could argue that it was not holding up agreement on changes which could occur if only seven other provinces agreed;

- if an amendment were adopted involving new federal expenditures, an "opting-out" province could press for financial compensation.

Ministers agreed to submit the report on the Alberta formula to the FMC [First Ministers' Conference].

(c)   <u>Delegation of Legislative Authority</u>

All governments have agreed in principle to a draft proposal respecting the delegation of legislative authority in relation to any matter or class of subjects from Ottawa to a province or vice versa.

(2)   <u>Significant Issues</u>

(a)   <u>Patriation</u>

It appears likely that one or more provinces would challenge the constitutionality of the federal government proceeding to patriate the Constitution with an amending formula without provincial consent.

(b)   <u>The Amending Formula</u>

Respecting the Alberta formula, the CCMC [Continuing Committee of Ministers on the Constitution] will draw two matters to the attention of First Ministers:

- how to deal with amendments of universal applicability which cannot be subject to "opting-out";

■   whether constitutional provision should be made for the financial implications of opting-out of amendments.

(c)   Delegation of Legislative Authority

Respecting the draft upon which governments are agreed in principle, the CCMC will draw to the attention of First Ministers the concern of British Columbia and Newfoundland that the draft does not oblige Parliament to delegate to any other province what it has agreed to delegate to one of them.

(3)   FMC Position

(a)   Patriation

The federal position has been clearly enunciated: Parliament may adopt a Joint Address to the Queen with or without the consent of the provinces. This should be maintained and articulated again.

(b)   The Amending Formula

(i)   If the provincial consensus on the Alberta amending formula holds, the federal government could consider joining the majority position. In those circumstances, however, the government would presumably wish to propose a limited change in the formula for matters of universal applicability with no opting-out (Parliament and 2/3 of the legislatures representing at least 50% of the population). Amendments to matters such as the Supreme Court and the use of English and French are demonstrably of particular concern to Quebec.

The government might propose, for this limited range of matters, that the Victoria formula, the "Toronto consensus" or 2/3 of the provinces including Quebec and representing 50% of the population of Canada be the amending procedure.

For other matters of universal applicability the government would resist any attempt to make the formula more rigid (i.e., the government would not support P.E.I.'s desire to make amendments to the Senate subject to unanimity or the consent of each province whose representation in the Senate might be affected).

The government would also wish to resist any attempt to include provisions respecting the financial implications in the event that a province "opts out".

(ii)   If the current provincial consensus begins to dissolve at the FMC, and this seems more likely than not, the federal government could ask the FMC to re-examine the Victoria formula which had been acceptable to all governments in 1971, the Toronto consensus formula or a formula that would treat all provinces the same way, with no "opting-out" but that would provide special protection for Quebec with respect at least to the Supreme Court and the use of English and French (e.g., Parliament and 2/3 of the provinces representing 50% of the population would have to approve all matters except those respecting the Supreme Court and languages where the consent of Parliament and 2/3 of the provinces including Quebec or the consent of Parliament, Quebec and 2/3 of the remaining provinces would be required).

Whether a consensus forms around the Alberta proposal or another, the federal government may wish to raise the possibility of citizens being able to initiate referenda in the event of negative action or lack of action by Parliament or legislatures on an amendment proposal. This would support the view that sovereignty ultimately resides in the people.

For example, if seven provinces approved an amendment and Parliament did not, 3% of the federal electorate could initiate a national referendum; if a majority of electors voting approved, the result would be binding on Canada.

On the other hand, if Parliament approved an amendment and no province or an insufficient number of provinces approved it, 3% of the provincial electorate in each province that had not acted affirmatively could initiate a provincial referendum. If referenda were carried in a sufficient number of provinces to bring the total of assenting provinces to seven, the amendment would be adopted.

(c)   Delegation of Legislative Authority

The governments should continue to support the current agreed draft legislative text.

APPENDIX 7

THE CHÂTEAU CONSENSUS

FEDERAL-PROVINCIAL CONFERENCE
OF
FIRST MINISTERS ON THE CONSTITUTION

Proposal for a common stand
of the Provinces

QUÉBEC

Ottawa
September 8–12, 1980

The attached text has been prepared by Québec for the purpose of specifying the common stand of the provinces on the series of subjects discussed by the Conference.

It was distributed to the provincial delegations and discussed by the ministers on Thursday, September 11, and served as a basis for the discussion by the First Ministers of the Provinces on Friday morning, September 12.

The appendices have been added to assist in understanding the text.

Québec Delegation
Ottawa, September 13, 1980.

DISCUSSION DRAFT

The Provinces of Canada unanimously agree in principle to the following changes to be made to the Constitution of Canada. It is understood that these changes are to be considered as a global package and that this agreement is a common effort to come to a significant first step towards a thorough renewal of the Canadian federation.

1.   <u>Natural resources</u>

    1979 Best effort draft (APPENDIX A)

2.   <u>Communications</u>

    Provincial consensus draft, August 26, 1980 (APPENDIX B)

3.   <u>Upper Chamber</u>

    Best effort draft for a Council of the Provinces, as an interim solution (Weight of vote and implementation to be set after consensus reached on horizontal federal powers) (APPENDIX C)

4.   <u>Supreme court of Canada</u>

    Entrenchment
    6-5 at least on constitutional matters
    Alternate chief-justice
    Appointment procedure, consultation and consent (no dead-lock mechanism) (APPENDIX D)

4a.   <u>Judicature</u>

    Repeal of S.96

    Constitutional guarantees (APPENDIX E)

5.   <u>Family law</u>

    Sub-committee draft (APPENDIX F)

6.   <u>Fisheries</u>

    Provincial draft, July 21, 1980 (APPENDIX G)

7.   <u>Off-shore resources</u>

    Principle of equal treatment for on-shore and off-shore resources

8.   <u>Equalization</u>

    Manitoba - Saskatchewan draft less paragraph 3 (APPENDIX H)

9.   <u>Charter of rights</u>

    Fundamental freedoms   - all existing laws deemed valid

    Democratic rights

    Judicial rights   - non-obstante clause

    Discrimination rights

Official languages of Canada
Use of official languages in federal institutions & services
S.133 applicable to Ont., Qué, N.B., Man.

Multilateral reciprocity agreement to be concluded without delay (Bill 101: Canada clause).

10. Patriation

Alberta Amending Formula (APPENDIX I) for matter subject to opting-out, with provision for financial arrangements between governments.
Victoria formula for other matters (APPENDIX J)
Implementation of patriation delayed until unanimous approval (APPENDIX 1)

11. Powers over the economy

No new S.121 (or Saskatchewan draft) (APPENDIX K)
Part of new S.91(2)

12. Preamble

Quebec proposal (APPENDIX L)

If a satisfactory interprovincial consensus is reached in this way, it must be accompanied when tabled by an announcement of the following measures:

(1) As soon as the federal government has given its assent to this consensus, the matters will be returned to the ministers' committee for final drafting of the texts in their legal form.

(2) Another list of subjects must be established to be covered by constitutional discussions at the ministerial level in the following months:

- the horizontal powers of the federal government (spending power, declaratory power, power to act for "peace, order and good government", etc.);

- culture;

- social affairs;

- urban and regional affairs;

- regional development;

- transportation policy;

- international affairs;

- the administration of justice.

(3) Another conference of First Ministers must be called for December to approve the texts drafted on the twelve subjects (initial list) and to discuss the results of the work done on the new subjects (second list).

(4) If the results of this work are satisfactory, then the Canadian Parliament could adopt its address to the Queen at the beginning of 1981.

(5) Another Conference of First Ministers to be held in February 1981 to approve the texts drafted on the second list.

(6) From February 1981: adoption of the resolutions of the ten Legislatures and Parliament to bring patriation into effect and to implement the second list according to the amending formula.

(7) Final Act of the British Parliament to be adopted hopefully in June 1981 implementing the amendments of the first list.

APPENDIX 1

<u>SUSPENSIVE PATRIATION</u>

A patriation formula with delayed or suspensive effect could enable the federal government to go to London only once and yet at the same time respect the principle of provincial consent.

This formula would enable the British Parliament to enact a final amendment to the B.N.A. Act with the following effects:

a)   the law would decree that the Parliament of Westminster no longer legislates with respect to the B.N.A. Act which is henceforth to be amended in accordance with the amendment formula enacted. This provision would come into force only by proclamation of the Government of Canada issued once it has been ascertained that each of the Provinces of Canada, as well as the Federal Government, has approved it;

b)   the same law would give immediate effect to the amendments agreed upon with respect to the matters discussed during the current constitutional negotiations. These amendments would come into force immediately and, obviously, would not be subject to the suspensive effect of the provision respecting patriation.

<u>DRAFT</u>

1.   The B.N.A. Acts 1867 to 1975 shall be amended as follows: (Insert the amendments to take immediate effect.)

2.   Section 7 of the Statute of Westminster is repealed.

3.   The B.N.A. Acts 1867 to 1975 shall henceforth be amended as follows: (Insert the agreed-upon amendment formula.)

4.   This Act shall come into force the day of its sanction. Nevertheless, Sections 2 and 3 shall take effect by proclamation issued by the Governor General of Canada; such proclamation shall not be issued unless it is declared that it is in accordance with the resolutions adopted by each of the ten Legislatures and by the Parliament of Canada.

BEST EFFORTS DRAFT
AMENDMENTS TO THE CONSTITUTION OF CANADA

1. (1) Amendments to the Constitution of Canada may from time to time be made by proclamation issued by the Governor General under the Great Seal of Canada when so authorized by resolutions of the Senate and House of Commons and the assent by resolution of the Legislative Assembly in two-thirds of the provinces representing at least fifty percent of the population of Canada according to the latest general census.

   (2) Any amendment made under sub-section (1) affecting:

   (a) the powers of the legislature of a province to make laws,

   (b) the rights or privileges granted or secured by the Constitution of Canada to the legislature or the government of a province,

   (c) the assets or property of a province, or

   (d) the natural resources of a province,

   shall have no effect in any province whose Legislative Assembly has expressed its dissent thereto by resolution prior to the issue of the proclamation, until such time as that Assembly may withdraw its dissent and approve such amendment by resolution.

2. A proclamation shall not be issued under Section 1 before the expiry of one year from the adoption of the resolution initiating the amendment procedure thereunder, unless the legislative assembly in each province has previously adopted a resolution of assent or dissent.

3. Amendments to the Constitution of Canada in relation to any provision that applies to one or more, but not all, of the Provinces including any such amendment made to provincial boundaries may from time to time be made by proclamation issued by the Governor General under the Great Seal of Canada when so authorized by resolutions of the Senate and House of Commons and the assent by resolution of the Legislative Assembly of each Province to which an amendment applies.

4. An amendment may be made by proclamation under section 1, 3 or 9 without a resolution of the Senate authorizing the issue of the proclamation if within ninety days of the passage of a resolution by the House of Commons authorizing its issue the Senate has not passed such a resolution and at any time after the expiration of the ninety days the House of Commons again passes the resolution, but any period when Parliament is prorogued or dissolved shall not be counted in computing the ninety days.

5. The following rules apply to the procedures for amendment described in sections 1, 3 and 9

   1) either of these procedures may be initiated by the Senate or the House of Commons or the Legislative Assembly of a Province,

   2) a resolution of authorization or assent made for the purposes of this Part may be revoked at any time before the issue of a proclamation authorized or assented to by it,

   3) a resolution of dissent made for the purposes of this Part may be revoked at any time before or after the issue of a proclamation.

6. The Parliament of Canada may exclusively make laws from time to time amending the Constitution of Canada, in relation to the executive Government of Canada and the Senate and House of Commons.

7. In each Province the Legislature may exclusively make laws in relation to the amendment from time to time of the Constitution of the Province.

8. Notwithstanding Sections 6 and 7, the following matters may be amended only in accordance with the procedure in section 1(1):

    1) the office of the Queen, of the Governor General and of the Lieutenant-Governor,

    2) the requirements of the Constitution of Canada respecting yearly sessions of the Parliament of Canada and the Legislatures,

    3) the maximum period fixed by the Constitution of Canada for the duration of the House of Commons and the Legislative Assemblies,

    4) the powers of the Senate,

    5) the number of members by which a Province is entitled to be represented in the Senate and the residence qualifications of Senators.

    6) the right of a Province to a number of members in the House of Commons not less than the number of Senators representing the Province,

    7) the principles of proportionate representation of the Provinces in the House of Commons prescribed by the Constitution of Canada, and

    8) the use of the English or French language.

9. 1) No amendment to section 1 of this Part, this section, or to any provision in the Constitution with respect to the procedure for altering provincial boundaries shall come into force unless it is authorized in by resolutions of the Senate and House of Commons and assented to by resolution of the Legislative Assemblies of all the provinces.

    2) The procedure prescribed in section o of this Part may not be used to make an amendment when there is another provision for making such amendment in the Constitution of Canada but, subject to the limitations contained in subsection (1) of this section that procedure may nonetheless be used to amend any provision for amending the Constitution.

10. The enactments set out in the Schedule shall continue as law in Canada and as such shall, together with this Act, collectively be known as the Constitution of Canada, and amendments thereto shall henceforth be made only according to the authority contained therein.

APPENDIX J

CANADIAN CONSTITUTIONAL CHARTER 1971
PART IX
AMENDMENTS TO THE CONSTITUTION

Art. 49. Amendments to the Constitution of Canada may from time to time be made by proclamation issued by the Governor General under the Great Seal of Canada when so authorized by resolutions of the Senate and House of Commons and of the Legislative Assemblies of at least a majority of the Provinces that includes

    (1)   every Province that at any time before the issue of such proclamation had, according to any previous general census, a population of at least twenty-five per cent of the population of Canada;

    (2)   at least two of the Atlantic Provinces;

    (3)   at least two of the Western Provinces that have, according to the then latest general census, combined populations of at least fifty per cent of the population of all the Western Provinces.

Art. 50. Amendments to the Constitution of Canada in relation to any provision that applies to one or more, but not all, of the Provinces may from time to time be made by proclamation issued by the Governor General under the Great Seal of Canada when so authorized by resolutions of the Senate and House of Commons and of the Legislative Assembly of each Province to which an amendment applies.

Art. 51. An amendment may be made by proclamation under Article 49 or 50 without a resolution of the Senate authorizing the issue of the proclamation if within ninety days of the passage of a resolution by the House of Commons authorizing its issue the Senate has not passed such a resolution and at any time after the expiration of the ninety days the House of Commons again passes the resolution, but any period when Parliament is prorogued or dissolved shall not be counted in computing the ninety days.

Art. 52. The following rules apply to the procedures for amendment described in Articles 49 and 50:

    (1)   either of these procedures may be initiated by the Senate or the House of Commons or the Legislative Assembly of a Province;

    (2)   a resolution made for the purposes of this Part may be revoked at any time before the issue of a proclamation authorized by it.

Art. 53. The Parliament of Canada may exclusively make laws from time to time amending the Constitution of Canada, in relation to the executive Government of Canada and the Senate and House of Commons.

Art. 54. In each Province the Legislature may exclusively make laws in relation to the amendment from time to time of the Constitution of the Province.

Art. 55. Notwithstanding Articles 53 and 54, the following matters may be amended only in accordance with the procedure in Article 49:

    (1)   the office of the Queen, of the Governor General and of the Lieutenant-Governor;

    (2)   the requirements of the Constitution of Canada respecting yearly sessions of the Parliament of Canada and the Legislatures;

    (3)   the maximum period fixed by the Constitution of Canada for the duration of the House of Commons and the Legislative Assemblies;

(4)   the powers of the Senate;

(5)   the number of members by which a Province is entitled to be represented in the Senate, and the residence qualifications of Senators;

(6)   the right of a Province to a number of members in the House of Commons not less than the number of Senators representing the Province;

(7)   the principles of proportionate representation of the Provinces in the House of Commons prescribed by the Constitution of Canada; and

(8)   except as provided in Article 16, the requirements of this Charter respecting the use of the English or French language.

Art. 56. The procedure prescribed in Article 49 may not be used to make an amendment when there is another provision for making such amendment in the Constitution of Canada, but that procedure may nonetheless be used to amend any provision for amending the Constitution, including this Article, or in making a general consolidation and revision of the Constitution.

Art. 57. In this Part, "Atlantic Provinces" means the Provinces of Nova Scotia, New Brunswick, Prince Edward Island and Newfoundland, and "Western Provinces" means the Provinces of Manitoba, British Columbia, Saskatchewan and Alberta.

APPENDIX 8

CONSTITUTION ACT, 1980

(October 1980)

Part IV

INTERIM AMENDING PROCEDURE AND

RULES FOR ITS REPLACEMENT

Interim procedure for amending Constitution of Canada

33. Until Part V comes into force, an amendment to the Constitution of Canada may be made by proclamation issued by the Governor General under the Great Seal of Canada where so authorized by resolutions of the Senate and House of Commons and by the legislative assembly or government of each province.

Amendment of provisions relating to some but not all provinces

34. Until Part V comes into force, an amendment to the Constitution of Canada in relation to any provision that applies to one or more, but not all, provinces may be made by proclamation issued by the Governor General under the Great Seal of Canada where so authorized by resolutions of the Senate and House of Commons and by the legislative assembly or government of each province to which the amendment applies.

Rules applicable to amendment procedures

35. (1) The procedures for amendment described in sections 33 and 34 may be initiated either by the Senate or House of Commons or by the legislative assembly or government of a province.

Idem

(2) A resolution made or other authorization given for the purposes of this Part may be revoked at any time before the issue of a proclamation authorized by it.

Limitation on use of interim amending procedure

36. Sections 33 and 34 do not apply to an amendment to the Constitution of Canada where there is another provision in the Constitution for making the amendment, but the procedure prescribed by section 33 shall be used to amend the *Canadian Charter of Rights and Freedoms* and any provision for amending the Constitution, including this section, and may be used in making a general consolidation and revision of the Constitution.

Coming into force of Part V

37. Part V shall come into force

(a) with or without amendment, on such day as may be fixed by proclamation issued pursuant to the procedure prescribed by section 33, or

(b) on the day that is two years after the day this Act, except Part V, comes into force,

whichever is the earlier day but, if a referendum is required to be held under subsection 38(3), Part V shall come into force as provided in section 39.

Provincial alternative procedure

38. (1) The governments or legislative assemblies of eight or more provinces that have, according to the then latest general census, combined populations of a least eighty per cent of the population of all the provinces may make a single proposal to substitute for paragraph 41(1)(b) such alternative as they consider appropriate.

Procedure for perfecting alternative

(2) One copy of an alternative proposed under subsection (1) may be deposited with the Chief Electoral Officer of Canada by each proposing province within two years after this Act, except Part V, comes into force but, prior to the expiration of that period, any province that has deposited a copy may withdraw that copy.

Referendum

(3) Where copies of an alternative have been filed as provided by subsection (2) and, on the day that is two years after this Act, except Part V, comes into force, at least eight copies remain filed by provinces that have, according to the then latest general census, combined populations of a least eighty per cent of the population of all the provinces, the government of Canada shall cause a referendum to be held within two years after that day to determine whether

(a) paragraph 41(1)(b) or any alternative thereto proposed by the government of Canada by depositing a copy thereof with the Chief Electoral Officer at least ninety days prior to the day on which the referendum is held, or

(b) the alternative proposed by the provinces,

shall be adopted.

Coming into force of Part V where referendum held

39. Where a referendum is held under subsection 38(3), a proclamation under the Great Seal of Canada shall be issued within six months after the date of the referendum bringing Part V into force with such modifications, if any, as are necessary to incorporate the proposal approved by a majority of the persons voting at the referendum and with such other changes as are reasonably consequential on the incorporation of that proposal.

Rules for referendum Right to vote

40. (1) Subject to subsection (2), Parliament may make laws respecting the rules applicable to the holding of a referendum under subsection 38(3).

(2) Every citizen of Canada has, without unreasonable distinction or limitation, the right to vote in a referendum held under subsection 38(3).

PART V

PROCEDURE FOR AMENDING

CONSTITUTION OF CANADA

General procedure for amending Constitution of Canada

41. (1) An amendment to the Constitution of Canada may be made by proclamation issued by the Governor General under the Great Seal of Canada where so authorized by

(a)   resolutions of the Senate and House of Commons; and

(b)   resolutions of the legislative assemblies of at least a majority of the provinces that includes

(i)   every province that at any time before the issue of theproclamation had, according to any previous general census, a population of at least twenty-five per cent of the population of Canada,

(ii)   at least two of the Atlantic provinces that have, according to the then latest general census, combined populations of at least fifty per cent of the population of all the Atlantic provinces, and

(iii)   at least two of the Western provinces that have, according to the then latest general census, combined populations of at least fifty per cent of the population of all the Western provinces.

Definitions

(2)   In this section,

"Atlantic provinces"

"Atlantic provinces" means the provinces of Nova Scotia, New Brunswick, Prince Edward Island and Newfoundland;

"Western provinces"

"Western provinces" means the provinces of Manitoba, British Columbia, Saskatchewan and Alberta.

Amendment authorized by referendum

42. (1) An amendment to the Constitution of Canada may be made by proclamation issued by the Governor General under the Great Seal of Canada where so authorized by a referendum held throughout Canada under subsection (2) at which

(a)   a majority of persons voting thereat, and

(b)   a majority of persons voting thereat in each of the provinces, resolutions of the legislative assemblies of which would be sufficient, together with resolutions of the Senate and House of Commons, to authorize the issue of a proclamation under subsection 41(1),

have approved the making of the amendment.

Authorization of referendum

(2) A referendum referred to in subsection (1) shall be held where directed by proclamation issued by the Governor General under the Great Seal of Canada authorized by resolutions of the Senate and House of Commons.

Amendment of provisions relating to some but not all provinces

43. An amendment to the Constitution of Canada in relation to any provision that applies to one or more, but not all, provinces may be made by proclamation issued by the Governor General under the Great Seal of Canada where so authorized by resolutions of the Senate and House of Commons and of the legislative assembly of each province to which the amendment applies.

Amendments without Senate resolutions

44. An amendment to the Constitution of Canada may be made by proclamation under subsection 41(1) or section 43 without a resolution of the Senate authorizing the issue of the proclamation if, within ninety days after the passage by the House of Commons of a resolution authorizing its issue, the Senate has not passed such a resolution and if, at any time after the expiration of those ninety days, the House of Commons again passes the resolution, but any period when Parliament is prorogued or dissolved shall not be counted in computing those ninety days.

Rules applicable to amendment procedures

45. (1) The procedures for amendment described in subsection 41(1) and section 43 may be initiated either by the Senate or House of Commons or by the legislative assembly of a province.

Idem

(2) A resolution made for the purposes of this Part may be revoked at any time before the issue of a proclamation authorized by it.

Rules for referendum

46. (1) Subject to subsection (2), Parliament may make laws respecting the rules applicable to the holding of a referendum under section 42.

Right to vote

(2) Every citizen of Canada has, without unreasonable distinction or limitation, the right to vote in a referendum held under section 42.

Limitation on use of general amending formula

47. The procedures prescribed by section 41, 42 or 43 do not apply to an amendment to the Constitution of Canada where there is another provision in the Constitution for making the amendment, but the procedures prescribed by section 41 or 42 shall nevertheless be used to amend any provision for amending the Constitution, including this section, and section 41 may be used in making a general consolidation or revision of the Constitution.

Amendments by Parliament

48. Subject to section 50, Parliament may exclusively make laws amending the Constitution of Canada in relation to the executive government of Canada or the Senate or House of Commons.

Amendments by provincial legislatures

49. Subject to section 50, the legislature of each province may exclusively make laws amending the constitution of the province.

Matters requiring amendment under general formula

50. An amendment to the Constitution of Canada in relation to the following matters may be made only in accordance with a procedure prescribed by section 41 or 42:

    (a)   the office of the Queen, the Governor General and the Lieutenant Governor of a province;

    (b)   the *Canadian Charter of Rights and Freedoms;*

(c) the commitments relating to equalization and regional disparities set out in section 31;

(d) the powers of the Senate;

(e) the number of members by which a province is entitled to be represented in the Senate and the residence qualifications of Senators;

(f) the right of a province to a number of members in the House of Commons not less than the number of Senators representing the province; and

(g) the principles of proportionate representation of the provinces in the House of Commons prescribed by the Constitution of Canada.

Consequential amendments

51. Class 1 of section 91 and class 1 of section 92 of the *Constitution Act, 1867* (formerly named the *British North America Act, 1867),* the *British North America (No. 2) Act, 1949,* referred to in item 21 of Schedule I to this Act and Parts III and IV of this Act are repealed.

our Majesty's loyal subjects, the Hou
s of Canada in Parliament assembl
approach Your Majesty, requesting
graciously be pleased to cause to be
Parliament of the United Kingd
containing the recitals and
ter set forth :

An Act to give effect to a request by t
and House of Commons of C

Whereas Canada has requested a
the enactment of an Act of the Parl
United Kingdom to give effect to
ter set forth and the Senate an
nada in Parliament
Majest

APPENDIX 9

PROPOSED CONSTITUTIONAL ACCORD
OF
APRIL 16, 1981

Amending Formula
for the
Constitution of Canada

Text and Explanatory Notes

PART A

AMENDING FORMULA FOR THE CONSTITUTION OF CANADA

EXPLANATORY NOTES

General Comment

The amending formula which is part of the Canadian patriation plan agreed to by eight governments in Ottawa on April 16, 1981, is the result of intensive discussions among the governments of Alberta, British Columbia, Manitoba, Newfoundland, Nova Scotia, Prince Edward Island, Quebec and Saskatchewan.

In developing the formula several important principles were recognized:

1.	All amendments to the Constitution of Canada, except those related to the internal constitution of the provinces, require the agreement of the Parliament of Canada.

2.	Any formula must recognize the constitutional equality of provinces as equal partners in Confederation.

3.	Any amending formula must protect the diversity of Canada.

4.	Any constitutional amendment taking away an existing provincial area of jurisdiction or proprietary right should not be imposed on any province not desiring it.

5.	Any amending formula must strike a balance between stability and flexibility.

6.	Some amendments are of such fundamental importance to the country that all eleven governments must agree.

During discussions, it was recognized that more than one method of amending the Constitution would be necessary. Accordingly, this formula contains different methods depending on the nature of the amendment.

The eleven sections described as "Part A - Amending Formula for the Constitution of Canada" are designed to contain a full and complete procedure for the future amendment of the Constitution of Canada in all respects. The provisions contained in Part A would replace both the limited amending formulas now contained in sections 91(1) and 92(1) of the B.N.A. Act as well as the United Kingdom Parliament's residual responsibility for amending certain aspects of the Canadian Constitution.

This amending formula would apply not only to the B.N.A. Act, 1867, and amendments made to it since that date, but also to the other parts of the Constitution of Canada, including the constitutional statutes and Orders-in-Council which relate to the entry into Canada of particular provinces, for example, The Manitoba Act, 1870, the Terms of Union admitting British Columbia in 1871, and Prince Edward Island in 1873, The Alberta Act, 1905, The Saskatchewan Act, 1905, and the Terms of Union with Newfoundland, 1949.

This amending formula is clearly preferable to the one proposed by the federal government for a number of reasons: 1) it recognizes the constitutional equality of each of Canada's provinces; 2) it gives the Senate only a suspensive rather than an absolute veto over constitutional amendment; 3) it omits the referendum provision opposed by many as being inappropriate to the Canadian federal system.

PART A

AMENDING FORMULA FOR THE CONSTITUTION OF CANADA

EXPLANATORY NOTES

1. (1) Amendments to the Constitution of Canada may be made by proclamation issued by the Governor General under the Great Seal of Canada when so authorized by:

   (a) resolutions of the Senate and House of Commons; and

   (b) resolutions of the Legislative Assemblies of at least two-thirds of the provinces that have in the aggregate, according to the latest decennial census, at least fifty per cent of the population of all of the provinces

   (2) Any amendment made under subsection (1) derogating from the legislative powers, the proprietary rights or any other rights or privileges of the Legislature or government of a province shall require a resolution supported by a vote of a majority of the Members of each of the Senate, of the House of Commons, and of the requisite number of Legislative Assemblies.

   (3) Any amendment made under subsection (1) derogating from the legislative powers, the proprietary rights, or any other rights or privileges of the Legislature or government of a Province shall not have effect in any province whose Legislative Assembly has expressed its dissent thereto by resolution supported by a majority of the Members prior to the issue

1. (1) This provision is known as the general amending formula. It would apply to all amendments to the Constitution of Canada unless another method of amendment is specifically provided for elsewhere in Part A.

   This provision requires that an amendment be supported by the Parliament of Canada and by at least seven provincial Legislatures representing at least 50% of the total population of all of the provinces.

   (2) Any amendment which diminishes provincial rights or powers must be supported by a majority of the actual membership of each of the Senate, the House of Commons, and the requisite number of Legislatures.

   (3) If an amendment, proposed under the general amending formula, would diminish the existing legislative powers, proprietary rights or any other rights or privileges of provincial Legislatures or governments, a province has two decisions to make:

   (a) whether or not to approve the amendment, and

of the proclamation, provided, however, that Legislative Assembly, by resolution supported by a majority of the Members, may subsequently withdraw its dissent and approve the amendment.

(b) if the amendment is approved under subsection (1), whether to retain its existing powers, rights or privileges by dissenting from its application within that province.

In this case, the Legislature of the province would have to express its dissent by adopting a Resolution supported by a majority of the total number of members of the Assembly. Such a procedure is commonly designated an "opting-out" provision.

A province wishing to use this "opting-out" procedure must do so before the proclamation making the amendment is issued. Also the opting-out provision applies only where the proposed amendment derogates from, or diminishes, the legislative powers, proprietary rights or any other rights and privileges of the Legislature or government of a province. Proprietary rights includes natural resources and assets. Broadly speaking, those powers, rights and privileges are assigned to the provinces by sections 92, 93 and 109 of the British North America Act.

In summary, no single province should be able to block an amendment desired by at least seven other provinces and the federal government. Conversely, that particular province would not be required to have this kind of amendment apply to it if it found the amendment to be unacceptable.

2. (1) No proclamation shall issue under section 1 before the expiry of one year from the date of the passage of the resolution initiating the amendment procedure, unless the Legislative Assembly of every province has previously adopted a resolution of assent or dissent.

2. (1) This provision ensures that a proposed amendment cannot come into force before one year has expired from the time of initiation unless all provinces have expressed their views by resolution prior to that time, and the necessary consents have been obtained. Thus, no amendment can be made until all Legislatures have had an opportunity to debate the proposed amendment.

(2) No proclamation shall issue under section 1 after the expiry of three years from the date of the passage of the resolution initiating the amendment procedure.

(2) This provision ensures that a proposed amendment must gain the requisite level of support within a reasonable length of time from initiation or it will lapse.

(3) Subject to this section, the Government of Canada shall advise the Governor General to issue a proclamation forthwith upon the passage of the requisite resolutions under this Part.

(3) This provision ensures that a proposed amendment, enjoying the requisite level of support, is proclaimed.

3. In the event that a province dissents from an amendment conferring legislative jurisdiction on Parliament, the Government of Canada shall provide reasonable compensation to the government of that province, taking into account the per capita costs to exercise that jurisdiction in the provinces which have approved the amendment.

3. If a province dissents under section 1(2) from a constitutional amendment that confers legislative jurisdiction on Parliament, then this provision requires the Government of Canada to provide reasonable compensation to the government of that province. Such compensation would take into account the per capita costs incurred by the federal government in those provinces where the federal jurisdiction is exercised.

This provision is designed to prevent a taxpayer, resident in a province to which the amendment does not apply, from paying twice: first, in his or her federal tax bill and second, to the province which continues to exercise the jurisdiction.

4. Amendments to the Constitution of Canada in relation to any provision that applies to one or more, but not all, of the provinces, including any alter-

4. The purpose of this provision is to allow the Parliament of Canada and the Legislature of a province or provinces to amend the Constitution in relation to

ation to boundaries between provinces or the use of the English or the French language within that province may be made only by proclamation issued by the Governor General under the Great Seal of Canada when so authorized by resolutions of the Senate and House of Commons and the Legislative Assembly of every province to which the amendment applies.

any provision that applies to one or more, but not all, of the provinces. Such an amendment would only require the approval of the provincial Legislatures affected and Parliament. Instances of matters falling within that category are, for example, the provisions of the Manitoba Act, the Terms of Union of Prince Edward Island and British Columbia, The Saskatchewan Act, The Alberta Act, and the Terms of Union with Newfoundland. This provision ensures that any such amendment has the consent of the affected province or provinces.

Alterations to boundaries between provinces would also be dealt with under this section and could be made by the approval of the Legislatures of those provinces affected and the Parliament of Canada.

Any amendments to the Constitution in relation to the use of the English or French language within a province could be made by resolution of the Legislature of the province affected and the federal Parliament. This provision would apply to those portions of section 133 of the B.N.A. Act which relate to the province of Quebec and those language provisions of the Manitoba Act which apply to Manitoba. This provision could make section 133 applicable to a province where it does not apply now but which wishes it to be applicable therein.

5. An amendment may be made without a resolution of the Senate authorizing the issue of the proclamation if, within one hundred and eighty days after the passage by the House of Commons of a resolution authorizing its issue, the Senate has not passed such a resolution and if, after the expiration of those one hundred and eighty days, the House of Commons again passed the resolution, but any period

5. Under this provision, the Senate of Canada will have only a suspensive veto over constitutional amendments. If the Senate refuses or fails to authorize the issue of a proclamation within one hundred and eighty days of the House of Commons passing a resolution authorizing its issue, the amendment may still proceed provided the matter is again submitted to and passed by the House of Commons.

when Parliament is dissolved shall not be counted in computing the one hundred and eighty days.

6. (1) The procedures for amendment may be initiated by the Senate, by the House of Commons, or by the Legislative Assembly of a province.

   (2) A resolution authorizing an amendment may be revoked at any time before the issue of a proclamation.

   (3) A resolution of dissent may be revoked at any time before or after the issue of a proclamation.

7. Subject to sections 9 and 10, Parliament may exclusively make laws amending the Constitution of Canada in relation to the executive government of Canada or the Senate and House of Commons.

8. Subject to section 9, the Legislature of each province may exclusively make laws amending the constitution of the province.

6. (1) Self-explanatory.

   (2) This section permits either of the Houses of Parliament or any Legislature to revoke an affirmative resolution before the proclamation implementing the proposed amendment is issued. However, once the proclamation is issued, an affirmative resolution may not be revoked.

   (3) This provision allows a resolution disapproving a proposed amendment to be revoked at any time either before or after the issue of a proclamation. This is designed to allow provinces which have dissented from an amendment to revoke their dissent subsequently and be subject to the amendment.

7. This provision allows Parliament, acting alone, to amend those parts of the Constitution of Canada that relate solely to the operation of the executive government of Canada at the federal level or to the Senate or House of Commons. Some aspects of certain institutions important for maintaining the federal-provincial balance, such as the Senate and the Supreme Court, are excluded from this provision and are covered in sections 9 and 10. This provision is intended to replace section 91(1) of the B.N.A. Act.

8. This provision allows the Legislature of a province, acting alone, to amend the provincial Constitution and is intended to

replace section 92(1) of the B.N.A. Act. Exceptions to this provision include the office of the Lieutenant-Governor.

9. Amendments to the Constitution of Canada in relation to the following matters may be made only by proclamation issued by the Governor General under the Great Seal of Canada when authorized by resolutions of the Senate and House of Commons and of the Legislative Assemblies of all of the provinces:

9. This section recognizes that some matters are of such fundamental importance that amendments in relation to them should require the consent of all the provincial Legislatures and Parliament.

(a) the office of the Queen, of the Governor General or of the Lieutenant Governor;

(a) Self-explanatory

(b) the right of a province to a number of members in the House of Commons not less than the number of Senators representing the province at the time this provision comes into force;

(b) This clause relates to the protection provided to provinces under section 51A of the B.N.A. Act.

(c) the use of the English or French language except with respect to section 4;

(c) This clause would require any changes to the Constitution related to the use of the English or French language either within the institutions of the federal government or nationwide to require the unanimous approval of Parliament and all the Legislatures.

(d) the composition of the Supreme Court of Canada;

(d) This clause would ensure that the Supreme Court of Canada is comprised of judges a proportion of whom are drawn from the Bar or Bench of Quebec and are, therefore, trained in the civil law. Other aspects of the Supreme Court of Canada are dealt with in section 10.

(e) an amendment to any of the provisions of this Part.

(e) This clause provides that any amendment to the amending formula itself requires unanimous approval of Parliament and all of the provincial Legislatures.

10. Amendments to the Constitution of Canada in relation to the following matters shall be made in accordance with the provisions of section 1(1) of this Part and sections 1(2) and 1(3) shall not apply:

10. Amendments to the Constitution in respect of the matters listed in section 10 may be achieved if approved by 1) the House of Commons and Senate of Canada and 2) at least seven provinces having, in the aggregate, at least 50% of the total population of all the provinces according to the latest decennial census. The types of amendments listed in this section are not subject to provincial non-application and, therefore, apply nationwide.

(a) the principle of proportionate representation of the provinces in the House of Commons;

(a) Self-explanatory.

(b) the powers of the Senate and the method of selection of members thereto;

(b) Self-explanatory.

(c) the number of members by which a province is entitled to be represented in the Senate and the residence qualifications of Senators;

(c) Self-explanatory.

(d) the Supreme Court of Canada, except with respect to clause (d) of section 9.

(d) This clause refers to all amendments relating to the Supreme Court of Canada except the composition of the Court which is dealt with in section 9, clause (d). The Supreme Court of Canada is established by a law of Parliament under section 101 of the B.N.A. Act and not by the Constitution itself. This clause anticipates constitutional amendments relating to the Court. Such amendments would apply nationwide.

(e) the extension of existing provinces into the Territories;

(f) notwithstanding any other law or practice, the establishment of new provinces;

(e) and (f) The alteration of boundaries between provinces is dealt with in section 4. The extension of existing provinces or the establishment of new provinces are dealt with in clauses (e) and (f).

(g) an amendment to any of the provisions of Part B.

g) This clause deals with amendments to the delegation of legislative authority provisions contained in Part B.

11. A constitutional conference composed of the Prime Minister of Canada and the First Ministers of the provinces shall be convened by the Prime Minister of Canada within fifteen years of the enactment of this Part to review the provisions for the amendment to the Constitution of Canada.

11. This section provides that the First Ministers of Canada shall meet within fifteen years to review the amending formula itself. This is a minimum requirement and does not preclude other constitutional conferences.

PART B
DELEGATION OF LEGISLATIVE AUTHORITY
EXPLANATORY NOTES

General Comments

Part B allows for the delegation of legislative authority from one order of government to the other, something which is not now provided for in the B.N.A. Act. Delegation of legislative authority would add considerable flexibility to Canada's constitutional arrangements and could reduce the duplication of administrative services.

This Part would permit the Parliament of Canada to consent to the making of a provincial law in an area of federal responsibility. Conversely, it would permit one or more provinces to consent to the making of a federal law in an area of provincial responsibility. There is also provision for the consents to relate to all laws in relation to a particular matter of jurisdiction, as distinct from a particular statute. In the event of delegation, financial compensation is payable to the governments exercising delegated power.

Delegation could conceivably be used to test the effect of transferring responsibility for a certain jurisdictional area before proceeding in a more general way through the amending formula itself. Finally, a delegation of power may be revoked upon two years' notice.

PART B

| DELEGATION OF LEGISLATIVE AUTHORITY | EXPLANATORY NOTES |

1. Notwithstanding anything in the Constitution of Canada, Parliament may make laws in relation to a matter coming within the legislative jurisdiction of a province, if prior to the enactment, the Legislature of at least one province has consented to the operation of such a statute in that province.

1. This section permits one or more provinces to consent to Parliament enacting a law in an area of provincial jurisdiction.

2. A statute passed pursuant to section 1 shall not have effect in any province unless the Legislature of that province has consented to its operation.

2. Statutes passed by the federal Parliament pursuant to section 1 only have effect in those provinces that have consented to their operation.

3. The Legislature of a province may make laws in the province in relation to a matter coming within the legislative jurisdiction of Parliament, if, prior to the enactment, Parliament has consented to the enactment of such a statute by the Legislature of that province.

3. This is the converse of section 1. It permits Parliament to consent to one or more provinces enacting a law in an area of federal jurisdiction.

4. A consent given under this Part may relate to a specific statute or to all laws in relation to a particular matter.

4. This section provides that the delegation may be in respect to either a whole matter of constitutional jurisdiction or merely a specific statute.

5. A consent given under this Part may be revoked upon giving two years' notice, and

   (a) if the consent was given under section 1, any law made by Parliament to which the consent relates shall thereupon cease to have effect in the province revoking the consent, but the revocation of the consent does not affect the operation of that law in any other province;

   (b) if the consent was given under section 3, any law made by the Legislature of a province to which the consent relates shall thereupon cease to have effect.

5. This section allows for the delegation of authority to be revoked provided two years' notice is given. After the two years, the law ceases to have force and effect within those jurisdictions that have revoked the consent. In the case of a delegation to the Parliament of Canada by several provinces, the federal law ceases to have effect only in those provinces which have revoked the consent.

6. In the event of a delegation of legislative authority from Parliament to the Legislature of a province, the Government of Canada shall provide reasonable compensation to the government of that province, taking into account the per capita costs to exercise that jurisdiction.

7. In the event of a delegation of legislative authority from the Legislature of a province to Parliament, the government of the province shall provide reasonable compensation to the Government of Canada, taking into account the per capita costs to exercise that jurisdiction.

6. and 7. These are reciprocal sections which would provide that the order of government that acquires the right to pass a law through the delegation process is entitled to be provided with reasonable compensation from the other order of government for the exercise of that jurisdiction. The definition of reasonable compensation must take into account the per capita costs of exercising that jurisdiction.

our Majesty's loyal subjects, the Hou

s of Canada in Parliament assemb

approach Your Majesty, requesting

graciously be pleased to cause to be

Parliament of the United Kingd

containing the recitals and

ter set forth :

An Act to give effect to a request by t

and House of Commons of C

Whereas Canada has requested a

the enactment of an Act of the Par

United Kingdom to give effect to

in after set forth and the Senate ar

anada in Parliament

Her Majest

CONSTITUTION ACT, 1981

(April 23, 1981)

Part V

INTERIM AMENDMENT PROCEDURE AND
RULES FOR ITS REPLACEMENT

Interim procedure for amending Constitution of Canada

37. Until Part VI comes into force, an amendment to the Constitution of Canada may be made by proclamation issued by the Governor General under the Great Seal of Canada where so authorized by resolutions of the Senate and House of Commons and by the legislative assembly or government of each province.

Amendment of provisions relating to some but not all provinces

38. Until Part VI comes into force, an amendment to the Constitution of Canada in relation to any provision that applies to one or more, but not all, provinces may be made by proclamation issued by the Governor General under the Great Seal of Canada where so authorized by resolutions of the Senate and House of Commons and by the legislative assembly or government of each province to which the amendment applies.

Amendments respecting certain language rights

39. (1) Notwithstanding section 41, an amendment to the Constitution of Canada

    (a)   adding a province as a province named in subsection 16(2), 17(2), 18(2), 19(2) or 20(2), or

    (b   otherwise providing for any or all of the rights guaranteed or obligations imposed by any of those subsections to have application in a province to the extent and under the conditions stated in the amendment,

may be made by proclamation issued by the Governor General under the Great Seal of Canada where so authorized by resolutions of the Senate and House of Commons and the legislative assembly of the province to which the amendment applies.

Initiation of amendment procedure

(2) The procedure for amendment prescribed by subsection (1) may be initiated only by the legislative assembly of the province to which the amendment applies.

Initiation of amendment procedures

40. (1) The procedures for amendment prescribed by sections 37 and 38 may be initiated either by the Senate or House of Commons or by the legislative assembly or government of a province.

Revocation of authorization

(2) A resolution made or other authorization given for the purposes of this Part may be revoked at any time before the issue of a proclamation authorized by it.

Limitation on use of interim amendment procedure

41. Sections 37 and 38 do not apply to an amendment to the Constitution of Canada where there is another provision in the Constitution for making the amendment, but the procedure prescribed by section 37 shall be used to amend the *Canadian Charter of Rights and Freedoms* and any provision for amending the Constitution, including this section.

Coming into force of Part VI

42. Part VI shall come into force

    (a)   with or without amendment, on such day as may be fixed by proclamation issued pursuant to the procedure prescribed by section 37, or

    (b)   on the day that is two years after the day this Act, except Part VI, comes into force,

whichever is the earlier day but, if a referendum is required to be held under subsection 43(3), Part VI shall come into force as provided in section 44.

Provincial alternative procedure

43. (1) The legislative assemblies of seven or more provinces that have, according to the then latest general census, combined populations of at least eighty per cent of the population of all the provinces may make a single proposal to substitute for paragraph 46(1)(b) such alternative as they consider appropriate.

Procedure for perfecting alternative

(2) One copy of an alternative proposed under subsection (1) may be deposited with the chief Electoral Officer of Canada by each proposing province within two years after this Act, except Part VI, comes into force but, prior to the expiration of that period, any province that has deposited a copy may withdraw that copy.

Referendum

(3) Where copies of an alternative have been deposited as provided by subsection (2) and, on the day that is two years after this Act, except Part VI, comes into force, at least seven copies remain deposited by provinces that have, according to the then latest general census, combined populations of at least eighty per cent of the population of all the provinces, the government of Canada shall cause a referendum to be held within two years after that day to determine whether

    (a)   paragraph 46(1)(b) or any alternative thereto approved by resolutions of the Senate and House of Commons and deposited with the Chief Electoral Officer at least ninety days prior to the day on which the referendum is held, or

    (b)   the alternative proposed by the provinces,

shall be adopted.

Coming into force of Part VI where referendum held

44. Where a referendum is held under subsection 43(3), a proclamation under the Great Seal of Canada shall be issued within six months after the date of the referendum bringing Part VI into force with such modifications, if any, as are necessary to incorporate the proposal approved by a majority of the persons voting at the referendum and with such other changes as are reasonably consequential on the incorporation of that proposal.

Right to vote

45. (1) Every citizen of Canada has, subject only to such reasonable limits prescribed by law as can be demonstrably justified in a free and democratic society, the right to vote in a referendum held under subsection 43(3).

Establishment of Referendum Rules Commission

(2) If a referendum is required to be held under subsection 43(3), a Referendum Rules Commission shall forthwith be established by commission issued under the Great Seal of Canada consisting of

(a) the Chief Electoral Officer of Canada, who shall be chairman of the Commission;

(b) a person appointed by the Governor General in Council; and

(c) a person appointed by the Governor General in Council

(i) on the recommendation of the governments of a majority of the provinces, or

(ii) if the governments of a majority of the provinces do not recommend a candidate within thirty days after the Chief Electoral Officer of Canada requests such a recommendation, on the recommendation of the Chief Justice of Canada from among persons recommended by the governments of the provinces within thirty days after the expiration of the first mentioned thirty day period or, if none are so recommended, from among such persons as the Chief Justice considers qualified.

Duty of Commission

(3) A Referendum Rules Commission shall cause rules for the holding of a referendum under subsection 43(3) approved by a majority of the Commission to be laid before Parliament within sixty days after the Commission is established or, if Parliament is not then sitting, on any of the first ten days next thereafter that Parliament is sitting.

Rules for referendum

(4) Subject to subsection (1) and taking into consideration any rules approved by a Referendum Rules Commission in accordance with subsection (3), Parliament may enact laws respecting the rules applicable to the holding of a referendum under subsection 43(3).

Proclamation

(5) If Parliament does not enact laws under subsection (4) respecting the rules applicable to the holding of a referendum within sixty days after receipt of a recommendation from a Referendum Rules Commission, the rules recommended by the Commission shall forthwith be brought into force by proclamation issued by the Governor General under the Great Seal of Canada.

Computation of period

(6) Any period when Parliament is prorogued or dissolved shall not be counted in computing the sixty day period referred to in subsection (5).

Rules to have force of law

(7) Subject to subsection (1), rules made under this section have the force of law and prevail over other laws made under the Constitution of Canada to the extent of any inconsistency.

PART VI
PROCEDURE FOR AMENDING
CONSTITUTION OF CANADA

General procedure for amending Constitution of Canada

46. (1) An amendment to the Constitution of Canada may be made by proclamation issued by the Governor General under the Great Seal of Canada where so authorized by

    (a)   resolutions of the Senate and House of Commons; and

    (b)   resolutions of the legislative assemblies of at least a majority of the provinces that includes

        (i)   every province that at any time before the issue of the proclamation had, according to any previous general census, a population of at least twenty-five per cent of the population of Canada,

        (ii)   two or more of the Atlantic provinces, and

        (iii)   two or more of the Western provinces.

Definitions

(2) In this section,

"Atlantic provinces"

"Atlantic provinces" means the provinces of Nova Scotia, New Brunswick, Prince Edward Island and Newfoundland;

"Western provinces"

"Western provinces" means the provinces of Manitoba, British Columbia, Saskatchewan and Alberta.

Amendment authorized by referendum

47. (1) An amendment to the Constitution of Canada may be made by proclamation issued by the Governor General under the Great Seal of Canada where so authorized by a referendum held throughout Canada under subsection (2) at which

    (a)   a majority of persons voting thereat, and

    (b)   a majority of persons voting thereat in each of the provinces, resolutions of the legislative assemblies of which would be sufficient, together with resolutions of the Senate and House of Commons, to authorize the issue of a proclamation under subsection 46(1),

have approved the making of the amendment.

Authorization of referendum

(2) A referendum referred to in subsection (1) shall be held where directed by proclamation issued by the Governor General under the Great Seal of Canada, which proclamation may be issued where

    (a)   an amendment to the Constitution of Canada has been authorized under paragraph 46(1)(a) by resolutions of the Senate and House of Commons;

(b)   the requirements of paragraph 46(1)(b) in respect of the proposed amendment have not been satisfied within twelve months after the passage of the resolutions of the Senate and House of Commons; and

(c)   the issue of the proclamation has been authorized by the Governor General in Council.

Time limit for referendum

(3) A proclamation issued under subsection (2) in respect of a referendum shall provide for the referendum to be held within two years after the expiration of the twelve month period referred to in paragraph (b) of that subsection.

Amendment of provisions relating to some but not all provinces

48. An amendment to the Constitution of Canada in relation to any provision that applies to one or more, but not all, provinces may be made by proclamation issued by the Governor General under the Great Seal of Canada where so authorized by resolutions of the Senate and House of Commons and of the legislative assembly of each province to which the amendment applies.

Amendments respecting certain language rights

49. (1) Notwithstanding section 55, an amendment to the Constitution of Canada

(a)   adding a province as a province named in subsection 16(2), 17(2), 18(2), 19(2) or 20(2), or

(b)   otherwise providing for any or all of the rights guaranteed or obligations imposed by any of those subsections to have application in a province to the extent and under the conditions stated in the amendment,

may be made by proclamation issued by the Governor General under the Great Seal of Canada where so authorized by resolutions of the Senate and House of Commons and the legislative assembly of the province to which the amendment applies.

Initiation of amendment procedure

(2) The procedure for amendment prescribed by subsection (1) may be initiated only by the legislative assembly of the province to which the amendment applies.

Initiation of amendment procedures

50. (1) The procedures for amendment prescribed by subsection 46(1) and section 48 may be initiated either by the Senate or House of Commons or by the legislative assembly of a province.

Revocation of authorization

(2) A resolution made for the purposes of this Part may be revoked at any time before the issue of a proclamation authorized by it.

Right to vote

51. (1) Every citizen of Canada has, subject only to such reasonable limits prescribed by law as can be demonstrably justified in a free and democratic society, the right to vote in a referendum held under section 47.

Establishment of Referendum Rules Commission

(2) Where a referendum is to be held under section 47, a Referendum Rules Commission shall forthwith be established by commission issued under the Great Seal of Canada consisting of

(a) the Chief Electoral Officer of Canada, who shall be chairman of the Commission;

(b) a person appointed by the Governor General in Council; and

(c) a person appointed by the Governor General in Council

    (i) on the recommendation of the governments of a majority of the provinces, or

    (ii) if the governments of a majority of the provinces do not recommend a candidate within thirty days after the Chief Electoral Officer of Canada requests such a recommendation, on the recommendation of the Chief Justice of Canada from among persons recommended by the governments of the provinces within thirty days after the expiration of the first mentioned thirty day period or, if none are so recommended, from among such persons as the Chief Justice considers qualified.

Duty of Commission (3) A Referendum Rules Commission shall cause rules for the holding of a referendum under section 47 approved by a majority of the Commission to be laid before Parliament within sixty days after the Commission is established or, if Parliament is not then sitting, on any of the first ten days next thereafter that Parliament is sitting.

Rules for referendum (4) Subject to subsection (1) and taking into consideration any rules approved by a Referendum Rules Commission in accordance with subsection (3), Parliament may enact laws respecting the rules applicable to the holding of a referendum under section 47.

Proclamation (5) If Parliament does not enact laws under subsection (4) respecting the rules applicable to the holding of a referendum within sixty days after receipt of a recommendation from a Referendum Rules Commission, the rules recommended by the Commission shall forthwith be brought into force by proclamation issued by the Governor General under the Great Seal of Canada.

Computation of period (6) Any period when Parliament is prorogued or dissolved shall not be counted in computing the sixty day period referred to in subsection (5).

Rules to have force of law (7) Subject to subsection (1), rules made under this section have the force of law and prevail over other laws made under the Constitution of Canada to the extent of any inconsistency.

Limitation on use of general amendment procedure **52.** (1) The procedures prescribed by section 46, 47 or 48 do not apply to an amendment to the Constitution of Canada where there is another provision in the Constitution for making the amendment, but the procedures prescribed by section 46 or 47 shall, nevertheless, be used to amend any provision for amending the Constitution, including this section.

Idem

(2) The procedures prescribed by section 46 or 47 do not apply in respect of an amendment referred to in section 48.

Amendments by Parliament

53. Subject to section 55, Parliament may exclusively make laws amending the Constitution of Canada in relation to the executive government of Canada or the Senate or House of Commons.

Amendments by provincial legislatures

54. Subject to section 55, the legislature of each province may exclusively make laws amending the constitution of the province.

Matters requiring amendment under general amendment procedure

55. An amendment to the Constitution of Canada in relation to the following matters may be made only in accordance with a procedure prescribed by section 46 or 47:

(a) the office of the Queen, the Governor General and the Lieutenant Governor of a province;

(b) the *Canadian Charter of Rights and Freedoms;*

(c) the rights of the aboriginal peoples of Canada set out in Part II;

(d) the commitments relating to equalization and regional disparities set out in section 35;

(e) the powers of the Senate;

(f) the number of members by which a province is entitled to be represented in the Senate;

(g) the method of selecting Senators and the residence qualifications of Senators;

(h) the right of a province to a number of members in the House of Commons not less than the number of Senators representing the province; and

(i) the principles of proportionate representation of the provinces in the House of Commons prescribed by the Constitution of Canada.

Consequential amendments

56. (1) Class 1 of section 91 and class 1 of section 92 of the *Constitution Act, 1867* (formerly named the *British North America Act, 1867),* the *British North America (No. 2) Act, 1949,* referred to in item 22 of Schedule 1 to this Act and Parts IV and V of this Act are repealed.

Idem

(2) When Parts IV and V of this Act are repealed, this section may be repealed and this Act may be renumbered, consequential upon the repeal of those Parts and this section, by proclamation issued by the Governor General under the Great Seal of Canada.

our Majesty's loyal subjects, the Ho...
...s of Canada in Parliament assemb...
approach Your Majesty, requesting...
graciously be pleased to cause to be...
Parliament of the United Kingd...
containing the recitals and...
...ter set forth :

An Act to give effect to a request by t...
and House of Commons of C...

Whereas Canada has requested a...
the enactment of an Act of the Par...
United Kingdom to give effect to...
...ter set forth and the Senate an...
...nada in Parliament...
Majest...

APPENDIX 11

LETTER FROM PREMIER LÉVESQUE TO PRIME MINISTER TRUDEAU

November 25, 1981

Dear Prime Minister:

On behalf of the Government of Quebec, I am officially forwarding to you the Order by which Quebec formally exercises its right of veto of the resolution concerning patriation and amendment of the Canadian Constitution, as tabled in the House of Commons by the Minister of Justice on November 18, 1981.

I wish to point out in this connection that the Government of Quebec has always maintained that the assent of Quebec was constitutionally required to any agreement that would allow patriation of the Constitution and establishment of the amending formula for the future.

The discussions that resulted in the interprovincial Accord of April 16, 1981 related solely to the method of amending the Constitution after patriation. Since that Accord is now null and void, Quebec is no longer bound by it and we have returned to the previous situation. There has therefore never been any question of affecting the right of veto that Quebec has always possessed and still possesses concerning patriation and the amending formula as such.

With respect to Quebec's right of veto over the distribution of jurisdictions referred to in the interprovincial Accord dated April 16, 1981, we have always said that only a right to opt out together with full and obligatory compensation could be an acceptable substitute. Since this quid pro quo has been denied, we retain our traditional right of veto unchanged.

Accordingly, I would ask that you take the same action as you took in 1971 when Quebec objected to the Victoria agreement, and suspend your project until an agreement exists not only with the Anglophone provinces but also with Quebec. I would also ask you to table the text of this letter and attachment in the House of Commons and the Senate, so that Canadian parliamentarians are formally advised of the official position of Quebec. For my part, I intend to table a copy in the National Assembly of Quebec.

On the substance of the issue, I repeat that Quebec is prepared to sign any agreement that meets the minimum conditions set forth in the motion I tabled in the National Assembly on November 17, 1981, of which you have already received a copy. Those are reasonable conditions representing for Quebec the essential minimum it requires in order to protect its distinctiveness and its historic rights.

Yours truly,

[Signed René Lévesque]

René Lévesque

Encl.

ORDER
GOVERNMENT OF QUEBEC

NUMBER 3215-81   November 25, 1981

CONCERNING a reference to the Court of Appeal

--- oooOooo ---

WHEREAS the Minister of Justice of Canada, on behalf of the Government of Canada, has laid before the Senate and the House of Commons of Canada a Proposed Resolution regarding the Constitution of Canada;

WHEREAS this Proposed Resolution requests the introduction in the Parliament of the United Kingdom of a bill entitled the Canada Act which, if adopted by the Parliament of the United Kingdom, will most notably have the effect of enacting for Canada the Constitution Act, 1981;

WHEREAS the proposed legislation has the effect of making significant changes in the status and role of Quebec within the Canadian federal system;

WHEREAS Quebec forms a distinct society within the Canadian federation;

WHEREAS the Supreme Court of Canada stated on September 28, 1981 that the consent of the provinces is constitutionally necessary for the adoption of this proposal;

WHEREAS Quebec has not agreed and has objected to the proposed changes;

WHEREAS no change of a similar significance to that proposed in this Proposed Resolution has to date been made without the consent and over the objection of Quebec;

WHEREAS it is expedient to submit to the Court of Appeal for hearing and consideration, pursuant to the Court of Appeal Reference Act, the question herein below set out;

ACCORDINGLY, it is ordered, upon the proposal of the Minister of Justice, that the following question be submitted to the Court of Appeal for hearing and consideration:

Is the consent of the Province of Quebec constitutionally required, by convention, for the adoption by the Senate and the House of Commons of Canada of a resolution the purpose of which is to cause the Canadian Constitution to be amended in such a manner as to affect:

i)   the legislative competence of the Legislature of the Province of Quebec in virtue of the Canadian Constitution;

ii)   the status or role of the Legislature or Government of the Province of Quebec within the Canadian federation;

and, does the objection of the Province of Quebec render the adoption of such resolution unconstitutional in the conventional sense?

[Signed Louis Bernard]

Louis Bernard
Clerk of the Executive Council

LETTER FROM PRIME MINISTER TRUDEAU
TO PREMIER LÉVESQUE

December 1, 1981

My dear Premier:

This is in reply to your letter of November 25, 1981, transmitting the order of the executive council of the Quebec government which expressed the formal opposition of that government to the constitutional resolution now before the House of Commons, and which I acknowledged receiving on November 27. Your opposition is based on Quebec's alleged right of veto over patriation and amendments to the Constitution of Canada.

The alleged right of veto by Quebec with respect to patriation and amendment of the Constitution of Canada is, in my view, not substantiated either by law or by constitutional convention in light of the judgment of the Supreme Court of Canada rendered on September 28, 1981, in what is commonly known as the *Patriation Reference.*

On the question of whether the consent of the provinces is *legally* required for the adoption of a resolution by the two Houses of Parliament requesting the adoption by the United Kingdom of an amendment to the Constitution of Canada, the court stated unequivocally that "the law knows nothing of any requirement of provincial consent, either to a resolution of the federal Houses or as a condition of the exercise of the United Kingdom legislative power."

With respect to the question of a constitutional *convention* requiring provincial consent to seeking and obtaining constitutional amendments by the United Kingdom, while the Court did find that a convention existed in the nature of "a substantial measure of provincial consent," I would suggest that a close examination of the reasons for judgment discloses no suggestion that any one province, including Quebec, possesses a right of veto over such a constitutional amendment.

Indeed, in reaching the conclusion that the existing conventional rule was one of "a substantial measure of provincial consent," the Court was expressly rejecting the argument of the unanimity principle advanced by all provinces except New Brunswick, Ontario and Saskatchewan. In doing so, the Court spoke in terms of a particular number of provinces whose consent was required, without any reference to a need to consider other factors such as the size or character of the provinces in question. Consequently, in my view, the decision of the Supreme Court provides no basis for the assertion by your government that Quebec possesses a veto with respect to the present resolution.

What, then, can we say about the amending formula contained in the resolution and of which you spoke in the third and fourth paragraphs of your letter of November 25? In this regard, let me be clear about one thing: the Government of Canada had advocated the adoption of regional vetoes, at least since I became Prime Minister. Let me briefly recite the history underlying this assertion.

First, the Victoria Charter amending formula of 1971, which the federal government supported, would have provided regional vetoes, including a veto for Quebec.

Second, on April 19, 1975, when I wrote to all the premiers suggesting that we should take early action to patriate the Constitution, the amending formula I proposed was the one contained in the Victoria Charter of 1971. On October 14, 1976, Premier Lougheed informed me that, while the Victoria formula was acceptable to eight provinces, his government and that of Premier Bennett no longer accepted it.

Third, on January 19, 1977, I wrote to you and to the other premiers noting that the Victoria formula had been agreed to by all eleven governments in 1971 and by eight in 1976. Given this high degree of consensus, I proposed that we should make one more try to patriate the Constitution and I suggested that we adopt the Victoria formula, which, I repeat, gave Quebec a veto.

Fourth, when the first ministers met at the constitutional conference in October 1978, my government still supported the Victoria formula. However, to gain greater provincial support for an amending procedure, we were willing to consider the "Toronto consensus" which emerged in 1978. That formula provided that constitutional amendments would require the consent of Parliament and seven provinces representing at least 85 percent of the population. Because of the 85 percent population requirement, this "Toronto consensus" formula would have in practice provided a veto for Quebec.

Fifth, the draft constitutional resolution presented by the Government of Canada to Parliament in October 1980 would also have provided for a veto for Quebec.

Sixth, the formal resolution presented by my government to Parliament in February 1981, following more than three months of study in the Joint Committee of the Senate and House of Commons, carried forward this proposal.

Seventh — and finally — when I met with you and the other premiers on November 2nd last, I was still arguing for the Victoria formula, which provided a veto to Quebec.

This review of the Canadian government's position over a period of thirteen years makes it abundantly clear that the consistent desire of the Government of Canada to protect the interests of Quebec cannot be challenged. Sadly, the history of that period also shows that the successive governments of Quebec refused in every case to support the packages of constitutional proposals put forward by the Government of Canada, and which, in every case, included a Quebec veto in the amending formula.

Let us now examine the manner in which the "provincial equality" principle for an amending formula developed.

At a meeting of the Continuing Committee of Ministers on the Constitution in Toronto in December 1978, the Government of Alberta, reflecting views that had been formally advanced by that province in October 1976, argued that each province should have an equal voice in any amending formula and that there should not be a veto for any one province. It was decided at the meeting that this idea should be pursued.

Accordingly, during the winter of 1979, Alberta developed a new amending formula proposal based on this principle. This proposal, with a successive series of refinements, became the Vancouver consensus advocated by several provinces, including Quebec, at the constitutional conference in September 1980. This Vancouver consensus — without a veto for Quebec — was also proposed by the Conservative Party in a motion put to the House of Commons on October 22, 1980, by Mr. Joe Clark.

Finally, the Vancouver formula was contained in the "Premiers' Accord" of April 1981. As you well know, that accord — signed by yourself — included an amending procedure which did not give Quebec a veto. It was that formula which you again advocated during the November 2, 3, 4, and 5 meetings and which finally found its way into the agreement signed by the Government of Canada and nine provinces on November 5, 1981.

It is therefore clear that, from September 11, 1980, to November 5, 1981, you subscribed to the view first put forward by Alberta in 1976 — a view which forms the basic premise of the amending formula now in the resolution before Parliament — namely that each province should have an equal voice in any amending formula and that no single province should have a veto.

Ontario and New Brunswick were not parties to the accord of April 1981 but, in the interests of reaching "a substantial measure of provincial consent" at the November 1981 First Ministers' Conference, they agreed to support the principle already accepted by your government in the Premiers' Accord. The government of Canada then concurred in this view on November 5, though as I have explained above, we would have preferred a proposal that provided a veto for all regions, including the province of Quebec.

In brief, from 1971 to November 5, 1981, all the governments I led advocated an amending formula which provided for a veto for Quebec. We only abandoned this principle after your government did.

The only element of the amending formula contained in the Premiers' Accord which is not reflected completely in the resolution now before Parliament is the financial compensation provision. It is instructive to review the evolution of this idea in various amending formula proposals.

During discussions in the summer of 1980, your government advanced the principle that a province should not be penalized financially if it opted out of a constitutional amendment which transferred provincial powers to Parliament. But it was the general view of the other governments that financial compensation was a matter that should be addressed on the merits of each case as the need arose and that there should be no rigid constitutional obligation in this regard.

You will recall that on September 11, 1980, during the First Ministers' Conference on the Constitution, your government distributed a document entitled "Proposal for a common stand of the Provinces" — subsequently referred to as the "Château consensus." Although that proposal provided for the Alberta amending formula "with provision for financial arrangements between governments," the legal drafts attached to it to assist in understanding the proposal did not contain a provision to give constitutional effect to the notion of "financial arrangements." Provisions respecting financial arrangements did not appear in any agreed text until the Premiers' Accord was published in April of this year, at which time they appeared in the form of a constitutional obligation.

On November 5, 1981, you maintained that your agreement to the constitutional amending formula now in the resolution before Parliament was dependent upon including provisions respecting financial compensation. In response, I have repeatedly expressed my willingness to discuss this matter with you, yet you have refused to do so.

Nevertheless, despite your persistent refusal, the Government of Canada, with the agreement of the other nine provinces, modified the amending formula agreed upon on November 5 to provide for financial compensation to a province which opts out of an amendment related to education or other cultural matters. This was obviously designed to protect matters of special concern to the people of Quebec.

In summary, then, it is clear that your government dropped any claim for a Quebec veto in any amending formula as early as September 1980. True, this abandonment of principle was linked to "financial arrangements;" but then, it was not so much the principle of a veto as the assurance of compensation that was at stake.

Nevertheless, if you are no longer certain that the Alberta proposal, which you supported for over a year, meets your needs, it will be open to you after patriation to propose to the other provinces and to the Government of Canada that the amending formula itself be changed.

This, then, my dear Premier, is my understanding of the constitutional law and history respecting the claim for a provincial veto. Whether we are talking of patriation or of the amending formula, it is hard to understand how — by Order in Council or otherwise — you can maintain that a Quebec veto exists by law or custom.

Yours sincerely,

[Signed P. E. Trudeau]

APPENDIX 13

TELEX FROM PREMIER LÉVESQUE
TO PRIME MINISTER TRUDEAU

December 2, 1981

Dear Prime Minister:

I was very sorry but not surprised to read your letter of December 1, 1981, in which you explicitly deny Quebec a right of veto that generations of Quebecers have always regarded as a minimum degree of protection under the present system and that they have exercised on many occasions. The fact that this letter was signed by a Quebecer says a great deal about the loss of roots for which the present federal system is responsible.

I do not intend to respond, point by point, to the many inaccuracies in your letter. I will merely point out that in its decision of September 28, 1981, the Supreme Court expressly reserved its opinion concerning the "degree of consent" required from the provinces. Although it did not explicitly recognize Quebec's right of veto, the Supreme Court did not dismiss it: it simply did not express a view on this point.

I also wish to note a glaring contradiction between your present attitude and the historical process described in your letter. You provide a long list of the various proposals you have made since you became Prime Minister regarding the amending formula; and you state that it was not possible to adopt any of them, since "the successive governments of Quebec refused in every case to support the packages of constitutional proposals put forward by the Government of Canada." Could you then explain to me why the situation is any different today? If Quebec was able to block your previous formulas, why could it not block your present formula, especially since, in addition to contradicting what Quebecers understood to be your referendum promises, it threatens the rights and powers of Quebec as no other formula has ever done?

Since you are unwilling to respect a right that has always been respected since the beginning of Confederation, we have no choice but to have that right recognized by the Courts. The Government of Quebec has therefore decided to refer the matter to its Court of Appeal and to take the legislative action required for it to be referred thereafter to the Supreme Court of Canada. A copy of the Order adopted for this purpose is attached. [See Appendix 11.]

I would therefore ask you to suspend your project until a final decision on this matter is issued, as you agreed to do when the more general issue of the consent required from the provinces was referred to the Supreme Court early this year. Failure to agree to this request would be equivalent to preventing Quebec from exercising its rights at the proper time.

[Signed René Lévesque]

our Majesty's loyal subjects, the Ho... s of Canada in Parliament assembl... approach Your Majesty, requesting graciously be pleased to cause to be Parliament of the United Kingd containing the recitals and c ter set forth :

An Act to give effect to a request by t and House of Commons of C

Whereas Canada has requested a the enactment of an Act of the Par United Kingdom to give effect to in after set forth and the Senate an ...anada in Parliament ...Her Majest

APPENDIX 14

LETTER FROM PRIME MINISTER TRUDEAU
TO PREMIER LÉVESQUE

December 4, 1981

My dear Premier:

In reply to your telex of December 2, 1981, let me remind you that it was you who signed the Premiers' Accord of April 16, 1981, and, in so doing, *you* abandoned a veto for Quebec in the constitutional amending formula.

In the news release last April 16 which described the meaning and the importance of the agreement, you and your colleagues stated: "This establishes legal equality amongst all provinces," and, further, "This amending formula is demonstrably preferable for all Canadians to that proposed by the federal government because it recognizes the equality of provinces within Canada."

That a premier of Quebec subscribed to such an affirmation will seem aberrant and, indeed, irresponsible, especially when one remembers that the federal formula I proposed to you contained a right of veto for Quebec.

Let us be clear, then. On April 16, your government subscribed to the notion of the equality of the provinces and there was no question then of Canadian duality or even of a special status for Quebec! If Quebec, then, were to have a veto, one would also have to say that each of the other provinces had a veto too, and the amending formula would have to be unanimity to respect the equality of the provinces. But the Supreme Court in its decision on the *Patriation Reference* stated that unanimity is *not* required for constitutional amendments. Therefore, if the provinces are equal and unanimity is not required, there is no veto either for Quebec or for any other province. This is precisely the position you agreed to on April 16.

In your telex you assert that the Supreme Court of Canada expressly reserved its opinion on the degree of provincial consent required by the convention. It seems to me that this is not so. The Court indicated precisely that it was *not* its role to determine what constituted this measure of consent. The Court stated: "Conventions by their nature develop in the political field and it will be for the political actors, *not this Court*, to *determine the degree* of provincial consent required."

In light of the foregoing, I see no justification for your request that the process of adopting the constitutional resolution should be suspended pending the outcome of the court proceedings. These same courts have already told us that we should settle the matter among the political actors and that is precisely what we did at the federal-provincial conference and during the parliamentary debate, among other things.

Finally, I note that you declined in your telex of December 2, 1981, to respond to the numerous points set forth in my letter of December 1, while alleging that my letter contains numerous "inexactitudes." You must admit that's a rather hasty judgment! Until you have explained what you mean by "inexactitudes," I will continue to believe my letter to be an accurate reflection of the historical, political and legal developments during the past thirteen years.

Yours sincerely,

[*Signed P. E. Trudeau*]

acious

our Majesty's loyal subjects, the Ho

s of Canada in Parliament assemble

approach Your Majesty, requesting

graciously be pleased to cause to be

Parliament of the United Kingd

containing the recitals and

ter set forth :

An Act to give effect to a request by t

and House of Commons of C

Whereas Canada has requested a

the enactment of an Act of the Par

United Kingdom to give effect to

after set forth and the Senate and

nada in Parliament

Majest

LETTER FROM PREMIER LÉVESQUE
TO PRIME MINISTER TRUDEAU

December 17, 1982

Dear Prime Minister:

I believe that the time has come to express to you very clearly our position here in Quebec City with regard to a constitutional situation that is in essence the result of your actions, especially since the recent opinion of the Supreme Court has just contributed a conclusion that is so far the most logical and at the same time the most unacceptable.

Thus, as the Court has told us, Quebec does not possess, and has never possessed, a right of veto, by convention or otherwise, that would protect it from constitutional amendments made without its consent and affecting its rights, powers and jurisdictions.

This statement, which at least has the merit of clarity, denies a right whose existence had never been doubted and that had always been considered essential to defend the identity of Quebecers, who are the cornerstone of the North American Francophone community. If the representatives of Lower Canada in 1865 had realized that their agreement to the proposed Confederation would result in removing all protection against constitutional amendments imposed by others, there is no doubt that such agreement would never have been given.

In September 1981, the same Supreme Court confirmed that Quebec had no legal protection against unilateral actions designed to modify the powers of its National Assembly without its consent and despite its strongest objections. Now, fourteen months later, Quebecers have also learned that they have never had any protection based on convention. In other words, since 1867 Quebecers have been living under the illusion that they had an insurance policy; today, after the violation of certain of their most vital collective rights, they find that in fact they have never been protected.

This not only denies a past during which we relied on an illusion that has now vanished, but promises an even more perilous future. Now stripped of their illusions, Quebecers must learn to live at the mercy of the governments of English Canada. On November 5, 1981, following decisions made behind our back, we saw what this situation might mean for the constitutional future of Quebec.

If the Supreme Court wishes to give its legal blessing to this agreement reached under cover of night and signed just over a year ago between the Anglophone governments of Canada and your government, so be it. But I am obliged to inform you that the Canada Bill is nonetheless basically illegitimate and therefore absolutely unacceptable to Quebec and its government and, I am sure, to the very great majority of Quebecers. It will therefore be impossible for any government worthy of the name in Quebec to accept such a drastic and unilateral reduction of the powers of our National Assembly and to have imposed on it an amending formula that provides it with no real protection for the future.

The National Assembly already stated, in December 1981, the conditions under which this British constitutional statute might become acceptable. First, the Constitution Act must recognize not only the equality of the founding peoples but also the distinctiveness of Quebec society. Second, to ensure the vitality of that society, the amending formula of the Constitution of Canada must provide Quebec with a general right of veto or a right to opt out together with full financial compensation in all cases (a specific right of veto, or a "qualified" right of veto, to use the term employed by the federal Minister of Justice). Last, any Canadian Charter of Rights must not in any way alter the legislative jurisdiction of the National Assembly, particularly as regards the language of instruction and mobility rights. (A true copy of the resolution of the National Assembly is attached.)

In view of the opinion issued by the Supreme Court, all these conditions are more relevant than ever. But in the present situation, two of them have become more urgent: Quebec's (general or specific) right of veto, and the language of instruction.

On April 26, 1982, you said the following: "If Mr. Lévesque were to say tomorrow, let us work together and try to obtain for Quebec the right of veto provided at Victoria, I would give him my hand and I would say, very well, let us do that together." And on December 8, your Minister of Justice said that he was again ready to co-operate with Quebec to attempt to obtain for it a general or specific right of veto.

I would therefore ask you, as evidence of good faith and your apparent wish to grant Quebec its rightful place in Canada, to table a resolution to amend the Constitution as soon as possible and have it passed by both federal Houses, as provided by the Canada Bill.

Pursuant to the conditions indicated by the National Assembly, such a resolution would provide the Government of Quebec with either a general right of veto or a specific right of veto, that is, a right to opt out combined with full compensation in all cases. In addition, such a resolution would exempt Quebec from the application of Section 23 of the Canada Bill regarding the right of instruction in the minority language, thus entrenching Quebec's exclusive jurisdiction with respect to the language of education.

Since no constitutional amendment can be passed without the agreement of the federal government, you will understand that early tabling and passage of such a resolution in Ottawa constitute a necessity for Quebec and its government. I therefore trust that, as you hinted, you will be prepared to prove to the Quebec community that you can once again act to promote its rights and interests, even after injuring them to an extent that your predecessors would never have dared contemplate.

Your response, which we wish to receive as soon as possible, will certainly influence the outcome of the constitutional issue, at least with respect to Quebec.

Yours truly,

[*Signed René Lévesque*]

Encl.

c.c.: Provincial Premiers

RESOLUTION

L'Assemblée nationale du Québec,

rappelant le droit du peuple québecbécois à disposer de lui-même,

et exerçant son droit historique à être partie prenante et à consentir à tout changement dans la constitution du Canada qui pourrait affecter les droits et les pouvoirs du Québec,

déclare qu'elle ne peut accepter le projet de rapatriement de la constitution sauf si celui-ci rencontre les conditions suivantes :

1. on devra reconnaître que les deux peuples qui ont fondé le Canada sont foncièrement égaux et que le Québec forme à l'intérieur de l'ensemble fédéral canadien une société distincte par la langue, la culture, les institutions et qui possède tous les attributs d'une communauté nationale distincte;

2. le mode d'amendement de la constitution

a) ou bien devra maintenir au Québec son droit de veto,

b) ou bien sera celui qui a été convenu dans l'Accord constitutionnel signé par le Québec le 16 avril 1981 et confirmant le droit du Québec de ne pas être assujetti à une modification qui diminuerait ses pouvoirs ou ses droits et de recevoir, le cas échéant, une compensation raisonnable et obligatoire;

3. étant donné l'existence de la Charte québécoise des droits et libertés de la personne, la charte des droits inscrite dans la constitution canadienne ne devra inclure que :

a) les droits démocratiques;

b) l'usage du français et de l'anglais dans les institutions et les services du gouvernement fédéral;

c) l'égalité entre les hommes et les femmes, pourvu que l'Assemblée nationale conserve le pouvoir de faire prévaloir ses lois dans les domaines de sa compétence;

The National Assembly of Québec,

mindful of the right of the people of Québec to self-determination,

and exercising its historical right of being a full party to any change to the Constitution of Canada which would affect the rights and powers of Québec,

declares that it cannot accept the plan to patriate the Constitution unless it meets the following conditions:

1. It must be recognized that the two founding peoples of Canada are fundamentally equal and that Québec, by virtue of its language, culture and institutions, forms a distinct society within the Canadian federal system and has all the attributes of a distinct national community;

2. The constitutional amending formula

(a) must either maintain Québec's right of veto or

(b) be in keeping with the Constitutional Accord signed by Québec on April 16, 1981 whereby Québec would not be subject to any amendment which would diminish its powers or rights, and would be entitled, where necessary, to reasonable and obligatory compensation;

3. Given that a Charter of Human Rights and Freedoms is already operative in Québec, the Charter of Rights and Freedoms to be entrenched in the Canadian Constitution must limit itself to:

(a) democratic rights;

(b) use of French and English in federal government institutions and services;

(c) equality between men and women provided the National Assembly retains the power to legislate in matters under its jurisdiction;

d) les libertés fondamentales, pourvu que l'Assemblée nationale conserve le pouvoir de faire prévaloir ses lois dans les domaines de sa compétence;

e) les garanties quant à l'enseignement dans la langue des minorités anglaise ou française, pourvu que le Québec reste libre d'y adhérer volontairement, puisque sa compétence exclusive en cette matière doit demeurer totale et inaliénable et que la situation de sa minorité est déjà la plus privilégiée au Canada;

4. on donnera suite aux dispositions déjà prévues dans le projet du gouvernment fédéral concernant le droit des provinces à la péréquation et à un meilleur contrôle de leurs richesses naturelles.

COPIE CONFORME DE LA RÉSOLUTION ADOPTÉE PAR L'ASSEMBLÉE NATIONALE DU QUÉBEC LE 1er DÉCEMBRE 1981.

Signé à Québec ce

16 décembre 1982

(d) fundamental freedoms provided the National Assembly retains the power to legislate in matters under its jurisdiction; and

(e) English and French minority language guarantees in education, provided Québec is allowed to adhere voluntarily considering that its power in this area must remain total and inalienable and that its minority is already the most privileged in Canada.

4. Effect must be given to the provisions already prescribed in the federal proposal in respect of the right of the provinces to equalization and to better control over their natural resources.

TRUE COPY OF THE RESOLUTION PASSED BY THE NATIONAL ASSEMBLY OF QUEBEC ON 1 DECEMBER 1981.

Signed in Québec City on the

16 December 1982

[*Signed René Blondin*]

RENÉ BLONDIN

Secrétaire général de l'Assemblée nationale

TELEX FROM PRIME MINISTER TRUDEAU
TO PREMIER LÉVESQUE

December 24, 1982

My dear Premier:

In your telex of December 17, you requested that I ask the Parliament of Canada to adopt "a resolution which would recognize the right of the Government of Quebec to either a general veto or a specific veto, that is, a right to opt out with full compensation in all cases." You also insisted that this resolution should exempt Quebec from the Canada clause contained in section 23 of the Canadian Charter of Rights and Freedoms.

This request strikes me as somewhat curious coming from a government which only yesterday was denouncing federal unilateralism and which has declined to participate in any way in the preparatory work for the constitutional conference scheduled for March. I am wondering therefore if you have made similar requests of the premiers of the other provinces since, as you well know, the Parliament of Canada cannot now, any more than it could before patriation, act alone to determine or to change the amending formula in our constitution.

If we had this power, you would not today have to seek special measures to protect the Quebec identity, since we all know that the federal Parliament would have opted for the Victoria formula, which recognized a veto for Quebec. Since the federal government has been on record as favouring this formula for more than 10 years — and thus already subscribes to the principle of a veto — you would be better advised to direct your request in the first instance to your colleagues of the other provinces.

You place great importance in your telex on the recent Supreme Court judgement which, in your view, denies "a right of veto the existence of which has never been doubted and which has always been considered essential for the protection of the people of Quebec, cornerstone of the Francophones of North America."

I would like to ask you a simple question. If this right was so indisputable and so indispensable, why was it that you made no mention of it in the agreement you signed in April, 1981, with the other provinces, which opposed the constitutional initiatives of the federal government, Ontario and New Brunswick?

In rejecting out-of-hand the Victoria formula and its veto for Quebec, you chose instead to accept "opting-out," declaring that this formula "ensured the legal equality of all provinces" and, for this very reason, was "clearly preferable, for all Canadians, to the formula proposed by the federal government."

Similarly, when Quebec appeared in 1981 before the Supreme Court in company with the other dissenting provinces and sought to have the proposals for constitutional reform submitted by the Parliament of Canada declared unconstitutional, at no point did you claim a veto for Quebec or that Quebec's participation was indispensable to any consensus to amend the Constitution.

To keep intact a common front to which Quebec was totally committed, Quebec made itself into a province like the others, while, by an extraordinary paradox, it was the federal government which defended to the very end the principle that Quebec should have a right of veto over constitutional amendments.

Faced with this common front of eight provinces of which you were part, and faced too with the Supreme Court's decision of September 1981, the federal government and the two provinces which supported it had to give way before the notion of the equality of the provinces, and stopped insisting on the constitutional veto for Quebec which, for our part, we had always sought. As I have recently stated, if Quebec did not obtain a right of veto, that is because the Government of Quebec did not want one. Think of the strong support there would have been if the Government of Quebec had joined with Ontario, New Brunswick and the federal government in favour of an amending formula which would have given Quebec a veto. But you chose otherwise.

Although forced to accept, in the November 1981 agreement, an amending formula which was far from its preferred option, the federal government was nonetheless the one that arranged to modify the formula in order to take account of the interests of Quebecers. In fact, with the support of other provinces, we included a provision in the Constitution which guarantees reasonable compensation to any province which dissents from an amendment transferring power to the Canadian Parliament in the area of education and culture.

Furthermore, as regards the language of education, I have offered, publicly, to re-word section 23 if this should be necessary to arrive at a Canada clause acceptable to the Government of Quebec.

This offer still holds, as does my suggestion to you that we should unite in our efforts to return again to the right of veto which the federal government and all the other provinces were prepared to recognize for Quebec in Victoria in 1971.

I think it is reasonable, however, to ask you the following two questions:

First, will Quebec agree to participate in good faith in the current constitutional process? The veto question obviously cannot be settled by the federal and Quebec governments alone. We must discuss this matter with our colleagues of the other provinces if we really want to achieve a new amending formula according to the procedures which are now part of our country's constitution.

Second, in return for the veto, or its equivalent, is the Quebec government prepared to give formal acceptance to the Constitution Act, 1982? It would be unthinkable for the federal government and the governments of the other provinces to devote a great deal of time and effort to the search for an amending formula capable of meeting the needs of Quebecers, only to discover afterwards that the Government of Quebec still found other excuses for not accepting the new Constitution.

If, however, you accept these two reasonable conditions, I am fully prepared to explore with you and our colleagues all the available options which could give better protection to the legitimate interests of Quebecers as far as future amendments to the Canadian constitution are concerned.

As far as opting out is concerned, you are of course aware that, as I mentioned above, we have already included this concept in the Constitution by providing reasonable compensation in the fields of education and culture. I must tell you frankly, however, that it does not seem to me at this point either necessary or desirable to extend this concept to other fields. To go further would be to encourage the gradual balkanization of the country and thereby put its future in doubt.

As for the Canada clause provided in section 23 of the Canadian Charter of Rights and Freedoms, your government stated that it was willing to accept such a provision at the meetings of provincial premiers held in St. Andrews in 1977, and in Montreal in 1978, provided that the other provinces agreed, on a reciprocal basis, to guarantee the same rights to Francophones outside Quebec. You even inserted this principle of reciprocity in section 86 of Bill 101. Now that the other provinces have all adopted the Canada clause, it is incumbent on your government to respect its commitment, all the more so since this clause, like the Charter itself, enjoys the support of the vast majority of Quebecers, and since we are ready to re-word it if necessary to make it more acceptable to the Government of Quebec. Besides, as you know, our fellow Quebecers are interested not only in the development of the French language in Quebec, but also in the broadening of language rights of Francophones wherever they happen to live in Canada.

Finally, I would remind you that in your letter of August 19, you informed me that the Government of Quebec was waiting to consult with the Aboriginal communities before "engaging in a constitutional process concerning them." I hope that concern for Quebec's rights, which are already well protected and which we can strengthen in future, will not prevent us from rendering justice to our Aboriginal peoples, who have greater need than anyone to see their rights better defined and protected in the Canadian constitution.

Yours sincerely,

Pierre Elliott Trudeau

acious

our Majesty's loyal subjects, the Ho

s of Canada in Parliament assembl

approach Your Majesty, requesting

graciously be pleased to cause to be

Parliament of the United Kingd

containing the recitals and

ter set forth :

An Act to give effect to a request by t

and House of Commons of C

Whereas Canada has requested a

the enactment of an Act of the Parl

United Kingdom to give effect to

alter set forth and the Senate an

nada in Parliament

Majest

CONSTITUTION ACT, 1982

PART V

PROCEDURE FOR AMENDING THE CONSTITUTION OF CANADA

General procedure for amending Constitution of Canada

38. (1) An amendment to the Constitution of Canada may be made by proclamation issued by the Governor General under the Great Seal of Canada where so authorized by

    (a)   resolutions of the Senate and House of Commons; and

    (b)   resolutions of the legislative assemblies of at least two-thirds of the provinces that have, in the aggregate, according to the then latest general census, at least fifty per cent of the population of all the provinces.

Majority of members

(2) An amendment made under subsection (1) that derogates from the legislative powers, the proprietary rights or any other rights or privileges of the legislature or government of a province shall require a resolution supported by a majority of the members of each of the Senate, the House of Commons and the legislative assemblies required under subsection (1).

Expression of dissent

(3) An amendment referred to in subsection (2) shall not have effect in a province the legislative assembly of which has expressed its dissent thereto by resolution supported by a majority of its members prior to the issue of the proclamation to which the amendment relates unless that legislative assembly, subsequently, by resolution supported by a majority of its members, revokes its dissent and authorizes the amendment.

Resolution of dissent

(4) A resolution of dissent made for the purposes of subsection (3) may be revoked at any time before or after the issue of the proclamation to which it relates.

Restriction on proclamation

39. (1) A proclamation shall not be issued under subsection 38(1) before the expiration of one year from the adoption of the resolution initiating the amendment procedure thereunder, unless the legislative assembly of each province has previously adopted a resolution of assent or dissent.

Idem

(2) A proclamation shall not be issued under subsection 38(1) after the expiration of three years from the adoption of the resolution initiating the amendment procedure thereunder.

Compensation

40. Where an amendment is made under subsection 38(1) that transfers provincial legislative powers relating to education or other cultural matters from provincial legislatures to Parliament, Canada shall provide reasonable compensation to any province to which the amendment does not apply.

Amendment by unanimous consent

41. An amendment to the Constitution of Canada in relation to the following matters may be made by proclamation issued by the Governor General under the Great Seal of Canada only where authorized by resolutions of the Senate and House of Commons and the legislative assembly of each province:

(a) the office of the Queen, the Governor General and the Lieutenant Governor of a province;

(b) the right of a province to a number of members in the House of Commons not less than the number of Senators by which the province is entitled to be represented at the time this Part comes into force;

(c) subject to section 43, the use of the English or the French language;

(d) the composition of the Supreme Court of Canada; and

(e) an amendment to this Part.

Amendment by general procedure

42. (1) An amendment to the Constitution of Canada in relation to the following matters may be made only in accordance with subsection 38(1):

(a) the principle of proportionate representation of the provinces in the House of Commons prescribed by the Constitution of Canada;

(b) the powers of the Senate and the method of selecting Senators;

(c) the number of members by which a province is entitled to be represented in the Senate and the residence qualifications of Senators;

(d) subject to paragraph 41(d), the Supreme Court of Canada;

(e) the extension of existing provinces into the territories; and

(f) notwithstanding any other law or practice, the establishment of new provinces.

Exception

(2) Subsections 38(2) to (4) do not apply in respect of amendments in relation to matters referred to in subsection (1).

Amendment of provisions relating to some but not all provinces

43. An amendment to the Constitution of Canada in relation to any provision that applies to one or more, but not all, provinces, including

(a) any alteration to boundaries between provinces, and

(b)   any amendment to any provision that relates to the use of the English or the French language within a province,

may be made by proclamation issued by the Governor General under the Great Seal of Canada only where so authorized by resolutions of the Senate and House of Commons and of the legislative assembly of each province to which the amendment applies.

Amendments by Parliament

44.   Subject to sections 41 and 42, Parliament may exclusively make laws amending the Constitution of Canada in relation to the executive government of Canada or the Senate and House of Commons.

Amendments by provincial legislatures

45.   Subject to section 41, the legislature of each province may exclusively make laws amending the constitution of the province.

Initiation of amendment procedures

46.   (1) The procedures for amendment under sections 38, 41, 42 and 43 may be initiated either by the Senate or the House of Commons or by the legislative assembly of a province.

Revocation of authorization

(2) A resolution of assent made for the purposes of this Part may be revoked at any time before the issue of a proclamation authorized by it.

Amendments without Senate resolution

47.   (1) An amendment to the Constitution of Canada made by proclamation under section 38, 41, 42 or 43 may be made without a resolution of the Senate authorizing the issue of the proclamation if, within one hundred and eighty days after the adoption by the House of Commons of a resolution authorizing its issue, the Senate has not adopted such a resolution and if, at any time after the expiration of that period, the House of Commons again adopts the resolution.

Computation of period

(2) Any period when Parliament is prorogued or dissolved shall not be counted in computing the one hundred and eighty day period referred to in subsection (1).

Advice to issue proclamation

48.   The Queen's Privy Council for Canada shall advise the Governor General to issue a proclamation under this Part forthwith on the adoption of the resolutions required for an amendment made by proclamation under this Part.

Constitutional conference

49.   A constitutional conference composed of the Prime Minister of Canada and the first ministers of the provinces shall be convened by the Prime Minister of Canada within fifteen years after this Part comes into force to review the provisions of this Part.

our Majesty's loyal subjects, the Hou
of Canada in Parliament assembl
approach Your Majesty, requesting
graciously be pleased to cause to be
Parliament of the United Kingd
containing the recitals and c
ter set forth :

An Act to give effect to a request by t
and House of Commons of C

Whereas Canada has requested a
the enactment of an Act of the Parl
United Kingdom to give effect to
inafter set forth and the Senate an
Canada in Parliament
Majesty

APPENDIX 18

LETTER FROM PRIME MINISTER MULRONEY TO
SECRETARY OF STATE BENOÎT BOUCHARD

April 22, 1986

Dear Colleague:

There is already an agreement in principle between the Government of Canada and the governments of some provinces regarding three constitutional amendments which apply only to the provinces in question. These are proposed amendments regarding the educational rights of Pentecostal Assemblies in Newfoundland, the boundary between Manitoba and Saskatchewan, and the boundary between Alberta and British Columbia.

Her Excellency the Governor General may therefore be authorized during the year to issue a proclamation to amend the Constitution, and in these circumstances it would be appropriate to agree immediately on certain associated procedures.

With respect to the proclamation document itself, I think that the precedent established on June 21, 1984, at the time of the first proclamation following patriation of the Constitution, should be followed; that is, the wording of any amendment should be printed on fine paper with the Arms of Canada in colour. The Government will then not be required to make ad hoc decisions regarding the quality of the document to be preserved in the National Archives whenever a constitutional amendment is proclaimed.

If an amendment is of some sectoral, regional or national importance, the minister or ministers sponsoring the proposed amendment may wish to have additional copies of the signed document produced. This is a decision for the sponsoring ministers, who will be responsible for the costs.

Last, it is for the sponsoring minister or ministers to determine, in co-operation with the staff of the Governor General, the Department of Secretary of State and my office, the type of ceremony, if any, which should be associated with signature of any future proclamation.

Yours truly,

Prime Minister

our Majesty's loyal subjects, the Hon
s of Canada in Parliament assembl
approach Your Majesty, requesting,
graciously be pleased to cause to be
Parliament of the United Kingd
containing the recitals and c
ter set forth :

An Act to give effect to a request by t
and House of Commons of C

Whereas Canada has requested a
the enactment of an Act of the Parl
United Kingdom to give effect to
inafter set forth and the Senate an
Canada in Parliament
Her Majesty

MEECH LAKE ACCORD

June 3, 1987

(Excerpt)

9. Sections 40 to 42 of the Constitution Act, 1982 are repealed and the following substituted therefor:

Compensation

"**40.** Where an amendment is made under subsection 38(1) that transfers legislative powers from provincial legislatures to Parliament, Canada shall provide reasonable compensation to any province to which the amendment does not apply.

Amendment by unanimous consent

41. An amendment to the Constitution of Canada in relation to the following matters may be made by proclamation issued by the Governor General under the Great Seal of Canada only where authorized by resolutions of the Senate and House of Commons and of the legislative assembly of each province:

    (a) the office of the Queen, the Governor General and the Lieutenant Governor of a province;

    (b) the powers of the Senate and the method of selecting Senators;

    (c) the number of members by which a province is entitled to be represented in the Senate and the residence qualifications of Senators;

    (d) the right of a province to a number of members in the House of Commons not less than the number of Senators by which the province was entitled to be represented on April 17, 1982;

    (e) the principle of proportionate representation of the provinces in the House of Commons prescribed by the Constitution of Canada;

    (f) subject to section 43, the use of the English or the French language;

    (g) the Supreme Court of Canada;

    (h) the extension of existing provinces into the territories;

    (i) notwithstanding any other law or practice, the establishment of new provinces; and

    (j) an amendment to this Part."

10. Section 44 of the said Act is repealed and the following substituted therefor:

Amendments by Parliament

"**44.** Subject to section 41, Parliament may exclusively make laws amending the Constitution of Canada in relation to the executive government of Canada or the Senate and House of Commons."

11. Subsection 46(1) of the said Act is repealed and the following substituted therefor:

Initiation of
amendment
procedures

"**46.** (1) The procedures for amendment under sections 38, 41 and 43 may be initiated either by the Senate or the House of Commons or by the legislative assembly of a province."

12. Subsection 47(1) of the said Act is repealed and the following substituted therefor:

Amendments
without Senate
resolution

"**47.** (1) An amendment to the Constitution of Canada made by proclamation under section 38, 41 or 43 may be made without a resolution of the Senate authorizing the issue of the proclamation if, within one hundred and eighty days after the adoption by the House of Commons of a resolution authorizing its issue, the Senate has not adopted such a resolution and if, at any time after the expiration of that period , the House of Commons again adopts the resolution."

APPENDIX 20

LETTER FROM THE SECRETARY TO THE CABINET
FOR FEDERAL-PROVINCIAL RELATIONS
TO HIS PROVINCIAL COUNTERPARTS

June 20, 1988

Dear   :

The *Constitution Act, 1982* makes clear the role of the Senate, the House of Commons, the Queen's Privy Council for Canada and the Governor General in the constitutional amendment process. However, the Act is silent on the communications among the various political actors to make the procedure operational.

Since there continues to be some uncertainty respecting the transmission of constitutional resolutions once they have been duly authorized by a Legislative Assembly, I am writing you and our other colleagues to set out a standard procedure which, I trust, will be acceptable to all.

Following adoption of a constitutional resolution by a legislative assembly, the Speaker is the appropriate person to communicate the fact that a proclamation amending the Constitution in both official languages has been authorized by the Assembly. A certified copy of the resolution, signed by the Clerk of the Legislative Assembly, should be attached to the Speaker's letter.

The proper recipient of the Speaker's letter is the Clerk of the Privy Council (and not the Prime Minister of the Governor General), since it is he who must inform the Queen's Privy Council when the conditions for an amendment have been met.

The essential information that should appear in the Speaker's letter has been set out in the attached suggested draft.

I hope that this procedure will establish clear lines of communication and avoid possible confusion.

Yours sincerely,

Norman Spector

(Suggested draft letter)

Mr. Paul Tellier
Clerk of the Privy Council
and Secretary to the Cabinet,
Langevin Block, Room 332
Ottawa, Ontario.
K1A 0A3

Dear Mr. Tellier:

The Legislative Assembly of (name of the province) adopted a resolution on (date) that an amendment to the Constitution of Canada be authorized to be made in English and in French by proclamation issued by Her Excellency the Governor General under the Great Seal of Canada in accordance with the schedule to the resolution.

I have the pleasure of forwarding to you herewith for consideration by the Queen's Privy Council for Canada a certified copy of the resolution adopted by the Legislative Assembly.

Yours sincerely,

[Speaker]

APPENDIX 21

THE CONSTITUTION AMENDMENT, 1987: RECORD OF RATIFICATION, 1987–90

LEGISLATIVE BODY	STATUS OF RESOLUTION	COMMENTS
House of Commons	Adopted October 26, 1987, and June 22, 1988	First vote 242 to 16. Second vote 200 to 7
Senate	Adopted *amended* resolution April 21, 1988	Vote: 47 to 28
Quebec	Adopted June 23, 1987	Vote: 95 to 18
Saskatchewan	Adopted September 23, 1987	Vote: 43 to 3
Alberta	Adopted December 7, 198	Vote: 43 to 0
Prince Edward Island	Adopted May 13, 1988	No recorded vote (only one member voiced dissent)
Nova Scotia	Adopted May 25, 1988	Vote: 35 to 7
Ontario	Adopted June 29, 1988	Vote: 112 to 8

LEGISLATIVE BODY	STATUS OF RESOLUTION	COMMENTS
British Columbia	Adopted June 29, 1988	Vote: 42 to 5
Newfoundland	Adopted July 7, 1988 Motion to rescind March 22, 1990 Rescinded April 5, 1990	Vote: 28 to 10 Vote: Carried without division
New Brunswick	Adopted June 15, 1990	Vote: Carried without division (unanimous)
Manitoba	Tabled December 16, 1988 Withdrawn December 19, 1988 Reintroduced June 20, 1990	No vote

APPENDIX 22

THE CONSTITUTION AMENDMENT, 1987: RECORD OF PUBLIC HEARINGS, 1987–90

LEGISLATIVE BODY	HEARINGS	COMMENTS
House of Commons	Joint Committee (August 4–September 1, 1987: Ottawa – 15 days) Special Committee (April 9–May 4, 1990: Canada-wide – 18 days)	Hearings on Accord of June 3, 1987 (131 groups and individuals, 183 additional submissions) Hearings on 1990 N. B. Companion Resolution (161 groups and individuals, 755 additional submissions)
Senate	Committee of the Whole (June 26, 1987–March 31, 1988: Ottawa –15 days) Task Force (October 24–November 2, 1987: Yukon/NWT – 4 days) Subcommittee on Submissions (February 29–March 18, 1988 – 5 days)	All hearings on Accord of June 3, 1987 (Committee of the Whole – 41 witnesses; Task Force – 59 groups and individuals, 47 additional submissions; Subcommittee – 43 groups and individuals)
Quebec	May 12–25, 1987: Quebec – 8 days	Hearings on Agreement of April 30, 1987 (17 individuals and 20 groups)
Saskatchewan	Nil	

LEGISLATIVE BODY	HEARINGS	COMMENTS
Alberta	Nil	
Prince Edward Island	April 25–May 10, 1988: Charlottetown — 4 days, Wellington —1 day	Hearings on Accord of June 3, 1987 (approx. 31 witnesses and submissions)
Nova Scotia	Nil	
Ontario	February 2–May 4, 1988: Toronto —28 days, Ottawa — 4 days, London — 1 day	Hearings on Accord of June 3, 1987 (142 groups and individuals, 306 submissions)
British Columbia	Nil	
New Brunswick	January 25–February 16, 1989: Fredericton — 8 days	Hearings on Accord of June 3, 1987 (106 groups and individuals, 75 additional submissions)
Manitoba	April 6–May 2, 1989: province-wide — 12 days	Hearings on Accord of June 3, 1987 (341 groups and individuals, 39 additional submissions)

CHARLOTTETOWN ACCORD
October 9, 1992
(Excerpt — Draft Legal Text)

32. Sections 40 to 42 of the said Act [Constitution Act, 1982] are repealed and the following substituted therefor:

Compensation

"**40.** Where an amendment is made under subsection 38(1) that transfers legislative powers from provincial legislatures to Parliament, Canada shall provide reasonable compensation to any province to which the amendment does not apply.

Amendment by unanimous consent

41. An amendment to the Constitution of Canada in relation to the following matters may be made by proclamation issued by the Governor General under the Great Seal of Canada only where authorized by resolutions of the Senate and House of Commons and of the legislative assembly of each province:

(a) the office of the Queen, the Governor General and the Lieutenant Governor of a province;

(b) the powers of the Senate and the selection of Senators;

(c) the number of senators by which a province or territory is entitled to be represented in the Senate and the qualifications of senators set out in the *Constitution Act, 1867;*

[(c.1)* the number of senators by which the Aboriginal peoples of Canada are entitled to be represented in the Senate and the qualifications of such senators;]

(d) an amendment to section 51A of the *Constitution Act, 1867;*

(e) subject to section 43, the use of the English or the French language;

(f) subject to section 42(1), the Supreme Court of Canada;

(g) an amendment to section 2 or 3 of the *Constitution Act, 1871;* and

(h) an amendment to this Part.

Amendments by general procedure

42. (1) An amendment to the Constitution of Canada in relation to the method of selecting judges of the Supreme Court of Canada may be made only in accordance with subsection 38(1).

Exception

(2) Subsections 38(2) to (4) do not apply in respect of amendments in relation to the matter referred to in subsection (1).

---

*The issue of Aboriginal representation is to be discussed in the autumn of 1992, according to the Consensus Report.

New provinces

42.1. Subsection 38(1) and sections 41 and 42 do not apply to allow a province that is established pursuant to section 2 of the *Constitution Act, 1871* after the coming into force of this section to authorize amendments to the Constitution of Canada and, for greater certainty, all other provisions of this Part apply in respect of such a province."

[**33.** The said Act is further amended by adding thereto, immediately after section 45 thereof, the following section:

Amendments where Aboriginal peoples of Canada directly referred to

"**45.1*.** (1) An amendment to the Constitution of Canada that directly refers to, or that amends a provision that directly refers to, one or more of the Aboriginal peoples of Canada or their governments, including

> (a) section 2, as it relates to the Aboriginal peoples of Canada,** class 24 of section 91, and sections 91A, 95E and 127 of the *Constitution Act, 1867*, and
>
> (b) section 25 and Part II of this Act and this section,

may be made by proclamation issued by the Governor General under the Great Seal of Canada only where the amendment has been authorized in accordance with this Part and has received the substantial consent of the Aboriginal peoples so referred to.

Initiation of amendment procedures

(2) Notwithstanding section 46, the procedures for amending the Constitution of Canada in relation to any matter referred to in subsection (1) may be initiated by any of the Aboriginal peoples of Canada directly referred to as provided in subsection (1)."]

---

* A mechanism for obtaining Aboriginal consent would be worked out prior to the tabling of a constitution resolution in Parliament.
** A reference to any provision relating to Aboriginal representation in the Senate would be added here.

APPENDIX 24

Provincial Constitutional Amendment Resolutions April 17, 1982– June 1993

Province	Constitutional Amendment Resolutions	Days of Debate	Hearings	Passed/Failed	Vote
Newfoundland	1. *Constitution Amendment Proclamation, 1983.* Introduced on November 8, 1983.	2	No	Passed on December 2, 1983.	No recorded vote.
	2. *Constitution Amendment, year of proclamation (Neufoundland Act).* Introduced April 8, 1987.	1	No	Passed on April 10, 1987.	Carried unanimously.
	3. *Constitution Amendment, 1987.* Introduced March 15, 1988. [Meech Lake]	14	No	Passed on July 7, 1988.	For, 27. Against, 10. 52 seats in the Assembly.
	4. Resolution to rescind the *Constitution Amendment, 1987.* Introduced March 22, 1990.	7 sitting days of debate. The resolution was adopted on April 5, 1990, by a motion of closure.		Passed on April 5, 1990	For, 29. Against, 15.
	5. *Constitution Amendment, 1987.* Introduced June 13, 1990.	3 days of debate, including June 22, 1990, when debate was adjourned.	No formal hearings. (House was adjourned between June 13 and June 20 "to enable Members to canvass the views and opinions of their constituents.")	Failed. Debate adjourned on June 22, 1990, and resolution died on the Order Paper.	N/A

Province	Constitutional Amendment Resolutions	Days of Debate	Hearings	Passed/Failed	Vote
Newfoundland (continued)	6. *Constitution Amendment, year of proclamation.* Introduced June 13, 1990. [Companion resolution]	See above	See above	Failed. Debate adjourned on June 22, 1990, and resolution died on the Order Paper.	N/A
Nova Scotia	1. *Constitution Amendment Proclamation, 1983.* Introduced May 27, 1983.	1	No	Passed on May 31, 1983.	For, 36. Against, 4. 52 seats in Legislature.
	2. *Constitution Amendment, 1987.* Introduced February 26, 1988.	9	No	Passed on May 25, 1988.	For, 35. Against, 7.
	3. *Constitution Act, year of* proclamation. Introduced June 13, 1990. [Companion resolution]	2	No	Passed on June 19, 1990.	Passed on division (no recorded vote).
Prince Edward Island	1. *Constitution Amendment Proclamation, 1983.* Introduced June 16, 1983.	1	No	Passed on June 16, 1983.	Carried unanimously.
	2. *Constitution Amendment, 1987.*	3	Four sessions held in Charlottetown. Committee heard from 30 individual and group witnesses.	Passed on May 13, 1988.	No recorded division.

Province	Constitutional Amendment Resolution	Days of Debate	Hearings	Passed/Failed	Vote
Prince Edward Island (continued)	3. *Constitution Amendment, 1993 (Prince Edward Island).* Introduced June 15, 1993.	1	No	Passed on June 15, 1993.	Carried unanimously.
New Brunswick	1. Constitution Amendment Resolution. Introduced April 29, 1983. [Property rights]	3	No	Passed on June 28, 1983	No recorded division.
	2. *Constitution Amendment Proclamation, 1983.* Introduced June 16, 1983.	2	No	Passed on June 28, 1983.	For, 41. Against, 1. 58 seats in the Legislature.
	3. *Constitution Amendment, 1987.* Introduced March 21, 1990.	4	Select Committee on the 1987 Constitutional Accord. Nine days of public hearings were held, 182 briefs including 75 from individuals and 107 from groups were received. Forty individual briefs and 66 from groups were presented in person, 75 were received by mail.	Passed on June 15, 1990.	Carried unanimously.
	4. *Constitution Amendment, year of proclamation.* Introduced March 21, 1990. [Equality of English and French communities]	3	Resolution reflected recommendations made during hearings of the Select Committee on the 1987 Constitutional Accord. Nine days of public hearings were held; 182 briefs were received, including 75 from individuals and 107 from groups. Forty individual briefs and 66 from groups were presented in person, 75 were received by mail.	Withdrawn because of the signing by first ministers of a constitutional agreement, June 9, 1990.	N/A

Province	Constitutional Amendment Resolution	Days of Debate	Hearings	Passed/Failed	Vote
New Brunswick (continued)	5. *Constitution Amendment*, year of proclamation. Introduced June 9, 1990. [Companion resolution]	4	See above	Passed on June 15, 1990.	Carried unanimously.
	6. *Constitution Amendment*, year of proclamation *(New Brunswick)* Introduced June 9, 1990.	4	See above	Passed on June 15, 1990.	Carried unanimously.
	7. *Constitution Amendment*, year of proclamation *(New Brunswick)* Introduced December 4, 1992. [Equality of English and French linguistic communities]	2	September 10, 1990, months after the demise of Meech, the New Brunswick Commission on Canadian Federalism sought public input through written submissions, focus groups, personal interviews and presentations. It reported on January 14, 1992. February 12, 1992. Select Committee on the Constitution was appointed by the Legislative Assembly. Six days of public hearings were held, including a citizens' assembly. Forty-four presenters appeared, 51 briefs submitted. Final report, tabled March 27, 1992, recommended constitutional protection of two language groups.	Passed on December 8, 1992.	For, 37. Against, 8. 58 seats in the Assembly.
Quebec	1. *Constitution Amendment*, 1987. Introduced June 18, 1987. [Meech Lake]	4	No, but 8 days of hearings had been held between May 12 and May 25 on the Meech Lake principles.	Passed on June 23, 1987.	For, 95. Against, 18. 125 seats in the Assembly.

Province	Constitutional Amendment Resolution	Days of Debate	Hearings	Passed/Failed	Vote
Ontario	1. *Constitution Amendment Proclamation, 1985.* Introduced October 13, 1983.	4	No	Passed on October 18, 1983.	Carried unanimously.
	2. *Constitution Amendment* Resolution. Introduced November 27, 1986. [Property rights]	1	No	Passed on November 27, 1986.	For, 44. Against, 20. 130 seats at Queen's Park.
	3. *Constitution Amendment, 1987.* Introduced June 29, 1988.	1	No	Passed on June 29, 1988.	For, 112. Against, 8.
	4. *Constitution Amendment,* year of proclamation. Introduced June 20, 1990. [Companion resolution]	1	No	Passed on June 20, 1990.	For, 95. Against, 10.
Manitoba	1. *Constitution Amendment Proclamation, 1983* Introduced June 27, 1983.	4	On August 18, 1983, the Standing Committee on Elections and Privileges heard from eight groups and witnesses, and received eight briefs. The Committee tabled its report later that day prior to adoption of the resolution.	Passed on August 18, 1983.	Carried unanimously.
	2. *Constitution Amendment Proclamation, 1983 (Manitoba Act).* Introduced July 4, 1983.	16	Conducted 17 days of hearings, heard submissions from 305 delegations and received an additional 99 written submissions.	Failed. Died on the Order Paper. Last day of debate was February 1, 1984.	N/A

Province	Constitutional Amendment Resolution	Days of Debate	Hearings	Passed/Failed	Vote
Manitoba (continued)	3. *Constitution Amendment, 1987.* Introduced December 16, 1988.	1	No	Withdrawn December 19, 1987.	N/A
	4. *Constitution Amendment, 1987.* Reintroduced June 20, 1990. (Attempts to reintroduce the resolution had been denied on June 12, June 13, June 15, June 18 and June 19.)	2	No	Failed when time period for ratification of the amendment expired.	N/A
Saskatchewan	1. *Constitution Amendment Proclamation, 1983.* Introduced November 30, 1983.	1	No	Passed on November 30, 1983.	For, 54. Against, 0. 61 seats.
	2. *Constitution Amendment, 1987.* Introduced July 9, 1987.	6	No	Passed on September 23, 1987.	For, 43. Against, 3.
Alberta	1. *Constitution Amendment Proclamation, 1983.* Introduced June 3, 1983.	1	No	Passed on June 3, 1983.	No recorded vote.
	2. *Constitution Amendment, 1987.* Introduced June 17, 1987.	9	No	Passed on December 7, 1987.	For, 43. Against, 0. 83 seats in the Legislature.

Province	Constitutional Amendment Resolution	Days of Debate	Hearings	Passed/Failed	Vote
British Columbia	1. Constitution Amendment Resolution. Introduced September 21, 1982. [Property rights]	1	No	Passed on September 21, 1982.	Carried unanimously.
	2. *Constitution Amendment Proclamation, 1983.* August 11, 1983.	1	No	Passed on October 21, 1983.	For, 34. Against, 0. 57 seats in the Legislature.
	3. *Constitution Amendment, 1987.* Introduced June 29, 1988.	1	No	Passed on June 29, 1988.	For, 42. Against, 5.

our Majesty's loyal subjects, the Hou
s of Canada in Parliament assembl
approach Your Majesty, requesting
graciously be pleased to cause to be
Parliament of the United Kingd
containing the recitals and
ter set forth:

An Act to give effect to a request by t
and House of Commons of C

Whereas Canada has requested a
the enactment of an Act of the Par
United Kingdom to give effect to
in after set forth and the Senate an
Canada in Parliament
Her Majeste

BIBLIOGRAPHY

Books

Alberta. Constitutional Reform Task Force. *Restructuring Federalism (Roundtable III)*. Edmonton, 1990.

———. *'The Amending Process' and 'The Economics of Federalism' (Roundtable IV)*. Edmonton, 1990.

———. *Alberta in a New Canada: A Discussion Paper from the Constitutional Reform Task Force of Alberta*. Edmonton, 1990.

———. *Alberta in a New Canada: Visions of Unity*. Report of the Alberta Select Special Committee on Constitutional Reform. Edmonton, 1992.

Balthazar, Louis, Guy Laforest and Vincent Lemieux, eds. *Le Québec et la restructuration du Canada, 1980-1992 : enjeux et perspectives*. Sillery, Quebec: Septentrion, 1991.

Banting, Keith G., and Richard Simeon, eds. *And No One Cheered: Federalism, Democracy and the Constitution Act*. Toronto: Methuen, 1983.

———. *Industrial Nations: Redesigning the State: The Politics of Constitutional Change*. Toronto: University of Toronto Press, 1985.

Bayefsky, Anne F. *Canada's Constitution Act 1982 and Amendments: A Documentary History*. 2 vols. Toronto: McGraw-Hill Ryerson, 1989.

Beaudoin, Gérald A. *La Constitution du Canada : institutions, partage des pouvoirs, droits et libertés*. Montreal: Wilson & Lafleur, 1990.

Beck, Stanley, and Ivan Bernier, eds. *Canada and the New Constitution*. 2 vols. Montreal: Institute for Research on Public Policy, 1983.

Behiels, Michael D., ed. *The Meech Lake Primer: Conflicting Views of the 1987 Constitutional Accord*. Ottawa: University of Ottawa Press, 1989.

Breton, Raymond. *Why Meech Failed*. Toronto: C. D. Howe Institute, 1992.

British Columbia Special Committee on Constitutional Matters. *British Columbia and the Canadian Federation*. Victoria, 1992.

Brooke, Jeffrey. *Strange Bedfellows, Trying Times: October 1992 and the Defeat of the Powerbrokers*. Toronto: Key Porter Books, 1993.

Cairns, Alan C. *Charter Versus Federalism: The Dilemmas of Constitutional Reform*. Montreal: McGill-Queen's University Press, 1992.

———. *Disruptions: Constitutional Struggles, from the Charter to Meech Lake*. Edited by Douglas E. Williams. Toronto: McClelland and Stewart, 1991.

Canada. Canadian Intergovernmental Conferences Secretariat. *Constitutional Review, 1968–1971: Secretary's Report*. Ottawa, 1974.

———. Canadian Intergovernmental Conferences Secretariat. *Proposals on the Constitution, 1971-1978*. Ottawa, 1978.

———. Citizens' Forum on Canada's Future. *Report to the People and Government of Canada*. Ottawa, 1991.

———. *Consensus Report on the Constitution, Charlottetown, August 28, 1992: Final Text*. Ottawa, 1992.

———. *Draft Legal Text for the Charlottetown Accord*. Ottawa, 1992.

———. Federal-Provincial Relations Office. *Amending the Constitution of Canada: A Discussion Paper*. Ottawa, 1990.

———. Federal-Provincial Relations Office. *The Canadian Constitution and Constitutional Amendment*. Ottawa, 1978.

———. *A Guide to the Meech Lake Constitutional Accord*. Ottawa, 1987.

———. *Renewal of Canada Conferences: Compendium of Reports*. Ottawa: Constitutional Conferences Secretariat, 1992.

———. *Shaping Canada's Future Together: Proposals*. Ottawa, 1991.

———. Special Committee to Study the Proposed Companion Resolution to the Meech Lake Accord. *Report*. Ottawa, 1990.

———. Special Joint Committee of the Senate and of the House of Commons on the Constitution of Canada. *Constitution of Canada: Final Report*. Ottawa, 1972.

———. Special Joint Committee of the Senate and the House of Commons on the 1987 Constitutional Accord. *The 1987 Constitutional Accord*. Ottawa 1987.

———. Special Joint Committee of the Senate and the House of Commons on the Process of Amending the Constitution of Canada. *The Process for Amending the Constitution of Canada: The Report of the Special Joint Committee*. Ottawa, 1991.

———. Special Joint Committee of the Senate and the House of Commons. *Report of the Special Joint Committee on a Renewed Canada*. Ottawa, 1992.

———. Task Force on Canadian Unity. *A Future Together: Observations and Recommendations*. Ottawa, 1979.

Canadian Bar Association. *Rebuilding a Canadian Consensus: An Analysis of the Federal Government's Proposals for a Renewed Canada*. Ottawa, 1991.

Cheffins, Ronald I., and Patricia A. Johnson. *The Revised Canadian Constitution: Politics as Law*. Toronto: McGraw-Hill Ryerson, 1986.

Chrétien, Jean. *The Role of the United Kingdom in the Amendment of the Canadian Constitution: Background Paper*. Ottawa: Queen's Printer, 1981.

Clyne, J.V. *Citizens and Constitutions: A Constituent Assembly as a Means to Citizen Participation in Constitutional Change: A Report*. Calgary: Canada West Foundation, 1981.

Cohen, Andrew. *A Deal Undone: The Making and Breaking of the Meech Lake Accord*. Vancouver: Douglas & McIntyre, 1990.

Cook, Curtis, ed. *Constitutional Predicament: Canada After the Referendum of 1992*. Montreal: McGill-Queen's University Press, 1994.

Courchene, Thomas J. *In Praise of Renewed Federalism*. Toronto: C. D. Howe Institute,1991.

———. *The Community of the Canadas*. Kingston, Ontario: Institute of Intergovernmental Relations, Queen's University, 1991.

Coyne, Deborah M. R. *Roll of the Dice: Working With Clyde Wells During the Meech Lake Negotiations*. Toronto: James Lorimer, 1992.

Davenport, P., and R. H. Leach, eds. *Reshaping Confederation: The 1982 Reform of the Canadian Constitution*. Durham, N.C.: Duke University Press, 1984.

Delacourt, Susan. *United We Fall: The Crisis of Democracy in Canada*. Toronto: Viking, 1993.

Equality Party. *Quebec in Canada: One Nation — One Future*. Montreal, 1991.

Fafard, Patrick, and Darrel R. Reid. *Constituent Assemblies: A Comparative Survey*. Kingston, Ontario: Institute of Intergovernmental Relations, Queen's University, 1991.

Fallis, George. *The Costs of Constitutional Change: A Citizen's Guide to the Issues*. Toronto: James Lorimer, 1992.

Favreau, Guy. *The Amendment of the Constitution of Canada*. Ottawa: Queen's Printer, 1965.

Forsey, Eugene A. *The Royal Power of Dissolution of Parliament in the British Commonwealth*. Toronto: Oxford University Press, 1943.

Gérin-Lajoie, Paul. *Constitutional Amendment in Canada*. Toronto: University of Toronto Press, 1950.

Harrison, Peter. *The Constitutional Conferences Secretariat: A Unique Response to a Public Management Challenge*. Ottawa: Canadian Centre for Management Development, 1992.

Hawkes, David C. *Aboriginal Peoples and Constitutional Reform: What Have We Learned?* Kingston, Ontario: Institute of Intergovernmental Relations, Queen's University, 1989.

Heard, Andrew David. *Canadian Constitutional Conventions: The Marriage of Law and Politics*. Toronto: Oxford University Press, 1991.

Herperger, Dwight, and R. L. Watts. *Looking Forward, Looking Back: Constitutional Proposals of the Past and Their Relevance in the Post-Meech Era*. Montreal: Council for Canadian Unity, 1990.

Hogg, Peter W. *Canada Act 1982 Annotated*. Toronto: Carswell, 1982.

———. *Is the Canadian Constitution Ready For the 21st Century?* North York, Ontario: York University Centre for Public Law and Public Policy, 1991.

———. *Meech Lake Constitutional Accord Annotated*. Companion volume to the author's *Constitutional Law of Canada*. Second edition. Toronto: Carswell, 1988.

Howse, Robert. *Economic Union, Social Justice, and Constitutional Reform: Towards a High But Level Playing Field*. North York, Ontario: York University Centre for Public Law and Public Policy, 1992.

Hurley, James Ross. *The Canadian Constitutional Debate: From the Death of the Meech Lake Accord of 1987 to the 1992 Referendum*. "Revised text of a paper presented at the 1992 Conference of the Association for Canadian Studies in Australia and New Zealand. Wellington, New Zealand, December 16, 1992." Ottawa: Supply and Services Canada, 1994.

Kennedy, W. P. M. *The Constitution of Canada 1534–1937: An Introduction to Its Development, Law and Custom*. Second edition. Toronto: Oxford University Press, 1938.

Latouche, Daniel, and Alain-G. Gagnon, eds. *Allaire, Bélanger, Campeau et les autres : Les Québécois s'interrogent sur leur avenir*. Montreal: Québec/Amérique, 1991.

Lisée, Jean-Francois. *Le Naufrageur: Robert Bourassa et les Québécois, 1990–1991*. Montreal:Boréal, 1994.

———. *Le Tricheur: Robert Bourassa et les Québécois, 1990–1991*. Montreal: Boréal, 1994.

Livingston, William S. *Federalism and Constitutional Change*. Westport, Connecticut: Greenwood Press, 1974.

Lyon, Noel. *Aboriginal Peoples and Constitutional Reform in the 90s.* North York, Ontario: York University Centre for Public Law and Public Policy, 1991.

Manitoba Constitutional Task Force. *Report of the Manitoba Constitutional Task Force.* Winnipeg, 1991.

McRoberts, Kenneth, and Patrick J. Monahan eds. *The Charlottetown Accord, the Referendum and the Future of Canada.* Toronto: University of Toronto Press, 1993.

McWhinney, Edward. *Canada and the Constitution 1979–1982: Patriation and the Charter of Rights.* Toronto: University of Toronto Press, 1982.

———. *Constitution-Making: Principles, Process, Practice.* Toronto: University of Toronto Press, 1981.

Meekison, Peter J., Roy Romanow and William D. Moull. *The Origins and Meaning of Section 92a: The 1982 Constitutional Amendment on Resources.* Montreal: Institute for Research on Public Policy, 1985.

Milne, David. *The New Canadian Constitution.* Toronto: James Lorimer, 1982.

———. *The Canadian Constitution: From Patriation to Meech Lake.* Toronto: James Lorimer, 1989.

Monahan, Patrick J. *Meech Lake: The Inside Story.* Toronto: University of Toronto Press, 1991.

Monahan, Patrick J., and Lynda Covello. *An Agenda For Constitutional Reform.* North York, Ontario: York University Centre for Public Law and Public Policy, 1992.

Monahan, Patrick J., Lynda Covello and Nicola Smith. *A New Division of Powers For Canada.* North York, Ontario: York University Centre for Public Law and Public Policy, 1992.

Morin, Claude. *Le combat québécois.* Montreal: Boréal Express, 1973.

———. *Le pouvoir québécois...en négociation.* Montreal: Boréal Express, 1972.

———. *Lendemains piégés : du référendum à la nuit des longs couteaux.* Montreal: Boréal, 1988.

———. *Quebec versus Ottawa: The Struggle for Self-Government 1960–72.* Toronto: University of Toronto Press, 1976.

New Brunswick Legislative Assembly. *Final Report of the Select Committee on the Constitution.* Fredericton, 1992.

Newfoundland and Labrador Committee on the Constitution. *Final Report of the Newfoundland and Labrador Committee on the Constitution.* St. John's, 1992.

Nova Scotia Working Committee on the Constitution. *Finding Common Ground: The Nova Scotia Discussion Paper on the Constitution.* Halifax, 1991.

Ontario. Select Committee on Ontario in Confederation. *Changing for the Better: An Invitation to Talk About a New Canada.* Toronto, 1991.

———. Select Committee on Ontario in Confederation. *Final Report: Select Committee on Ontario in Confederation.* Toronto, 1992.

Prince Edward Island. *Report of the Special Committee of the Legislative Assembly of Prince Edward Island on the Constitution of Canada.* Charlottetown, 1991.

Quebec Liberal Party. Commission politique du Parti libéral du Québec. *Maîtriser l'avenir.* Montreal, 1985

———. Constitutional Committee. *A New Canadian Federation.* Montreal, 1980.

———. *A Quebec Free to Choose.*[Allaire Report]. Québec, 1991.

Quebec. *Éléments d'analyse économique pertinents à la révision du statut politique et constitutionnel du Québec.* Québec, 1991.

———. *Éléments d'analyse institutionnelle, juridique et démolinguistique pertinents à la révision du statut politique et constitutionnel du Québec.* Québec, 1991.

———. *La nouvelle entente Québec–Canada, Proposition du Québec pour une entente d'égal à égal : la souveraineté-association* [Livre blanc sur le référendum]. Québec, 1979.

———. *Les avis des spécialistes invités à répondre aux huit questions posées par la Commission.* Québec, 1991.

———. Commission on the Political and Constitutional Future of Quebec. *Report.* [Bélanger–Campeau Report]. Québec 1991.

Rémillard, Gil. *Le fédéralisme canadien : Le rapatriement de la constitution. t. II:* Montreal: Québec/Amérique, 1985.

Resnick, Philip. *Toward a Canada–Quebec Union.* Montreal: McGill-Queen's University Press, 1991.

Romanow, Roy, John Whyte and Howard Leeson. *Canada Notwithstanding: The Making of the Constitution 1976–1982.* Toronto: Methuen, 1984.

Russell, Peter H. *Constitutional Odyssey: Can Canadians Become a Sovereign People?* Second edition. Toronto: University of Toronto Press, 1993.

———. *The Court and the Constitution: Comments on the Supreme Court Reference on Constitutional Amendment.* Kingston, Ontario: Institute of intergovernmental Relations, Queen's University, 1982.

Saskatchewan Constitutional Unit. *The Charlottetown Agreement: A Saskatchewan Perspective.* Regina, 1992.

Schwartz, Bryan. *Fathoming Meech Lake.* Winnipeg: Legal Research Institute of the University of Manitoba, 1987.

———. *First Principles: Constitutional Reform with Respect to the Aboriginal Peoples of Canada, 1982-1984.* Kingston, Ontario: Institute of Inter-governmental Relations, Queen's University, 1985.

Sheppard, R., and M. Valpy. *The National Deal: The Fight for a Canadian Constitution.* Toronto: Macmillan, 1982.

Simeon, Richard. *A Citizen's Guide to the Constitutional Question.* Toronto: Gage, 1980.

Simeon, Richard, and Mary Janigan, eds. *Toolkits and Building Blocks: Constructing a New Canada.* Policy Study No.14. Toronto: C. D. Howe Institute, 1991.

Smith, David E., Peter MacKinnon and John C. Courtney, eds. *After Meech Lake: Lessons for the Future.* Saskatoon: Fifth House, 1991.

Smith, Melvin H. *The Renewal of the Federation: A British Columbia Perspective.* [Study commissioned by the Government of British Columbia]. Victoria: Queen's Printer for British Columbia, 1991.

Stein, Michael B. *Canadian Constitutional Renewal, 1968-1981: A Case Study in Integrative Bargaining.* Kingston, Ontario: Institute of Inter-governmental Relations, Queen's University, 1989.

Thomas, Clive Robert. *Navigating Meech Lake: The 1987 Constitutional Accord.* Kingston, Ontario: Institute of Intergovernmental Relations, Queen's University, 1988.

Trudeau, Pierre Elliott. *Fatal Tilt: Speaking Out About Sovereignty.* Toronto: Harper Collins, 1991.

———. *Lac Meech : Trudeau parle...* Textes réunis et présentés par Donald J. Johnston. LaSalle, Quebec: Hurtubise, 1989.

———. *With a Bang, Not a Whimper: Pierre Trudeau Speaks Out.* Edited by Donald J. Johnston. Toronto: Stoddart, 1988.

Watts, Ronald L., and Douglas M. Brown, eds. Options For a New Canada. Toronto: University of Toronto Press, 1991.

Articles

Ackerman, Bruce A., and Robert E. Charney. "Canada at the Constitutional Crossroads." *University of Toronto Law Journal,* 34 (Spring 1984): 117-35.

Aitken, Jonathan. "A British View of Canada's Repatriation Efforts." *University of New Brunswick Law Journal,* 33 (1984): 319-28.

Beaudoin, Gérald A. "Les Accords Meech-Langevin." *Revue de droit de l'Université du Nouveau-Brunswick,* 38 (1989): 227-50.

———."Le rapatriement : la fin du commencement?" *Revue de l'Université d'Ottawa,* 52 (July-September 1982): 287-301.

———. "La révision de la constitution du Canada et l'avenir du Québec : problèmes et perspectives." *Revue générale de droit,* 13 (1982): 477-97.

Blache, Pierre. "La Cour suprême et le rapatriement de la constitution : l'impact des perceptions différentes de la question." *Cahiers de droit,* 22: 3-4 (December 1981): 649-66.

Blais, André. "The Constitutional Game in Quebec: Options, Interests, Strategies, Outcomes." In *Confederation in Crisis*, edited by Robert Young, 65-74. Toronto: James Lorimer, 1991.

Boardway, Robin. "Constitutional Design in a Federation." In *Options for a New Canada*, edited by Ronald L. Watts and Douglas M. Brown, 237-57. Toronto: University of Toronto Press, 1991.

Boisvenu, Gérard. "When More Is Too Much: Quebec and the Charlottetown Accord." In *Canada: The State of the Federation 1993,* edited by Ronald L. Watts and Douglas M. Brown, 45-60. Kingston, Ontario: Institute of Intergovernmental Relations, Queen's University, 1993.

Bonin, Daniel. "Le Québec de l'après-Meech : entre le beau risque nouvelle manière et la souveraineté." In *Canada: The State of the Federation 1991,* edited by Douglas M. Brown, 19-56. Kingston, Ontario: Institute of Intergovernmental Relations, Queen's University, 1991.

Breton, Albert. "An Analysis of Constitutional Change, Canada, 1980-82." *Public Choice,* 44:1 (1984): 251-272.

Brock, Kathy L. "The Politics of Process." In *Canada: The State of the Federation 1991,* edited by Douglas M. Brown, 57-87. Kingston, Ontario: Institute of Intergovernmental Relations, Queen's University, 1991.

Burnside, Joyce D. "Implications of Quebec's 'Distinct Society' as recognized in the Meech Lake Accord. "*Queen's Law Journal*, vol. 13 (Winter 1988): 29-53.

Cairns, Alan C. "The Charter, Interest Groups, Executive Federalism, and Constitutional Reform." In *After Meech Lake: Lessons for the Future,* edited by David E. Smith, Peter MacKinnon and John C. Courtney, 13-31. Saskatoon: Fifth House, 1991.

―――. "Constitutional Change and the Three Equalities." In *Options for a New Canada,* edited by Ronald L. Watts and Douglas M. Brown, 77-100. Toronto: University of Toronto Press, 1991.

―――. "Passing Judgement on Meech Lake." In *Disruptions: Constitutional Struggles, from the Charter to Meech Lake,* edited by Douglas E. Williams, 223-63. Toronto: McClelland and Stewart, 1991.

―――. "Roadblocks in the Way of Constitutional Change." *Constitutional Forum,* 2:2 (Winter 1991): 54-8.

―――."Citizens (Outsiders) and Governments (Insiders) in Constitution-Making: The Case of Meech Lake." *Canadian Public Policy,* 14:3 (September 1988 Supplement): S121-S145.

Cairns, Robert D. "Economic Assessment of the Resource Amendment (to the Constitution Act)." *Canadian Public Policy,* 13:4 (December 1987): 502-14.

Careless, Anthony G., and Donald W. Stevenson. "Canada: Constitutional Reform as a Policy-Making Instrument." *Publius,*12 (Summer 1982): 85-98.

Cheffins, Ronald I. "The Constitution Act, 1982 and the Amending Formula: Political and Legal Implications." *Supreme Court Law Review,*4 (Special Edition 1982): 43-54.

Christian, Timothy. "Sweeping Constitutional Changes in Canada." *International and Comparative Law Quarterly,* 36:1 (1987): 139-142.

Courchene, Thomas J., and John N. McDougall. "The Context for the Future Constitutional Options." In *Options for a New Canada,* edited by Ronald L. Watts and Douglas M. Brown, 33-51. Toronto: University of Toronto Press, 1991.

Craig, T. "Canadian and Foreign Constitutional Amending Procedures." *University of Toronto Faculty of Law Review,* 36:1 (Spring 1978): 159-190.

Dafoe, John Wesley. "Revising the Constitution." *Queen's Quarterly,*37:1 (Winter 1930): 1-17.

Dellinger, Walter. "The Amending Process in Canada and the United States: A Comparative Perspective." *Law and Contemporary Problems,* 45:4 (1982): 283-302.

Demontigny, Yves. "Preuve d'une convention constitutionnelle devant les tribunaux : modification de l'Acte de l'Amérique du Nord : rôle du Québec." *Revue du Barreau,* 43 (November–December 1983): 1133-50.

Dion, Stéphane. "L'Obsession a assez sévi." *Policy Options politiques,* 14:3 (April 1993): 3-5.

D'Onorio, Joël-Benoît. "Le rapatriement de la constitution canadienne." *Revue internationale de droit comparé,* 35ᵉ année (January–March 1983): 69-108.

Driedger, Elmer A. "Constitutional Amendment in Canada." *Canadian Bar Association Journal,* vol. 5:1 (February 1962): 52-59.

Duplé, Nicole. "La Cour suprême et le rapatriement de la constitution : la victoire du compromis sur la rigueur." *Cahiers de droit,* vol. 22: 3-4 (December 1981): 619-48.

Favreau, Guy. "Constitutional Amendment in a Canadian Canada." *McGill Law Journal,* 12:4 (1966/67): 384-393.

Fournier, Pierre. "L'échec du Lac Meech : un point de vue québécois." In *Canada: The State of the Federation 1990,* edited by Ronald L. Watts and Douglas M. Brown, 41-68. Kingston, Ontario: Institute of Intergovernmental Relations, Queen's University, 1990.

Fraser, Graham. "Slouching Towards Canada." In *Canada: The State of the Federation 1991,* edited by Douglas M. Brown, 89-104. Kingston, Ontario: Institute of Intergovernmental Relations, Queen's University, 1991.

Frémont Jacques. "Le droit international, la souveraineté du Canada et le 'rapatriement' de la Constitution canadienne." *Revue québécoise de droit international,*1 (1984): 327-43.

Gagnon, Alain-G. "Everything Old Is New Again: Canada, Quebec and Constitutional Impasse." In *How Ottawa Spends 1991-92: The Politics of Fragmentation,* edited by Abel Francis, 63-106. Ottawa: Carleton University Press, 1991.

———. "Other Federal and Nonfederal Countries: Lessons for Canada." In *Options for a New Canada,* edited by Ronald L. Watts and Douglas M. Brown, 207-33. Toronto: University of Toronto Press, 1991.

Gérin-Lajoie, Paul. "Du pouvoir d'amendement constitutionnel au Canada." *Canadian Bar Review,* 29:10 (December 1951): 1136-1179.

Hawkes, David C., and Marina Devine. "Meech Lake and Elijah Harper: Native-State Relations in the 1990s." In *How Ottawa Spends 1991-92: The Politics of Fragmentation,* edited by Abel Francis, 33-62. Ottawa: Carleton University Press, 1991.

Hawkes, David C., and Bradford W. Morse. "Alternative Methods for Aboriginal Participation in Processes of Constitutional Reform." In *Options for a New Canada,* edited by Ronald L. Watts and Douglas M. Brown, 163-87. Toronto: University of Toronto Press, 1991.

Herman, Lawrence L. "International Law Aspects of Patriation." *University of New Brunswick Law Journal,* 31 (1982): 69-86.

Hogg, Peter W. "Comments on Legislation and Judicial Decisions, Constitutional Law — Amendment of the British North America Act — Role of the Provinces." *Canadian Bar Review,* 60 (June 1982): 307-34.

———. "Patriation of the Canadian Constitution: Has it Been Achieved?" *Queen's Law Journal,* 8 (Fall 1982/Spring 1983): 123-20.

Johnston, Richard, and André Blais. "Meech Lake and Mass Politics: The 'Distinct Society' Clause." *Canadian Public Policy,* 14:3 (September 1988 Supplement): S25-S42.

Johnston, Richard., et al. "The People and the Charlottetown Accord." In *Canada: The State of the Federation 1993,* edited by Ronald L. Watts and Douglas M. Brown, 19-43. Kingston, Ontario: Institute of Intergovernmental Relations, Queen's University, 1993.

Kallen, Evelyn. "The Meech Lake Accord: Entrenching a Pecking Order of Minority Rights." *Canadian Public Policy,* 14:3 (September 1988 Supplement): S107-S120.

Kay, Richard S. "Courts as Constitution-Makers in Canada and the United States." *Supreme Court Law Review,* 4 (Special Edition 1982): 23-41.

———. "The Creation of Constitutions in Canada and the United States." *Canada–United States Law Journal,* 7 (1984): 111-163.

Kilgour, D. Marc. "Distributing the Power to Amend Canada's Constitution." *Canadian Journal of Political Science,* 18:2 (June 1985): 389-396.

———. "A Formal Analysis of the Amending Formula of Canada's Constitutional Act, 1982." *Canadian Journal of Political Science,* 16:4 (December 1983): 771-777.

Kilgour, D. Marc, and Terrence J. Levesque.. "The Canadian Constitutional Amending Formula: Bargaining in the Past and the Future." *Public Choice,*.44:3 (1984): 457-480.

———."The Choice of a Permanent Amending Formula for Canada's Constitution." *Canadian Public Policy,* 10:3 (September 1984): 359-361.

Laforest, Guy. "Quebec Beyond the Federal Regime of 1867–1982: From DistinctSociety to National Community." In *Options for a New Canada,* edited by Ronald L. Watts and Douglas M. Brown, 103-22. Toronto: University of Toronto Press, 1991.

LaSelva, Samuel V. "Federation and Unanimity: The Supreme Court and Constitutional Amendment." *Canadian Journal of Political Science,* 16:4 (December 1983): 757-770.

Laskin, Bora. "Amendment of the Constitution." *University of Toronto Law Journal,* 15:1 (1963): 190-194.

Latouche, Daniel. "Problems of Constitutional Design in Canada: Quebec and the Issue of Bicommunalism." *Publius,* 18 (Spring 1988): 131-46.

Leach, Richard H. "Implications for Federalism of the Reformed Constitution of Canada." *Law and Contemporary Problems,* 45 (Autumn 1982): 149-64.

Lederman, William R. "Canadian Constitutional Amending Procedures: 1867-1982." *American Journal of Comparative Law,* 32:2 (Spring 1984): 339-360.

———. "Charter Influences on Future Constitutional Reform." In *After Meech Lake: Lessons for the Future,* edited by David E.Smith, Peter MacKinnon and John C. Courtney, 115-19. Saskatoon: Fifth House, 1991.

———. "The Constitutional Amendment and Canadian Unity." In *The Constitution and the Future of Canada,* 17-36. Toronto: Richard DeBoo, 1978.

———."Cooperative Federalism: Constitutional Revision and Parliamentary Government in Canada." *Queen's Quarterly,* 78:1 (Spring 1971): 7-17.

———. "The Process of Constitutional Amendment for Canada." *McGill Law Journal,* 12:4 (1966/67): 371-383

———. "The Process of Constitutional Amendment for Canada." In *New Developments in the Law of Remedies,* edited by Richard DeBoo, 91-106. Toronto: Butterworths, 1980.

———. "The Supreme Court of Canada and Basic Constitutional Amendment." In *The Court and the Constitution: Comments on the Supreme Court Reference on Constitutional Amendment,* 43-56. Kingston, Ontario: Institute of Intergovernmental Relations, Queen's University, 1982.

Leslie, Peter M. "Bicommunalism and Canadian Constitutional Reform." *Publius,* 18 (Spring 1988): 115-29.

————. "Options for the Future of Canada: The Good, the Bad and the Fantastic." In *Options for a New Canada,* edited by Ronald L. Watts and Douglas M. Brown, 123-40. Toronto: University of Toronto Press, 1991.

Levesque, Terrence J. "Citizens and Provincial Power Under Alternative Amending Formulae: An Extension of Kilgour's Analysis." *Canadian Journal of Political Science,* 17:1 (March 1984): 154-166.

Mahler, Gregory S. "Canadian Federalism and Constitutional Reform." *Journal of Commonwealth and Comparative Politics,* 25:2 (July 1987): 107-125.

Mallory, J. R. "Amending the Constitution by Stealth." *Queen's Quarterly,* 82:3 (Autumn 1975): 394-401.

————. "The Politics of Constitutional Change." *Law and Contemporary Problems,* 45:4 (Autumn 1982): 53-71.

Marshall, Geoffrey. "Canada's New Constitution (1982): Some Lessons in Constitutional Engineering." In *Constitutions in Democratic Politics,* edited by Vernon Bogdanor, 156-171. Aldershot, England: Gower Press, 1988.

McConnell, W.H. "Cutting the Gordian Knot: The Amending Process in Canada." *Law and Contemporary Problems,* 44:3 (Summer 1981): 195-230.

McMurtry, R. Roy. "The Search for a Constitutional Accord — A Personal Memoir." *Queen's Law Journal,* 8 (Fall 1982/Spring 1983): 28-73.

McWhinney, Edward. "Constitution Patriation as Prologue: Phase Two Constitution-Making and Reform of Federal Institutions." *Cahiers de droit,* 25 (March 1984): 165-71.

McWilliams, R.F. "Amendment of the Constitution." *Canadian Bar Review* 16:6 (June 1938): 466-475.

Meekison, Peter J. "The Amending Formula." *Queen's Law Journal,* 8 (Fall 1982/Spring 1983): 99-122.

————. "The Amending Formula and the Agenda for Change." *Constitutional Forum,* 2:4 (Summer 1991): 93-8.

————. "Constitutional Reform in Canada." In *Canadian Federalism: Myth or Reality,* edited by Peter J. Meekison (Second edition), 235-252. Toronto: Methuen, 1971.

————."Distribution of Functions and Jurisdiction: A Political Scientist's Analysis." In *Options for a New Canada,* edited by Ronald L. Watts and Douglas M. Brown, 259-84. Toronto: University of Toronto Press, 1991.

————. "Let There Be Light." In *Canada: The State of the Federation 1993,* edited by Ronald L. Watts and Douglas M. Brown, 61-86. Kingston, Ontario: Institute of Intergovernmental Relations, Queen's University, 1993.

Mercredi, Ovide. "Aboriginal Peoples and the Constitution." In *After Meech Lake: Lessons for the Future,* edited by David E.Smith, Peter MacKinnon and John C. Courtney, 219-22. Saskatoon: Fifth House, 1991.

Miller, D. R. "A Shapley Value Analysis of the Proposed Canadian Constitutional Amendment Scheme." *Canadian Journal of Political Science,* 6:1 (1973): 140-143.

Milne, David. "Equality or Asymmetry: Why Choose?" In *Options for a New Canada,* edited by Ronald L. Watts and Douglas M. Brown, 285-307. Toronto: University of Toronto Press, 1991.

Mintz, Eric. "Banzhaf's Power Index and Canada's Constitutional Amending Formula: A Comment on Kilgour's Analysis." *Canadian Journal of Political Science,* 18:2 (June 1985): 385-388.

Morin, Claude. "L'expérience canadienne et québécoise de révision constitutionnelle : leçons et perspectives." *Cahiers de droit,* 26:1(March1985): 29-55.

Morton, F. L. "Comment ne pas modifier la Constitution" *Revue parlementaire canadienne,* 12 (Winter 1989/90): 9-10.

Munro, Gary. "Constitutional Change in Canada: The Meech Lake Accord." *Commonwealth and Comparative Politics,* 27 (July 1989): 201-17.

Murray, Lowell. "The Process of Constitutional Change in Canada: The Lessons of Meech Lake." *Choices* (Institute for Research on Public Policy), (February 1988): 1-6.

Ninian, Stephen. "Constitutional Change in Canada: Lessons and Analogies From Across the Pacific." *Australian Journal of Public Administration,* 42 (March 1983): 173-86.

Nouailhat, Yves-Henri. "Les provinces atlantiques dans le débat sur le rapatriement de la Constitution." *Études canadiennes,* 13 (December 1982): 143-51.

Orban, Edmond. "Constitution and Regional Cleavages: A View from Québec." In *After Meech Lake: Lessons for the Future,* edited by David E. Smith, Peter MacKinnon and John C. Courtney, 83-97. Saskatoon: Fifth House, 1991.

Owram, Doug. "The Historical Context of Meech Lake." *Constitutional Forum* 2:2 (Winter 1991): 23-6.

Pal, Leslie A., and F. Leslie Seidle. "Constitutional Politics 1990-92: The Paradox of Participation." In *How Ottawa Spends 1993-94: A More Democratic Canada ...?* edited by Susan D. Phillips, 143-202. Ottawa: Carleton University Press, 1993.

Philip, Christian. "Le Québec et le rapatriement de la Constitution canadienne." *Revue du droit public et de la science politique en France et à l'étranger,* 98:6, (November-December 1982): 1567-600.

Rémillard, Gil, and Guylaine Bérubé."The Constitution Act, 1982: An Unfinished Compromise." *American Journal of Comparative Law,* 32 (Spring 1984): 269-81.

———. "Le contrôle de la constitutionnalité des lois au lendemain de la Loi constitutionnelle de 1982." *Revue du Barreau du Québec,* 42:4 (September-October 1982): 565-96.

———. "Historique du rapatriement." *Cahiers de droit,* 25:1 (March 1984): 15-97.

Rocher, François, and Daniel Salée. "Démocratie et réforme constitutionnelle: discours et pratique." *International Journal of Canadian Studies / Revue internationale d'études canadiennes,* 7-8 (Spring 1993): 167-85.

Robertson, Gordon. "The Amending Formula." *Policy Options politiques,* 3:1 (January/February 1982): 10-14.

Romanow, Roy. "Reworking the Miracle: The Constitutional Accord 1981." *Queen's Law Journal,* 8 (Fall 1982/Winter 1983): 74-98.

Russell, Peter H. "The Future Process of Canadian Constitutional Politics." In *Confederation in Crisis,* edited by Robert Young, 75-87. Toronto: James Lorimer, 1991.

———. "The Politics of Frustration: The Pursuit of Formal Constitutional Change in Australia and Canada." In *Federalism in Canada and Australia,* edited by Bruce W. Hodgins, John J. Eddy, Shelagh D. Grant and James Struthers, 59-85. Peterborough, Ontario: Frost Centre for Canadian Heritage and Development Studies, Trent University, 1989.

———. "Towards a New Constitutional Process." In *Options for a New Canada,* edited by Ronald L. Watts and Douglas M. Brown, 141-56. Toronto: University of Toronto Press, 1991.

Sabetti, Filippo. "The Historical Context of Constitutional Change in Canada." *Law and Contemporary Problems,* 45 (Autumn 1982): 11-32.

Schwartz, Bryan. "Refashioning Meech Lake." *Manitoba Law Journal,* 18:1 (1989): 19-70.

Scott, Stephen Allan. "The Canadian Constitutional Amendment Process: Mechanisms and Prospects." In *Recurring Issues in Canadian Federalism,* co-ordinated by Clare F. Beckton and A. Wayne MacKay, 77-111. Toronto: University of Toronto Press, 1986.

———. "The Constitutional Amendment Process." *Law and Contemporary Problems,* 45:4 (Autumn 1982): 249-282.

———. "No Dice: Two Cycles of Canadian Constitutional Crisis." *Policy Options politiques,* 14:3 (April 1993): 6-10.

———. "Pussycat, Pussycat or Patriation and the New Constitutional Amendment Process." *University of Western Ontario Law Review,* 20:2 (December 1982): 247-306.

Sharman, Campbell. "Parliamentary Federations and Limited Government: Constitutional Design and Re-design in Australia and Canada." *Journal of Theoretical Politics,* 2:2 (April 1990): 205-230.

Simeon, Richard. "Meech Lake and Shifting Conceptions of Canadian Federalism" *Canadian Public Policy,* 14:3 (September 1988 Supplement): S7-S24.

———. "Why Did the Meech Lake Accord Fail?" In *Canada: The State of the Federation 1990,* edited by Ronald L. Watts and Douglas M. Brown, 15-40. Kingston, Ontario: Institute of Intergovernmental Relations, Queen's University, 1990.

Singer, Howard L. "The Canadian Constitution and Constitutional Change." *Études canadiennes,* 5 (December 1978): 63-76.

Smith, Jennifer. "Origins of the Canadian Amendment Dilemma." *Dalhousie Review,* 61 (Summer 1981): 291-306.

———. "Representation and Constitutional Reform in Canada." In *After Meech Lake: Lessons for the Future,* edited by David E. Smith, Peter MacKinnon and John C. Courtney, 69-82. Saskatoon: Fifth House, 1991.

Smith, Lynn. "Could the Meech Lake Accord Affect the Protection of Equality Rights for Women and Minorities in Canada?" *Constitutional Forum,* 1 (Winter 1990): 12,17-20.

Smith, Miriam. "Constitutionalizing Economic and Social Rights in the Charlottetown Round." In *How Ottawa Spends 1993-94: A More Democratic Canada ...?* edited by Susan D. Phillips, 83-108. Ottawa: Carleton University Press, 1993.

Stein, Michael B. "Canadian Constitutional Reform, 1927-1982: A Comparative Case Analysis Over Time." *Publius,* 14:1 (1984): 121-140.

———. "Tensions in the Canadian Constitutional Process: Elite Negotiations, Referendums and Interest Group Consultations, 1980-1992." In *Canada: The State of the Federation 1993,* edited by Ronald L. Watts and Douglas M. Brown, 87-116. Kingston, Ontario: Institute of Intergovernmental Relations, Queen's University, 1993.

Thomas, Craig. "Canadian and Foreign Constitutional Amending Procedures." *University of Toronto Faculty Law Review.* 36:1 (Spring 1978): 159-190.

Tremblay, Arthur. "Les lendemains constitutionnels du rapatriement." *Policy Options politiques,* 3:5 (September-October 1982): 20-7.

Tremblay, Guy. "La procédure de modification de la Constitution du Canada et ses puzzles." *Revue du Barreau,* 43 (November-December 1983): 1151-9.

Ward, Norman. "The Realities of Constitutional Change." *Queen's Quarterly,* 86:2 (1979): 237-242.

Watts, Ronald L. "Canada's Constitutional Options: An Outline." In *Options For a New Canada,* edited by Ronald L. Watts and Douglas M. Brown, 15-30. Toronto: University of Toronto Press, 1991.

———. "Canadian Federalism in the 1990s: Once More in Question." *Publius,* 21:3 (Summer 1991): 169-90.

———. "The Federative Superstructure." In *Options For a New Canada,* edited by Ronald L. Watts and Douglas M. Brown, 309-36. Toronto: University of Toronto Press, 1991.

Wells, Clyde K. "Reforming the Amending Formula: The Case for Constitutional Convention." *Constitutional Forum,* 2:3 (Spring 1991): 69-73.

Woehrling, José. "La Cour suprême et les conventions constitutionnelles : les renvois relatifs au rapatriement de la constitution canadienne." *Revue de droit* (Université de Sherbrooke), 14:2 (1984): 391-440.